Satan's Mistress

More than 14,000 followers became disciples of Joanna Southcott, signing proclamations of loyalty, bearing her seal in red wax. These became known as "passports to Heaven" and often changed hands for a guinea each. They helped to make Joanna wealthy and famous and created a cult which survives today.

Replica of
Joanna's personal seal

Joanna Southcott

Satan's Mistress
by Val Lewis

Published by Nauticalia Ltd
The Ferry Point, Ferry Lane, Shepperton,
Middlesex TW17 9LQ, England
Tel. 01932 244396. Fax: 01932 241679
e-mail: vall@nauticalia.co.uk

A CIP record for this title is
available from the British Library

ISBN 0953045803

Printed in England by Biddles

Illustrations

Cover Illustration: Portrait of Joanna Southcott engraved January 7, 1812 by William Sharp. A print from it is on display at the National Portrait Gallery, London. According to Alice Seymour, who revived interest in her at the beginning of the 19th century, the Bible she is holding lies open at Isaiah 1, verses xv and xvi:
"And when ye spread forth your hands, I will hide mine eyes from you; yea, when ye make many prayers, I will not hear; Your hands are full of blood. Wash you, make you clean; put away the evil of your doings from before mine eyes; cease to do evil."

With special thanks to my husband, Lynn Lewis, for his love and guidance, to my children, Carol and Lindon, for their encouragement and to my grandson, Daniel, for his computer skills.

Chapters

When all its work is done,
The Lie shall rot!
The Truth is great
And shall prevail
When none cares whether
It prevail or not!

Coventry Patmore*
English poet (1823-1896)

*Uncle of Mabel Barltrop
(founder of the Panacea Society, Bedford)

Acknowledgements to:

Emily Nicholson: *granddaughter of Edwin Armstrong Jowett, for providing valuable information and photographs of the Jowett family.*

Picture of Harry Price opening fake Joanna Southcott Box (page 284) by courtesy of the Mary Evans Picture Library.

Editors: Ken Jackson and David Gurney.

Book Design: Daniel Hodge, of Austin Marketing Associates, Chertsey, Surrey.

Introduction

A psychic friend once assured me that no spirit, good or evil, can harm or influence you unless you allow it to. Although she wanted to be good, Joanna Southcott *allowed* herself to be influenced by an evil spirit. She knew she had special gifts which she longed to use to serve Jesus. But her fear of poverty proved stronger than her love of Jesus and she abandoned her pious intentions in exchange for fame and fortune and consequently Satan became her master.

However, she deluded herself that it was God influencing her. She believed, for instance, that comets were divinely sent to herald important news and that the Star of Bethlehem was one. A minor one showed up in the sky in 1750, the year she was born and Halley's Comet made a spectacular appearance when she was seven. In 1811 German astrologer, Johann Franz Encke, discovered one which was visible for about 18 months, during which time she announced she was to give birth to an immaculately conceived child.

Present day followers of Joanna Southcott are always looking out for signs and the Hale Bopp comet of 1997, with its impressive white tail and clearly visible to the naked eye, to them must have seemed conclusive evidence that Joanna's prophesy, that Judgement Day will be in the year 2004, is about to be proved and any time now Joanna and her "holy" son, Shiloh, will arrive to prepare the world for the Final Millennium.

Until now, those who have written about Joanna Southcott have either been enthusiastic followers or curious ecclesiastics, interested in her mostly as a visionary or a religious phenomenon. This book shows she was not only an extraordinary woman, a fascinating opportunist and a virulent feminist but also historically significant. For, in an age when few women of her class could read or write, let alone publish their own work, she wrote and published a 5,000 word book with her hard earned savings, revealing a ruthless determination out of keeping with her seemingly pious nature, which astonished her family and friends.

It was to be some years before George Elliott, Jane Austen and the Bronte sisters managed to get into print. Until Joanna, the only other popularly read professional English woman writer was Aphra Behn who, in the second half of the 17th century, made a good living writing erotic stories read mainly by men, although there were a few educated women who wrote for a selected readership, such as Mary Wollstonecraft, mother of Mary Shelley, who later wrote Frankenstein.

Religion was a subject that engrossed people of all classes and became the vehicle Joanna rode upon to achieve her aims. Within months of her first book being published, in 1801, Joanna was "discovered" by a group of religious enthusiasts on the look-out for a spiritual leader. A year later, her integrity abandoned and her future apparently assured, she left Exeter for a life of comparative ease in the homes of her new rich London friends, claiming that God had told her she would never want again.

The Strange Effects of Faith, which Joanna said God ordered her to write, became an unlikely best seller. It was an ungrammatical and tedious mixture of doggerel and prose relating to conversations she claimed to have had with God, but nonetheless thousands bought it, believing her to be a genuine Old Testament-style prophetess. The fact that the book contained slanderous references to many respectable people, including the royal family, probably also helped to sell it.

Exeter printer, Thomas Brice, refused to include any proper names, concerned that he might find himself liable. When Joanna protested about the omissions, he told her drily that he was full of admiration for her initiative and for having the courage of her convictions, and that he recognised she had a shrewd instinct for survival which he felt was akin to his own, but added he was a businessman and therefore obliged to put his own interests first.

As the sparsely educated fourth daughter of a poor 18th century Devonshire farming couple, Joanna Southcott would have been considered lucky if, like her sisters, she had married a local farmer. At the worst it might have been one of the farm hands. But, on discovering she had an uncanny gift of prophesy, she aimed high, claiming to be guided by God.

She developed into a highly-strung, charismatic woman, with a strong worldwide following even today, who ruined many lives, hoodwinked thousands of gullible people and eventually mesmerised Londoners by claiming to be the "Woman Clothed with the Sun", described in the *Book of Revelation*, who gave birth to a male child, destined to rule all nations.

The Napoleonic Wars were pushed right off the front page of *The Times* and the *Daily Monitor* to make room for day-by-day bulletins about Joanna Southcott's Holy Child, Shiloh, who was to be born in London's posh new suburb of Marylebone.

Despite her meagre education, Joanna Southcott had a detailed knowledge of even the most obscure books of the Bible. She also had an advantage over other prophets in that she claimed to have person-to-person conversations with God, who conveniently confirmed all her conclusions.

Her son, Shiloh, who she said was immaculately conceived through the Holy Ghost, was to have been born on Christmas Day, 1814. She was 64 at the time and claimed to be a virgin but had a hugely distended stomach and breasts bursting with milk. The thirty or so eminent doctors who examined her and confirmed the pregnancy, including the French Empress Josephine's own gynaecologist, were more impressed that any flesh and blood man would *want* to impregnate her, let alone the Holy Ghost. Unperturbed, Joanna wrote to the newspapers saying that if she was lying about her immaculate conception, then the Virgin Mary and Jesus were liars too.

Joanna may not be as well known as some prophets such as Nostradamus, the 15th century French astrologer, but her name strikes a chord with most people, mainly because of her *Sealed Box of Prophecies* which has remained in the jealous custody of her disciples since her death in 1814. It is supposed to contain vital facts about the approaching *Final Millennium*. Her modern disciples claim it has not been opened for 200 years. What keeps this *Box* in the public eye is an advertisement urging the Bishops of the Church of England to open it, which has appeared several times a year in national newspapers such as the *Daily Mail* and the *Daily Telegraph*, since about 1920, although a campaign for it to be officially opened and the contents studied, has been going on since well before Joanna's death.

These advertisements always bear the same chilling, enigmatic message: **"Crime, Banditry, Distress of Nations and Perplexity will continue until the Bishops of the Church of England agree to open Joanna Southcott's Box of Prophecies."**

It is astonishing that this invitation to open it has never been accepted. For how could the Bishops turn down such an opportunity? Even Bishops must have some sense of curiosity. A box that has been sealed up for two centuries has to contain *something* of interest, even if it is only an old postage stamp!

It emerged that Joanna strictly stipulated that her Box was only to be opened in the presence of 24 Bishops of the Church of England and 24 virgins dressed in white, and seven full days and nights had to be devoted to studying the contents. The joke amongst today's clergy is that they would be happy to attend, but the main problem is finding the virgins. Also the whereabouts of the *Box* and who has custody of it has been a kept secret since 1861.

Joanna claimed with pride that she was responsible for the madness of King George III. Because he didn't reply to her letters, she put a curse on him and the rest of the Royal Family. She worked the curse into a complicated patchwork quilt, in the centre of which she embroidered the date of his downfall, 1811, with threads of her own hair. This was the year he was declared insane and the Prince of Wales became Regent and poor mad King George spent the rest of his life in and out of a strait-jacket. The quilt incorporating her awful curse is today on show at the Royal Albert Museum, Exeter, with other of her relics.

When she announced to her 14,000 followers that she was pregnant and the Holy Ghost was the father, over 200,000 people believed her and flocked to London to await the birth. It was a big, long-running news-story at the time - if a holy child was going to be born, every newspaper in London wanted to make sure it had a first-hand account of the event.

"If the dome of St. Paul's had collapsed, or a fourth of the city had been destroyed by an earthquake, the excitement could not have been more intense," reported the *Sunday Monitor*, the paper with the biggest circulation in the country.

One ardent believer, Samuel Jowett described the euphoria of the moment: *"The idea of having one of the Godhead reign over us was so overwhelming that we could not calmly and deliberately consider what was delivered unto us, because of the bright, shining picture of the illustrious era which was present to our view."*

The holy child was to have been born on October 19, 1814, but failed to arrive! After this, Joanna's health rapidly deteriorated, although she was still considered pregnant. She died two months later, on December 27, 1814. Her disciples insisted she had in fact given birth two days earlier, on Christmas Day, to a spiritual child! They maintained that God had decided the world was not ready for a second Messiah and had snatched him back to Heaven - as described in Chapter 12 of the *Book of Revelation*. Before she died Joanna promised she would one day return to earth, with her holy son, to prepare the world for Judgement Day.

After taking what was little more than an idle interest in Joanna, I acquired access to thick batches of contemporary letters and papers relating to her and soon found myself hooked. She seemed so remarkable a woman, I felt I had to get to know her, to find out whether she was a total fraud or a genuine visionary.

Enthusiastically throwing myself into research, for hours I pored over faded handwriting written in the style of the day and very difficult to decipher, until my eyes were sore. Sometimes I forgot what century I was in and a feeling of unreality would often continue for days and at night my dreams became peopled with characters from Joanna's day.

The musty smelling letters often dealt with mundane subjects, which were infinitely more fascinating than the religious communications, claimed by Joanna to be directly from God, which her followers considered of vital importance but in fact were tedious and rambling. At the time, it was customary for hand-written copies to be made of every line she ever wrote, or was written about her, which her disciples then bound into books. Not only did these include large chunks of awful doggerel, but were further explained in dreary prose.

Robert Southey, the English poet, came across Joanna's writings when he was writing a travel book and said they were half a yard high, voluminous and dull. His opinion was that her prophecies were of the sort that popular English almanacs contained - threats concerning the fate of Europe and the successes of the French which were, in fact, the speculations of every newspaper and every politician in the country at that time.

Another of her contemporaries, William Blake, poet, artist and mystic, was also curious about her. He would have been only too happy to accept her divinity, but wanted absolute proof of her powers. His conclusion was that, since she had performed no proven miracles, nor had she accomplished anything superhuman but had merely made a few lucky guesses about bad harvests and people dying suddenly, he found himself "obliged to regard her as an ordinary mortal".

Yet her charisma persistently drew to her people who rated her powers so highly that many would not make a single decision of any importance without first consulting her. Having access to so many letters, personal and otherwise, written and circulated at the time amongst Joanna's believers, I tried to read between the lines to find out what the hold was she had over them. Their letters, notes and diaries revealed so much about them as people that they became as familiar to me as my own family. I also felt guilty for, although spellbound, I couldn't help feeling I shouldn't really be reading their private letters. They were not written for my eyes! I was not one of them! I was trespassing into their past.

I came to imagine I knew intimately not only how Joanna Southcott felt and thought, but how the people who shadowed her life felt and thought and when things went wrong in my own every day existence, I even fancied sometimes that Joanna was the cause.

It was a relief to find a friend I could discuss her with - eminent botanist, the late Dr. Arthur Exell, of Blockley, Gloucestershire, who had done careful research into Joanna's life, published his own book about her and was custodian to a large collection of literature about and by Joanna

Southcott and her followers. In his nineties, he was a mine of information and with more than a hint of humour. When I first visited him he commented wickedly: "It's a good job you caught me before I died."

To her present day believers - and she has an impressive following world-wide - Joanna Southcott is a divine being, equal to the Virgin Mary. To Dr. Exell and me she was just fascinating and extraordinary. We saw her as strong-willed and spirited - a survivor in what was then, for a simple peasant girl, a harsh world.

Even as a child she was determined to make her mark, to use whatever gifts she had, to her own advantage. She became an opportunist as she gradually realised she needed to take advantage of the times and circumstances to boost her growing reputation as a Wise Woman. At first she was content to be merely an issuer of curses, an interpreter of dreams, a white witch. There were dozens in Devon in those days, and still are today.

Dr. Exell recognised her ruthlessness in this respect and we shared the opinion that she succeeded beyond her wildest dreams in becoming a woman of power and influence, a woman respected if not by everyone, at the peak of her fame by over 14,000 people, all signed and sealed. But this was not enough to satisfy her. She wanted to be accepted and recognised by the Church and Royalty and this was to be her downfall for, as she came to believe she was invincible, she also became seriously emotionally unbalanced and eventually her claims were so absurd she ended up a laughing stock, the butt of cruel jokes.

From her own account of her life it seems that, as a child, it was she who held her large family together. Her father was a drunkard, a braggart and a wastrel. Her mother was superstitious, God-fearing and rather set herself above her neighbours. Joanna loved both but recognised their weaknesses and ended up a mixture of the two.

As a young girl, although she displayed a hearty interest in sex and enjoyed leading lads on, nonetheless she wanted to be considered virtuous and pure. This sanctimonious attitude might have had a lot to do with the sort of person she eventually became. She wouldn't admit to ever having had a sexual experience, claiming at 65 that she was a virgin yet having previously outlined in detail her many "love" affairs. How far these love affairs went is difficult to gauge. She was certainly no innocent! And, taking into account the life she led and the temptations constantly confronting her, she would have needed to be a saint to remain a virgin all her life - which, to give her her due, is what she claimed to be. Nevertheless, there were rumours early in her career that she had illegitimate or stillborn babies - with no suggestion that they might have been divinely conceived.

Today the *Panacea Society*, in Bedford, a bizarre sect of religious enthusiasts, believe Joanna was, and still is, divine. They owe their immense wealth to her. In the 1920's believers were persuaded to give all their money and worldly goods to the Society in return for a promise of not only a home, food and spiritual sustenance for the rest of their lives, but an assurance that their earthly bodies would be restored to them after death, on Judgement Day, when Joanna would return from the dead. In the 1920's, this attractive proposition drew thousands of recruits from all over the world and provided enough wealth to create a weird little thriving community in the centre of Bedford.

The *Panacea Society's* invested wealth enables them to place the advertisements which appear several times a year in national newspapers demanding that the Bishops open Joanna Southcott's Box. They believe Joanna to be equal to the Virgin Mary and that the spirit of her son, Shiloh, has been floating about in space for almost 200 years and will soon be manifest in a divinely chosen body, if it has not already done so, in time for the *Final Millennium.*

A 20-room mansion has even been prepared for him in the centre of Bedford, at present unoccupied but each day carefully dusted and cleaned so that, the minute he arrives, he will be able to settle in in a manner befitting a Prince of Peace.

Armed with the *First Book of Wonders*, Joanna's own brief account of her life, I set off to trace Joanna back to her roots in Devon, driving one wet Sunday to Ottery St. Mary from London, intent on finding Taleford Farm where she said she was born. Her actual date of birth is not known for sure, although modern day Southcottians believe it to be April 26, 1750. Records show she was baptised at St. Mary's Church, Ottery St. Mary, on June 6, 1750 and her parents, Hannah Godfrey and William Southcott, were married there on February 6, 1739.

Ottery St. Mary is a quiet, delightful village, built on a hill in a higgledy piggledy fashion, with the church perched on top dominating everything. In the churchyard, I found the name Godfrey, Joanna's mother's maiden name, featured on many of the old headstones, confirming they had once been a prominent established family in the village. It was a pleasant bonus when I got into conversation with a villager who said he had heard that Joanna Southcott used to live at a farm in Gosford Lane, only a mile away.

I found Taleford Farm a little way out of the village, one of its walls fronting Gosford Lane. It was big and gloomy and a notice on the gate stated it was a dairy farm specialising in Friesian cows. Knocking on the farmhouse door, I was startled when it opened ever so slightly, apparently by itself because I waited and nobody came! A slight chill ran down my spine and I had to tell myself not to be so jumpy. There were windows ajar and a radio playing, but no sign of real life, not even a passing car in the lane. It felt spooky and so, uneasy, I turned to go. Then I heard the sound of machinery starting up in the yard behind the house and my curiosity got the better of me. I went to investigate.

In the milking shed a mud-spattered farmhand was busy swilling down a Friesian cow's backside. He explained in a friendly way that all the family were at a wedding and wouldn't be back till very late. Obligingly he gave me the farmer's name and telephone number. Then I asked if he had ever heard of Joanna Southcott. His face darkened and the friendliness vanished as he turned and pretended to take an undue interest in the cow's udders. So I took the hint and left, shouting to him that I had to be back in London that evening, but would he please tell the farmer I would telephone later.

I already knew from Joanna's writings that Taleford Farm had been leased to the Godfrey family for generations, and became the Southcott home after William Southcott got into debt and couldn't pay the rent for his own small holding. The intention was for him to help old Mr. Godfrey run the farm in return for a home. But the old man died and William made such a mess of things that he ran into debt again and the family had to be evicted. As well as Grandmother Godfrey, Hannah and William had four daughters and a son to feed, so things must have looked pretty bleak for them.

They were lucky enough to be given the tenancy of a smallholding in Gittisham, only a few miles from Ottery St. Mary. The family would probably have walked there on the day of the eviction, their possessions piled onto a wagon. In my car I got there in ten minutes and was pleasantly surprised. Gittisham can't have changed much from Joanna's day! I felt I had arrived in a time-warp. In comparison to Ottery St. Mary, it is immaculate. The cottages, barns and other buildings are thatched and a clear stream runs alongside the village, with a stout wooden bridge placed at a convenient point to allow visitors to cross. In 1797 a Rev. Richard Powhele wrote a history of Devon, in which he described Gittisham as "delightfully situated and esteemed the cleanliest in the county - consisting of many trim cottages and the peop!e remarkably neat in their houses and in themselves". A description that could equally apply today.

Visitors to Gittisham are first drawn to the grand Elizabethan manor, Coombe House, which has been converted into an elite hotel. Surrounded by thick beech woods and stunningly beautiful parklands abounding with deer and other game, it is the ancestral home of the Putt family. The fearful Squire Thomas Putt, Lord of the Manor, died when Joanna was seven. He was said to have had a ferocious temper and all the village children would run in excited terror when they saw him approaching, striding across the bridge from Coombe House, brandishing a thick walking stick. They nicknamed him Black Tom.

Black Tom planted beech trees in the park lands and the lane outside the village "so that some fool would not want to cut them down", since beech trees are unsuitable for working with. So he was directly responsible for the dark, spooky lanes around Gittisham, where the branches of beech trees on either side meet, shutting out the light and forming gloomy avenues.

At the Manor he built a "pleasure ground" with terraces and an orangery. Some of the fruit found its way to the village children via Sarah Bridle, a servant at Coombe House for forty years, who died on December 1, 1765, aged 78, when Joanna was 15.

The Coombe estates originally belonged to the Beaumont family and the last of them, Sir Henry and his wife Elizabeth, died childless. In St. Michael's church, a cement covered building dressed in grey flint which dates back to 1244, is a touching memorial to them - two cold alabaster figures lying side by side with a carving of Elizabeth's stillborn baby placed poignantly beside her. The estate passed to the Putt family in 1615.

It was probably because the Putt family adopted the Beaumont tradition of taking a charitable interest in the village, that the Southcott family survived at all. Not only did the Putts give them a roof over their heads but the children received a basic education, personally supervised by the Rev. Mr. William Putt, a poorer member of the family. When times were hard, William Southcott's income was supplemented with grave-digging work.

A wander around an old church-yard can yield a wealth of information about the people who once lived in the vicinity. Judging from the gravestones at St. Michael's church, Gittisham, it seemed that in this tranquil place folks survived to a ripe old age. One inscription on a weathered old stone revealed that in May 1757, when Joanna was seven,

Edward Skinner died aged 100. His neighbour, Elizabeth Gosleigh, died six years later aged 103.

The church was central to village life and the Southcott family would have attended services each Sunday. Feeling an odd rapport with the long-dead Southcotts, I sat on one of the hard wooden benches at the back of the church - as they would have done - to read the church literature. It explained that the patron saint, Michael, was one of the seven Archangels mentioned in the *Book of Daniel. The Book of Revelation* describes St. Michael and the Angels fighting the dragon (the Devil) and casting him out of heaven. Often St. Michael is portrayed with a sword standing over, or fighting with, a dragon, the symbol of evil. Such stories may have given the young Joanna grand ideas of her own.

Searching the village for the house where the Southcott family settled I finally located it, exactly as described by Joanna in her book. Just outside the village, in a lane with a stream running alongside it, was the little farmhouse with its thatched roof, a dairy and a cowshed, protected from the lane by a wall of heaped up earth topped with a thick hedge. Now called Winsor Cottage, in Joanna's day it was just the Southcott farm.

The retired couple who lived there had only heard rumours about Joanna Southcott and knew little about her. The thought that her ghost might still be in residence delighted them. They showed me the old dairy, where Joanna and her sisters used to churn butter, which was now a smart laundry room. The cowshed was a garage. The upstairs bedroom was where Joanna's mother, Hannah, had died after telling her she had been singled out at birth by God for a divine purpose.

Devonshire folk are notoriously superstitious and even today there is an air of the supernatural in the narrow, damp lanes surrounding the village. Even from the security of my car I could sense it as I drove around that dark afternoon. The ground was covered with a carpet of moss and rotting leaves - the sort of eerie setting in which such beliefs easily ferment. Broad beams of light penetrated canopies of entwined branches overhead, creating theatrical patches perfect for supernatural beings to put in fleeting appearances and yet make you think it is a trick of the light. If such creatures exist at all, then these dark lanes would be a natural place for them to lurk.

An example of local superstition is a pagan sacred stone, known as the Rolling Stone, almost six feet long and over five feet wide and weighing about a ton, situated at Putt's Corner on Gittisham Hill. Its original purpose has long been forgotten but tantalising tales are still told about it. In pagan times, beautiful maidens and innocent children were said to have been tied to the stone and sacrificed. The stone probably once stood erect and it was said that at midnight, when the moon was full, it rolled down to the River Sid, where the waters washed away the blood stains remaining from human sacrifices. At the same time, at Ottery St. Mary, an armed statue in the parish church would slip from its pedestal and walk up and down the aisles to protect it from the evil spirits roaming abroad.

In Joanna's day, any remotely strange incident in the village was interpreted as an indication of doom. Dreams were analysed and discussed and deep significances read into them. Joanna's Grandmother Godfrey appears to have built up a fine reputation as a wise woman. Locals used to come to her for advice about how to ward off evil spirits and for interpretations of their dreams. Joanna would have learned a lot from her.

Before returning to London, my final call was Exeter, where Joanna spent a large part of her adult life and where her reputation was first established. Even today workmen, knocking down the walls of old houses, sometimes come across one of the thousands of lucky seals she issued to her followers, who regarded them as passports to heaven and a guarantee of earthly protection. The fact that they were concealed within walls as a protection from evil, is an indication of how highly prized they were. Although she insisted she never charged a penny for these seals, they often changed hands for up to a guinea a time. The English poet, Lord Byron, once remarked wittily to John Murray, his friend and publisher: "I would like to buy one of her seals. If salvation can be had for half a guinea, the landlord of the Crown & Anchor should be ashamed of charging double for a mere terrestrial feast."

I made a special point of visiting St. Peter's Cathedral, in the heart of the city, where Joanna said she always felt at home and would often sit on one of the hard wooden benches for hours. A plaque on the Cathedral wall commemorates the death of the unfortunate Bishop William Buller, who died in 1796 and is buried in the Cathedral. He was unwise enough to upset Joanna by not replying to her letters, so she put a curse on him. Although considered healthy, he died within a year aged 61. But he was in good company! Curses were also put on the Prime Minister, William Pitt, and his successor, Charles James Fox, who both died within months of each other in 1806.

I returned to London that evening feeling elated with the progress I had made. Although it was late, I couldn't resist telephoning the tenant farmer at Taleford Farm, just to round the day off. He was very courteous and didn't seem to mind the lateness of the hour, but politely said he preferred not to talk about Joanna Southcott because every time her name was mentioned, something sinister seemed to happen. Despite being frustratingly intrigued, I agreed to let the matter drop but gave him my phone number in case he changed his mind. Within an hour, he rang to say he had talked it over briefly with his family and they had agreed it would be better if "everything" was brought out into the open. He promised faithfully he would make a list of the inexplicable incidents which the family blamed on Joanna, and let me have it as soon as he could.

Six weeks went by without a word. I became impatient and eventually rang him. He was very apologetic, explaining that he had had every intention of making out the list for me, but for one unnerving incident. It was his custom to get up at about 4am to milk the cows and the morning after he spoke to me his best cow, healthy and young, suddenly dropped dead for no apparent reason. The vet who examined her could find nothing wrong. The farmer insisted he knew it had nothing to do with Joanna Southcott and that it was all in the mind. But for some reason the incident had put him off any desire to rake up the past. However, since he had promised me, he would write out the list as soon as he had a moment.

The next morning, at 8am, he rang again. He assured me he still felt that Joanna Southcott had no power whatsoever to reach out from the grave and create evil but he thought I would like to know that when he went into the field that morning, another healthy young cow had dropped dead right in front of him. It was just coincidence, of course, but he thought I might be amused. It wouldn't make any difference to his promise to me. He was a man of his word! He would still make out the list.

I didn't hear from him for a month and when I eventually rang, he again apologised for not contacting me. He said he had been so busy he just hadn't found the time to write anything down, so instead he was happy to tell me of a few of the strange incidents now, over the phone. He went on to explain how the family had taken over the farm before World War II. Inexplicable incidents included some uncles getting killed, and tractors starting up by themselves. He talked for an hour, while I made notes, and then excused himself, saying he had to be up at 4am. Early next day he was on the phone again, shocked but calm. He explained how he had gone out to the field that morning and the same unbelievable thing had happened - his best cow dropped dead in front of him! As was the case with the other animals, the vet could find nothing wrong with it. The farmer still felt it was ridiculous to think that it had anything to do with Joanna Southcott but, apart from the fact that he couldn't afford to lose any more cows, his daughter was pregnant and he was not prepared to risk providence. So he had decided to go back to the family's policy of not talking about "that woman". I felt extraordinarily responsible for the loss of his cows. I didn't contact him again - I didn't want to risk anything happening to his expected grandchild, no matter how remote the possibility. But it made me even more determined to find out more about Joanna Southcott.

A week later I moved house. My briefcase, stuffed with research notes about Joanna, mysteriously found its way into a packing case marked for OXFAM. An over-eager helper found the box and delivered it without checking the contents. The moment I realised what must have happened I rushed to the OXFAM shop to find they had already unpacked the box and, as is their policy, thrown the contents of the briefcase into the dustbin. Had Joanna somehow deliberately engineered the disposal of my notes, I found myself wondering. If she had, I smartly thwarted her by delving into the bags of rubbish, salvaging most of the papers, telling myself I was not prepared to be beaten by a long-dead witch.

Then, after I had almost completed the manuscript, I went away for a much needed holiday in Italy. The finishing touches were to be done the week I got back. Within an hour of my husband and I getting into our hire car at Brindisi, we had a terrible head-on crash and I ended up with a couple of crushed vertebrae. As I lay in agony flat on my back in the intensive care unit of a tiny hospital in Southern Italy, I wondered ruefully if Joanna had had a hand in our accident. It was five weeks before I could summon the strength to continue working on the manuscript and during this time I was very tempted to abandon it.

But I had by now formed a reluctant admiration for her. I felt I could understand the young Joanna's desire for that intangible something Shelley described as "the desire of the moth for the star, of the day for the morrow, the longing for something afar from the sphere of our sorrow". She didn't *want* to be corrupt but, at the time, circumstances demanded it. Afraid she might "rust unburnished" rather than "shine in use", like Tennyson's Ulysses, instinct told her she had something splendid within her and she longed to bring it out, to gleam! Her desire to make her mark in life was so strong that rather than end up a nobody, it seems she inadvertently sold her soul to the Devil. She would much rather have given it to Jesus!

She lived in constant fear that it was the Devil controlling her and not God. It was only towards the end of her life that she reluctantly faced the fact that it really was "all a delusion" and, as her enemies had been telling her for years, she had all along been under an evil influence. She claimed she once met Satan face to face and had a physical battle with him; that he looked like a pig and when she bit him, his flesh tasted sweet. He told her that her body was inhabited by one of his evil spirits who had loved her from childhood but found the only way to possess her was to pose as a divine being. Satan explained he was lively and cheerful, full of mirth and gaiety, which God couldn't tolerate. Whereas he wanted all men to lead an agreeable life, God wanted everyone to be self-denying and penitent, which was against man's natural inclination. Satan's personal opinion of her was that she was an infamous bitch who had a "damned eternal tongue which runneth so fast, all the devils in Hell cannot keep up with thee!"

Having decided that Joanna started off good and ended up devious and wicked, I contacted some of her present-day believers - not the cranky members of the *Panacea Society* in Bedford but sincere Christians. Their lives revolve round this unfathomable woman who has been dead for nearly two centuries, and they say they believe in her divinity without question. They speak about her with the same devout reverence normally reserved for the Virgin Mary. I found their very ordinariness baffling. They were kindly concerned that I should be given as much help as possible and supplied me with photocopies of letters, extracts from her writings, information about her mysterious *Box*. Consequently, I felt like a hypocrite! I would have dearly loved to have repaid their kindness by portraying Joanna in a more sympathetic light.

To discover that Joanna's character was not cut and dried, but a disturbing enigma, was disconcerting. What I have finally written about her will hurt and distress her modern followers, but I doubt that they will bear a grudge. On the contrary, they will conclude that, if it is unsympathetic, it is all part of God's divine plan to draw the world's attention to her.

Taleford Farm, Gosford Lane, Ottery St. Mary,
where Joanna was born on April 26, 1750

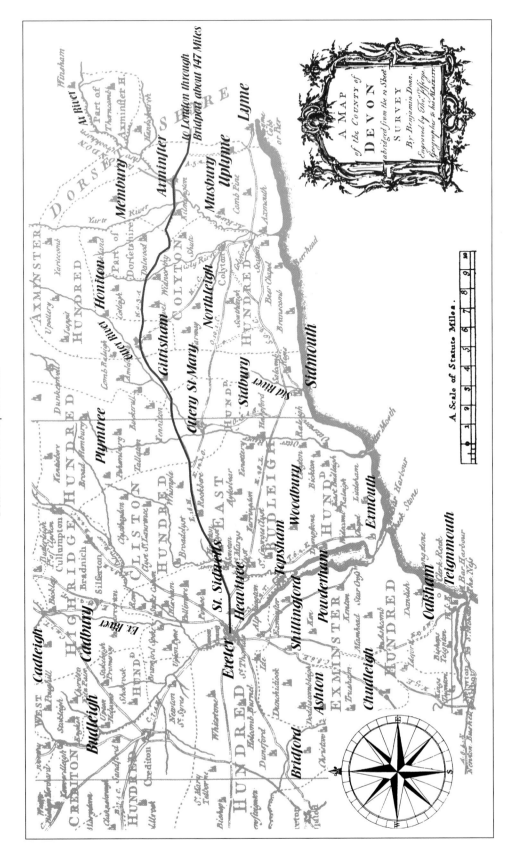

Detail from 1765 Map of Devon

Joanna Southcott
wearing a mob cap

Mezzotint (c.1800 artist unknown). Joanna's excuse for having her portrait painted was that so many unsavoury characters impersonated her, it was necessary for her picture to be distributed - at a price - throughout the country in order that everyone should know what she looked like. William Sharp's portrait of her (see front cover) sold at a guinea a time.

Chapter One

Girlhood in Gittisham

Joanna boasted that when she was born, on April 26, 1750, the angels in heaven rejoiced at her birth. She probably got this notion from *Moore's Almanac*, being an avid reader of back numbers in later life. The front cover of the 1750 edition has an illustration of a group of angels celebrating. She said that, at the same time, God sent a dazzling star to brighten up the sky in her honour. A minor comet did in fact show up that year, which caused some excitement. One of her followers remarked admiringly sixty years later that it was similar to "the one which denoted the birthplace of Christ".

Her father, William Southcott, born in 1717, was the second son of John Southcott, who was drowned at sea. Joanna loved to tell of the Southcott family's exciting history of lost inheritances and that, had not her grandfather been cut off without a penny because of a family feud, William would have been one of the landed gentry and Joanna an educated gentlewoman.

Her mother, Hannah Godfrey, was William's second wife. His first died in childbirth and her child, also William, was reared by Hannah. Joanna had three sisters and two younger brothers, John, born 1752, and Joseph, born 1755.

The key to Joanna's character probably lay in her early desperate desire to be good confounded by her longing to be famous. A misguided pride instilled in her in childhood by her mother, led her to believe she deserved better things in life than a girl in her position could normally expect. She wanted to be respected by educated and established people. Although basically well-intentioned, in the end there was no contest in the conflict between good and bad, and the Devil became her master earlier than Joanna could ever bring herself to admit.

In many ways, the Southcotts were a problem family. Their father, William, was irresponsible, emotional and, when he had too much to drink, explosive. He would erupt into foul rages for no good reason. When his children complained about him, their mother defended her husband by pointing out that, although life was a struggle, at least their father would never dream of sending them to work as apprentices for slave wages, a common practice then amongst poor families.

Hannah somehow managed to keep them all well-fed and decently clothed. She encouraged them to regard themselves as a cut above the rest and they were often told how Fate had been cruel to them, depriving their father of not one, or even two, but three fortunes. There were bizarre stories of how fortunes were lost in amazing circumstances utterly beyond William's, or his father's, control. But then, Hannah was a great storyteller. She treasured a book of hymns and verses, which she said had been written by a Great Aunt Sarah Southcott, who had been forbidden to marry a young suitor because he was not good enough for her. So, instead, she became a religious recluse, devoting her life to prayer and writing heavenly poetry until her death at the early age of 30. This story captured the imagination of the young Joanna and she proceeded to model herself on the saintly aunt. The treasured verses Joanna said were written by Sarah, are of a commendable standard.

> "Suppose my youth, in wit and beauty bloom,
> Should promise many a flattering year to come?
> What if I'm decked in Royal shirts,
> A darling Queen, by King I sit?
> What would it all avail?
> Why should my passions mix with earth,
> And thus debase my heavenly birth?
> Why should I cleave to things below,
> And let my God and Saviour go?"

Verses such as these inspired the young Joanna with the idea that she too would dedicate herself to Jesus and reject all earthly things, as Sarah had.

> "From earth's dull pleasures and senseless mirth,
> Come thou, my soul, in haste retire.
> Assume the grandeur of thy birth.
> And to thy native heaven aspire.
> 'Tis heaven alone can make thee blest,
> Can every wish and want supply.
> My endless comforts ever blest,
> Are all above the sky."

Hannah's main object in telling these stories was to instil a sense of family pride in her girls. Her own family history was dull. She came from a solid Devonshire farming family who had lived at Taleford Farm, Ottery St. Mary, for generations. William Southcott managed to destroy that solid background the Godfrey family had taken years to build up, in only a few months. When old Mr. Godfrey died and William took over, his fanciful management of the farm resulted in careless debts and there was soon a backlog of rent owing and no funds. It must have been a very sad day when the family were evicted, yet moving to Gittisham was to be their salvation. The Rev. William Putt, the conscientious rector of St. Michael's Church in Gittisham, recognised how difficult William was and decided to give the family the full protection of the parish.

So Joanna was born into this volatile family, full of false pride and piety and depending very much on the charity of the parish for survival. She inherited from her father his inconsistency, which she struggled to repress, pretending to herself that she was really sweet-tempered and tolerant. Her father found this aggravating. He once told her sarcastically: "No man but the Devil can fall out with you."

A thatcher called James Speerway, working on the roof of the Southcott home, one day heard William shouting angrily at Joanna and, recalling the remark, suggested that, by doing so, William had therefore made a devil of himself.

William was always sorry after his outbursts. Joanna said that "after a passion he would do anything to make amends". At a whim, he could change from an angry mood to tears of recrimination, particularly when the worse for drink. One morning, after drinking too much the night before, he woke up raving like a madman having remembered that he had upset Joanna earlier. He went to her room, full of maudlin remorse. Joanna said her father's face was like a pot when you take off a cover, covered in great drops of sweat. But she acted the dutiful daughter: "I took him and wiped off the sweat and sat hours by his bedside to comfort and compose him to sleep."

Another incident which made a lasting impression upon her, she described in detail many years later. After the whole family had worked all day making cider, Joanna stayed up doing her chores. William, who was in bed, called down to her to go to the orchard where the pound-house was, to check if the cider was running over. The shed, because it was sweetly pungent with rotting fruit, and therefore an attraction to flies and wasps, was "more than two fields from the house we lived in, or along the lane the other way round". The moon was hidden by heavy clouds when she set off and Joanna, who associated night with the Devil, found it a terrifying trek in the pitch dark across two fields to the cider shed.

She carried a small lantern with one candle inside, which cast shadows all round. The trees seemed to take on satanic shapes and the slightest noise she imagined was an evil spirit pursuing her. When she reached the shed she heard some apples drop with a thud onto the earth floor inside, which scared her. As she pushed open the door, an owl hooted and, at the same time, the moon appeared from behind the clouds, lighting up the building with a ghostly light which made her drop the lantern, causing the candle inside to go out.

Grandmother Godfrey once told her that the Devil lived in the Moon and the terrifying thought hit her that he had opened up his windows to spy on her. Leaving the door open, she turned tail and fled, not across the fields, but the long way back down the dark lane leading to the Southcott farm. The lane was flooded because the stream running alongside it had risen and overflowed its banks. "I thought I heard the footsteps of a spirit after me," she wrote. "For more than twenty yards, I ran through a river as the waters were then high." When she got to the house, she ran "as fast as I could, without bolting the door or locking the garden gate."

Her father heard her sobbing and called: "My love, what is the matter?" In her own account of her childhood, Joanna wrote that she reflected grimly that he might well say "my love" when he was responsible for the dreadful fright she had had. Nonetheless, she welcomed his concern and when he came down, gasped out the story of the evil spirit she thought had followed her, and he "pitied my weakness and did not blame me, but assured me I had seen no spirit and it was nothing but the moon that was hid in a cloud, that shined against the jambs."

Strange noises were often heard in the cider shed at night. Some said it was haunted, but others insisted that the wily William was making a bit of extra money on the side by allowing smugglers to use it. Squire Putt called him up to the Manor to explain. William maintained indignantly that the scuffling sounds were the noise of some rabbits his son Joseph kept there. The Squire chose to believe him and the matter was dropped.

If William was a charming braggart, Hannah, in her children's eyes at least, was a saint and the mainstay of the household. The youngest, Joseph, once described her fondly: "To all those who were in the habit of friendship with my Mother, it is well known that she lived and died in the fear of God with the hope of a glorious resurrection through the merits of our Blessed Saviour."

On her deathbed Hannah told Joanna that when she gave birth to her, God told her her child had been chosen for a divine purpose which would be revealed to her in later life. Joanna adored her mother and always referred to her with great tenderness. It was Hannah who, she said, had taught her to "genuinely love Christ and fear the Devil". She was warmly religious as well as being light-hearted and entertaining, at the same time displaying her curious sense of superiority over her neighbours, having convinced herself of the truth of her husband's lost inheritances.

If she was a bit haughty, she was not above joining in the local gossip and loved chewing over village hearsay. The real witch of the family, Grandmother Godfrey, was adept at issuing curses, interpreting dreams and mixing up potions. Any odd incident that occurred in the village was regarded as an indication of doom and Grandmother Godfrey was asked to explain it. Dreams were analysed and discussed and deep significances read into them.

"One day," wrote Joanna, "a maid came to my grandmother weeping. She had dreamt she had come across a cat sitting on a gate and the cat scratched her on the right breast and drew blood." The girl was later found raped and murdered "at the very same place she had dreamt the cat had met her".

Another young girl dreamt she was stung to death by a serpent while walking on Sidbury Hill. Joanna's grandmother, concerned at the fate of the previous girl, warned her not to wander. The advice was ignored and she was found murdered at the spot she dreamt she saw the serpent, and was "judged, like the former, to be ravished and murdered". Old Mrs. Godfrey was upset when yet another young villager, Molly Gardiner, also refused to listen. To impress upon Molly the wisdom of her words, she made up a rhyme for her:

> "Dreams are not fables, Moll,
> Though some wonders they do tell.
> For 'tis in dreams the Lord doth warn,
> A way that men do not discern."

Grandmother Godfrey sometimes gave young girls a piece of paper to tuck into their bosom to protect them against evil spirits. Messages were scribbled on them such as: "This is a sign against evil demons" or "This is a sign against putrid infection and sudden death". Later Joanna imitated her grandmother by supplying her believers with pieces of paper signed by her, on which an obscure message was written. Her followers came to regard them as passports to heaven and a protection from evil.

The Rev. William Putt considered it his duty to drum into the ears of the children of the village, the sombre message that Satan was always on the alert, ready to tempt them to commit sin. Joanna's dread of the Devil stemmed from this and from the stories that abounded in the village. Satan, spirits, witchcraft, sorcery and superstition all seemed to merge into one until to the young Joanna they became virtually indistinguishable.

When she was fourteen, Joanna was asked one night to sit with a dying neighbour called Mr. Follard. He had apparently become ill after telling Mr. Putt he didn't believe in God. His wife had exhausted herself looking after him and needed some relief. Joanna described the experience.

"At midnight, the room shook as though by thunder, and the dying man rose in his bed and spoke with a voice most dreadful, saying that there was a great black dog in the window." When Joanna went to calm him, the man became angry and insisted he was in his right mind but could still clearly see the Devil in the shape of a black dog. He began to tremble and Joanna said the bed shook under him. This continued for an hour before the room became silent and she realised the man was dead.

Any normal 14-year-old girl would surely have rushed from the room as soon as the dying man began to rave, but Joanna said she remained alone with him for another hour while the bed continued to shake "in a most unnatural manner". She wrote that the incident gave her the fright of her life and Satan became terrifyingly real to her and, as a result, she never ever again underestimated his powers. Only towards the end of her life did it occur to her that Satan might have been using her and that this incident could have been the very moment when he took over her body, assuming the character of a good spirit.

She later recalled, in her *First Book of Wonders,* how she once came face to face with the Devil and he told her that Mr. Follard had lusted after her for years and when he died his evil spirit was allowed by the Devil to return to possess her body.

Joanna learned to read and write at the church school, attached to St. Michael's church. She was not only an avid reader, but a compulsive scribbler too - although her writing was crude and almost illegible - and risked the money she had saved up for her old age to publish her vivid accounts of her childhood in Gittisham, making herself out to be as pure as the driven snow, a child so unbelievably good and bright, everyone adored her. According to Joanna, as a child there was not a spark of malice in her and she would have been prepared to martyr herself for the sake of others, particularly her wayward father who was constantly drunk and prone to flying into rages which upset the family. His saving grace was his natural charm and winning personality.

Gittisham   Julian Roebuck '75

St. Michael's Church, Gittisham, Devon, where Joanna was taught to read and write at the school attached to the church.

When bad luck hounded the Southcotts, it was blamed on evil spirits. One autumn, the apple crop was ridden with maggots. Another year sheep-rot attacked their flock of sheep, many of which died. But William on the whole was an optimist, believing that one day fortune would smile on him. To keep on the right side of God, he listened to the Rev. Putt's sermons with "awe and admiration" and sent his children to him to be taught "reading, writing, arithmetic, navigation and catechisms".

William made his children read one chapter of the Bible each day and then tell him what they had learned. He was exasperated when Joanna asked questions he was unable to answer. He would lose his temper and she would end up in tears.

The Rev. Putt was a strong influence on Joanna's life and it was he she had to thank for teaching her to know the Bible so well that, in later years, she always had an appropriate Biblical quotation to call to mind to illustrate a point. She probably had the rare gift of total recall. Learning chunks of the Bible was easy for her and she said she regarded it, not as a chore, but a pleasant pastime.

Playing at being good was a game she never grew out of. She wrote proudly of herself: "The fear of God was placed in me from a child. I not only feared sin, but hated it and found no pleasure in anything but the service of the Lord. My character will bear the strictest scrutiny and many said I had not my like amongst women, as my temper was mild and heavenly and my principles honest and upright in all things." She added that reading from the Gospel of Christ and of the persecutions He went through, made her love Him and fear to offend Him. "I felt my heart burn with indignation against His accusers and when I cried, I cried for Christ."

Glowing with all this piety and Great Aunt Sarah's shining example to model herself on, she decided to devote her life to God. Years later a critic remarked that, considering she had spent so much of her childhood reading the Bible, and therefore had a good beginning, he was filled with surprise and pity at her "present state of religious pursuits, since religious frenzy took possession of her".

He quoted from chapter 5 of St. Paul's address to the Galatians: "Ye did run well. Who did hinder ye, that ye should not obey the truth?" The answer, of course, was the Devil!

A fault she *was* prepared to admit to was of having a "resenting spirit". All her life she could never forget a slight and ruthlessly persecuted anyone who crossed her and as a result ruined many people's lives. She also admitted to being vain, more so than the average girl. "I delighted in vanity and dress, more than I saw in others, and was often reproved by my mother." Hannah would recite to her an exemplary verse written by the legendary Great Aunt Sarah.

> "Will thou take then the first morning water,
> To trim and make thee fine?
> 'Twill be but bitterness at last,
> If Christ be none of thine.
> How frail is beauty, in how short a time,
> 'Twill fade like roses which are past their prime.
> So wrinkled age, the fairest face will plough
> And cast deep furrows on the smoothest brow,
> Where's now the lovely, tempting face? Alas,
> Yourself will blush to view it in the glass.
> Unless adorned with beauty in the mind,
> And then an interest in the Saviour find."

She said her mother's reprimand had only a temporary effect and she was soon back to preening herself in front of the mirror. "So deeply was my heart fixed upon the vanity of dress, that I didn't care how hard I worked, early and late, so long as I could earn money to get clothes to appear smart in."

William was upset and told his daughter he was "ashamed to see me, for a farmer's daughter, to dress as I did. But it had no effect upon me. My heart was set upon it. And when I reflect upon my youthful days, I see how flattery hurts the mind. My heart was set on serious meditations and I felt great comfort and pleasure in learning hymns and repeating them to myself. But when I came to the age of fifteen and sixteen and began to be flattered by the world, I found vanity wise and I became vain."

It was when she reached fifteen that Little Miss Perfect discovered, to her delight, that she was pretty. She found it fun to dress provocatively and tease the boys. A great transformation took place. She lost interest in the Bible and learning hymns and instead sex became a fascination to her. There were lurid tales being told amongst her friends, that caught her youthful imagination and stirred her blood. One was about a Lord Burnet. While he was out hunting his wife was found in bed with Musgraves, his page, and an excited servant sent a message to Burnet telling him of his wife's infidelity. Lord Burnet returned home in a rage, threw open the door to find the couple still in bed.

> "Well, how dost thou like my bed, he cry'd
> And how dost thou like my sheets?
> And dost thou like my wedded lady
> That lies in thy arms, asleep?"

To which Musgraves merrily replied:

> "Oh, well I like thy bed, he cry'd
> And well I like thy sheets.
> But better I like thy wedded lady,
> That lieth in my arms asleep.
> So he killed the Lady and Musgrave
> So merrily sings the bonny thrush.
> So sadly sings the sparrow,
> So merrily sung Lord Burnet himself,
> For he shall be hanged tomorrow."

Not the sort of tale one would expect an aspiring saint to relate! But if the sexual element excited Joanna, cheap romance thrilled her just as much. Another of her favourite stories was about a knight who was told by his King that his bride would be "an infant born of mean parents". The knight could not bear to think his future bride would be a commoner and so he found out who she was and then tried to kill her. Eventually he accepted that the marriage was ordained by God and he married her "with raptures of joy and love".

> "To see a helpless child,
> Born of such parents that were mean,
> A knight's heart to beguile:
> Ladies of fame I thought to claim
> In title great with me:
> Therefore the heavens I judg'd unkind,
> To shew such destiny.
> As did appear to me then clear,
> To let myself down low;
> But by the wonders that are here,
> No knight so high can go."

The young Joanna hoped she too would find a high-born lover who would overlook the shortcomings of her family. She never did find him, and eventually in desperation invented a romance with the highest-born lover of all - God Himself!

Joanna's flightiness caused her father, William, so much concern, he decided to send her to keep house for her brother William at his farm in Sidmouth. Here she met the man she later boasted was the great romance of her life, Noah Bishop. In fact, it was a sordid, petty affair and Joanna behaved shamefully towards him, mercilessly teasing him while hiding behind a veil of piety. Noah was a pleasant young man with prospects of one day inheriting his father's farm and so was considered a good catch. Joanna set out to win him, but her soul was already tainted and she was unable to carry on a normal romance, although wildly in love. "I had many lovers," she commented immodestly, "but the first I indulged in the company of was Noah Bishop."

She said she admired the nobleness of his spirit and was "convinced his passion was love". Noah was a practical, simple soul, ill-equipped to deal with her mercurial shifts of mood. From a promising beginning, the courtship became complicated and stormy with Joanna behaving like a spoilt child and the very nice Noah ending up heartbroken. If, instead, he had fallen in love with pretty little Fanny Wickers, daughter of Captain Wickers of Sidmouth, he would have been more fortunate, for Fanny said she loved him every bit as much as Joanna and was not ashamed to admit it. Joanna was jealous of her. She said Fanny was forward and threw herself at Noah in a most unbecoming manner.

"Fanny Wickers was mad about Noah," she wrote petulantly. "She followed him wherever he went. One Sunday she followed him onto the beach and he stood talking to her. A friend told me about it, which fired my soul with jealousy."

She waited sulkily for Noah to call round, rehearsing to herself exactly how she would deal with him in such a way he would never dare look at another woman. She intended to be dignified and cool, but in the end behaved childishly.

"When I saw him enter the yard, I went upstairs and bade my sister to tell him that, where he had been, he might go again. He declared he detested Fanny and thought her a bad, loose girl but, as she followed him, he had to speak. This excuse did not do for me. I said I would not come down. Neither did I!"

Of course, she expected him to be round again next day, while she was doing the milking, but he didn't come. Angrily, she went home to Gittisham, with the intention of teaching him a lesson. But after a few days, finding she missed him, she returned to Sidmouth. He came to see her and refused to go until "he had convinced me that I was the only woman he loved". After he kissed her, she said she "gave up her jealousy".

But Joanna still wasn't happy. Things were going too smoothly for her liking. She had an unattractive vision of herself as a dull farmer's wife and, after a couple of months, began to question whether she was doing the right thing. Some perverse urge prompted her to upset her own applecart and, without any good reason, she accused Noah of going with another woman.

They had a flaming row and, according to Joanna, Noah "flew into a violent passion that astonished me". Joanna untruthfully maintained that some of her friends "were witness to his infidelity". He said he wished their tongues were in Hell burning and told her angrily she shouldn't listen to gossip from people out to cause trouble between them. Joanna refused to be pacified. "You might wish my tongue was in Hell, too, if I were your wife," she screamed at him.

Noah quietened down and said it was not love that provoked him, but anger with those that set her against him. However, having got the row going nicely, Joanna was not prepared to let him down lightly.

"I would not listen to him. I had seen his rage and so broke off the acquaintance, though I confess I had equal love for him. But thought - better once smart than always ache. Time and prudence would wear off love by keeping my thoughts for my Creator."

But that was not the end of the matter. She said friends "dinned into my ears that he was ill and determined to go to sea for he could not bear to see me the wife of another. This opened every wound of my heart afresh and kindled love stronger than ever." So she made up her mind to get him back at the Sidmouth Fair, which she knew Noah wouldn't miss for anything, not even a broken heart.

Confident of her charms, she set off, refusing invitations from friends to join them with the excuse that she was only there to look for her brother, who she eventually found in the company of Noah, who seemed pleased to see her and hopefully invited her to walk with them. Such a conquest was too easy to satisfy the haughty Joanna, yet even she couldn't understand why she behaved so icily.

"My hand and heart seemed bolted together and I asked my brother to go for the horse so that we could go home directly."

While her brother fetched the horse from the yard, Noah begged Joanna to at least have a drink with him at the pub, for old acquaintance if not for new.

"I told him I would not go either for old or for new, if he made as many words as there were stars in the sky or stones in the street."

His face registered such pain at her rejection, she professed to being cut to the core. But, like a cat with a mouse, she *still* wasn't prepared to let him go. The following Sunday he called at the farm with a friend called Richard Isaacs, and said her brother had given them permission to pick some pears. Joanna told them haughtily that it was all right for Richard to, but not Noah.

There had to be *some* sort of devil in her to make her behave so perversely. Even she thought so. "I said to myself, what a stubborn creature I was to plague myself, and to plague him."

Joanna fancied the intrigue was making her ill. A friend tried to mend the tiff by urging Noah to approach her once more, pointing out to him that she was very unhappy and still in love with him.

But by now Noah had had enough. "I have tried and it is always the same. If I die for her sake, I will try no more." He began courting a girl called Anne, and later married her. Joanna pretended not to mind and, to save face, boasted it was *she* who arranged the match.

> "While I his heart had surely got,
> His Anne I then did see.
> And told him then, his wife was come,
> The woman he should have.
> But mark how he did her despise.
> And said he'd never give,
> His hand to she, 'twas known to me
> But yet it so did burn,
> That afterwards his love was thus,
> The same for her did burn."

Even after this she said she wanted him back. "I wished to awaken his passion again, for I would die rather than live without him."

She threw herself into the role of the rejected maiden and, when her sisters begged her to return to Gittisham, replied soulfully, "No. You may kill me or you may drown me, but I will not leave this place where he is. I must see him, even if I cannot have him."

Joanna went to the Newton Fair, despite an injury to her eye, hoping to bump into him. She set off with her sisters, her eye streaming painfully and, when she spotted Noah, went wild with delight shouting "There he is! There he is!"

Her sisters laughed, especially when Noah totally ignored her. Cross and humiliated, she insisted on them all returning home immediately.

On their way they met his brother Nathaniel who, noticing Joanna's red eye from her injury and thinking it was caused by weeping, suggested Noah could cure it.

Joanna said bitterly: "If he can, he won't!" Her sisters were shocked, pointing out she had now made it clear to Nathaniel that she was still in love with Noah, even though he was married to someone else. She replied that she did not care, for she "wished to awaken his passion".

When William heard of the state she was in and the way she was behaving, he exploded. His daughter, Susanna, said he walked round the room raving like a madman: "My former sins are brought to my remembrance. How many women's hearts have I broken by love?   It is come home to me. For that maid, who is the delight of my soul, is now wounded the same." He said he rued the day he had courted any woman who loved him and he had not been true to.

She stayed in Sidmouth for some months, in the hope of seeing Noah but, finding he kept away from her, took a job as a servant. She never forgot him, or ever admitted it was *he* who eventually rejected *her*.

As an old woman, she convinced herself that the reason she had behaved so disgracefully was because God had singled her out for a special mission and told her it was vitally important that she remained unmarried until He decided otherwise.

She wrote that God explained to her that, at the time, she was unknowingly under the influence of the Devil. "The Devil had been working upon thee to make thee miserable and, for wise ends, I permitted it to shame and confuse him." The suggestion was that God appreciated how much she and Noah loved each other but He deliberately made her reject him because she was destined for greater things.

Joanna never really understood herself why she had been so mean to Noah. In lonely old age, when he was still married to Anne and with several fine sons, she must have often reflected upon what she gave up through her own foolishness. She yearned to invent a happy ending to what she considered was the great romance of her life, when she was young and uncorrupted and so, in her deluded state, persuaded herself that God had chosen a man for her to marry who looked exactly like Noah as a young man.

God apparently promised her: "If thou obeyest My commands in every direction I have given thee, the heart I took from thee in thy youthful days I will return to thee."

The best part of this promise was that she would be miraculously transformed from a fat, unattractive old woman into the beautiful girl she had been at eighteen.

It was becoming apparent that nothing was beyond the bounds of Joanna's versatile imagination. As she progressed through to periods of severe depression bordering on madness, her claims became more and more bizarre.

Chapter Two

Gaining Confidence

So Joanna went home to Gittisham! The good person she had resolved to become only a short while ago, was fast fading. She was dissatisfied and restless, but couldn't quite pinpoint what was wrong. Since home was not the best place to find out, she took a job in nearby Honiton, as a servant/shop assistant with the Brown family who were very fond of her, she said, and treated her like their own daughter.

Here a young man called John Thomas asked her to marry him. He was very well off, with fifty pounds a year coming in from two legacies. When Joanna pointed out that her father couldn't afford to give her a dowry, he apparently replied: "I would rather have you without a farthing than any other woman with five hundred pounds." Nonetheless, she turned him down.

In 1768, when she was still only 18, her mother was taken ill and Joanna went home to help nurse her. The night before she died, Joanna said she heard a gurgling in her mother's throat and asked what it was.

"My dear child," said Hannah. "Can't you hear the rattle is upon me?" Amazingly, even on the point of death, it seems she found the strength to sing this little verse to comfort her daughter:

> "Jesus can make a dying bed,
> As sweet as downy pillows are,
> While on His breast, I lay my head,
> And breathe my life out sweetly there."

"I was death-struck myself, to think I should lose a good parent," Joanna wrote. "I called my sister Susanna and we both sat by her side till morning when, thinking our mother was better, we returned to our dairy work and left a neighbour to sit by her, not supposing her end was so near."

Their neighbour, Mrs. Venn, sat with her until eight in the morning, when Hannah stirred and whispered that she thought her time was short. "As to my children," she said, "I must leave them to the Lord."

She asked for Joanna, who came immediately. Susanna, not realising her mother was close to death, stayed to finish her buttermaking. Hannah held Joanna's hand and said: "My dear child. Stand there and learn to die. Live in Christ, for to die in Him is great gain. You are a maid of lively spirits and great courage. Be strong in the Lord. Cast all thy care on Him, for He careth for thee. He will direct thy goings."

She was losing strength and, although Joanna said she seemed to want to say more, words failed her. Just as Susanna and their father William came into the room, she died with her hand clasped in Joanna's.

Hannah's death was a shock to them all, but particularly to Joanna. She said it "sunk deep into my heart and since then I have been desirous to live in the knowledge of the Lord, but to my shame I can reproach myself for forgetting Him for days without number. I am an unworthy object of His loving kindness."

Without her mother, Joanna found life bleak. There was no one to encourage her to be good, or to aspire to greater heights. Hannah had told her once that she had had "great faith, great comfort and great promises made to her, before I was born, and ever since".

Sorrow now unhinged her mind. She described how "rivers of water" seemed to flood her brain and fill her with foreboding. She was more conscious of the evil in the world and in herself and she wasn't sure she could fight it without Hannah's help. Her deepest fear was that Hannah might have been taken by the Devil and dragged down to Hell. She turned to the Scriptures for comfort.

"This is about the time I began to have a lively and strong faith in the Lord," she wrote years later.

Although followed a series of suitors, she wouldn't even consider them. Often hysterical and impossible to handle, her father eventually sent her to stay with a married sister in Black Torrington, ten miles north west of Okehampton, to see if a change might restore her to health. He hoped she might find a husband there, for he had no wish to be responsible for her for the rest of his life. He had enough trouble looking after himself.

His hopes were realised when a Mr. Rigsby fell in love with her "at first glance" as she sat in church one Sunday. William was impressed when Rigsby came to Gittisham to ask his permission to marry her, claiming he had a fortune of sixty pounds a year. Delighted with such a good match, William accepted on his daughter's behalf.

But Joanna didn't like Rigsby. She said she found out he had kept a common-law wife who, after she became pregnant, he persuaded to take a massive dose of savine (oil extracted from juniper berries) - to abort the child. Unfortunately it killed her too. Therefore, Joanna explained to William, she couldn't marry the man. William went berserk, for he considered Rigsby handsome, genteel and wealthy and couldn't believe Joanna could be so stupid as to turn him down.

"I don't know what the devil thou *do* like," he shouted, and accused her of treating her suitors like chalk drawings, rubbing them out when they no longer amused her.

Joanna replied haughtily: "The husband I choose will be of a more noble spirit than Rigsby." To which William retorted: "Well, I don't see any of these noble-spirited men going."

Two other prospective husbands came forward, a young serge-maker and then a middle-aged farmer with a "baseborn" child. She said that thoughts of Noah hardened her against them. Then William fell ill. Without Hannah's help, he found the farm difficult to run. There had been some mysterious incidents - cattle inexplicably poisoned and hayricks deliberately set on fire. William suspected a neighbour who had a grudge against him, but couldn't prove anything. Eventually depression got the better of him and he took to his bed and sent for Joanna.

Refreshed by her long break, she took over the management of the farm with gusto. Still only 21, the challenge appealed to her. "The Lord gave me courage and strength to act for my father's good," she said.

The first task she set herself was to find out who had poisoned the cattle and fired the hayricks. It turned out that a local farmer's son had been courting Joanna's sister for several years, when she suddenly accused him of "using every art to seduce her". When she rejected him he took his revenge on her father.

Joanna said "every invention he could think of to ruin my father, was practised until my father was brought into great distress. The agonies of his mind were so great that when he went to bed, meditating upon his sorrows, he would be in such agitation that I have been obliged to sit by him for hours of a night, wiping the perspiration from his face. In this manner, he continued, calling to me night after night to give him something, fearing he should be choked. He said his sorrows were greater than he could bear.

"I have seen the sweat running down his face, in a cold winter's night, like a man in the harvest day, that I have stood hours wiping his face. All the disappointments that he had gone through now crowded upon his mind.

The loss of his property, that he was heir to, now came upon him with double weight. When I entreated him not to grieve at the loss of his estates and said, supposing he had never been entitled to anything, he said then he should be as other poor men were, nothing to reflect about. But now old age and poverty were come upon him, he could not forget what he was entitled to."

William had never before shown much interest in the old tales. It was Hannah who had told their children about the lost inheritances. Now it began to haunt him. It was the beginning of an obsession that was to last for the rest of his life and make him bitter.

On Christmas Day, 1795, when Joanna was 45, she said her father told her he had hopes of getting all his land in Hertfordshire, because a voice in his head had called to him: "Southcott! Southcott! Thy name must spread far and wide. There is a lady in Hertfordshire who hath great possessions for thee." He was so certain about this voice, that he told the Rev. Putt, who laughed and called him old and foolish. So Joanna wasn't the only member of her family to hear voices.

Joanna enjoyed putting the farm to rights. She found she had natural managerial skills and, whether by divine guidance or her own good sense, she converted chaos to order. She said she worked early and late to save the expense of workmen. Threats of bankruptcy were averted and most of the farm's debts paid. That autumn the apple crop was the best the farm had ever produced.

William's health improved and soon he was well enough to notice how well she had done. But was he pleased? No, he was not! He became jealous and irritated and complained that Joanna had completely changed the methods he had always used to run the farm and he felt shown up, incompetent and useless.

His ungrateful attitude rankled Joanna and they argued. But, determined to finish the job, she remained on the farm and went on with the reorganisation, despite his surliness. It was a difficult time, which she described in verse:

"Thy father's passions, they were strong,
In his own way, he wished all to be done.
But his own way, by prudence thou didst see
If he did get it, would his ruin be.
Therefore, together, jangling you went on."

Once Joanna had decided she was right, then nothing could persuade her otherwise. All her life she insisted things were done her way and she would not consider anyone else's way. In this case, it seemed that her stubborn attitude paid dividends. William recovered not only his health and his good humour but they became on such fond terms that one day, in an enlightened moment, she said he realised how much she had done for him and cried out with grateful astonishment: "Too much oil puts out the lamp and too much goodness overcomes me!"

He became emotional and burst into tears, telling her that if only he had a faith like hers, he would freely consent to being burnt in the flames. The spirit of her mother, he said, had fallen upon her. Just the sort of remark the wily old man knew would please her. For this was the way the old rogue tackled life - always knowing which side his bread was buttered and acting accordingly. He died on January 21, 1802 when he was 85 and so witnessed, and took advantage of whenever he could, Joanna's astonishing rise to fame.

Joanna was at Gittisham for two years before she left to live again with her brother at Sidmouth. She liked Sidmouth. It was where she had met and fallen in love with Noah Bishop and perhaps she hoped she would again find romance there. A respectable farmer called Peter West courted her. Joanna found him attractive and was tempted to marry him. She said he was not only of good character, but very handsome, and they went walking together and even attended church as a couple - indicating publicly they had an understanding.

Joanna's brother sent hopeful reports back to William at Gittisham. But Joanna harboured doubts she couldn't identify. One Sunday she said she walked round the room "with war in my heart. I was thinking to myself, where is my foolish heart wandering? I asked the Lord not to permit the love of this creature to draw my heart from my Creator and that he would not permit me to keep company with any man that He had not ordained for my husband."

After struggling with her conscience she prayed for a sign and was told that, if Peter West failed to visit her for a whole month, then this was certain proof she should not marry him. Since the young man had been visiting her several times a week, pressing his suit, it seemed unlikely. Joanna decided it was a good test with few risks attached. "If he does not come for a month, it is the Will of God I should not marry him," she bargained with herself. However, he didn't visit her for four weeks.

Maybe his ardour had waned, or perhaps like Noah he had become exasperated by her contrariness. When he eventually did turn up at the farm he was told the relationship was finished.

Peter West was furious: "These upright men, get if you can. But I don't know where you will find them," were his parting words.

Joanna said at the time she reflected to herself, "True, I found his words as true as he did mine. For upright men are very scarce."

For the second time in her life, her heart was made to feel sore. She had once vowed she would rather die than marry anyone but Noah. Now she resolved to "wean my heart from the world and direct it heavenward in the manner of my Great Aunt Sarah".

Six years went by. Little is known about this period of her life, except she said she studied her Bible daily and had more offers of marriage. At one stage she had an affair with a man called Page.

"He first made love to me and then married my sister." Later in life she used to dream about him. "I dreamt last night I married my brother-in-law Page, that is dead."

She may well have survived all these affairs without losing her virginity which, when she was 65, she claimed was still intact. But being involved in so many courtships, many of them sordid, was not in keeping with a woman who claimed to be so saintly. By the time she was twenty-seven she must have been fairly knowing and the extra years, far from diminishing her charms, seemed to enhance them.

Her family now regarded the securing of a husband for her before it was too late, as a top priority. In an effort to escape the pressure, she took a job as a maid with a wealthy family but it seemed she couldn't avoid problems with men. Before she'd been there a month, an arrogant young footman tried to seduce her and pestered her so much she said her life was made miserable and "finding his base arts ineffectual, studied nothing but revenge". He set out to deliberately destroy her good character and she said she felt unsafe in the house with him. She described how, one Sunday, she went alone to a field and composed a prayer asking for help.

> "From this sad prison, set me free,
> And dangerous days to frame.
> Lord, Thou wilt sure deliver me,
> And I shall praise Thy name.
> And holy men will join with me,
> Thy praises to proclaim."

Whenever something traumatic, or dramatic, happened in her life, she would record it in verse. She may not even have actually written the words down, for she appeared to have a remarkable gift for retaining chunks of information in her head. She said God told her she would not need to spend another Sabbath in the house, which cheered her up enormously.

The lovelorn footman resented her going off by herself, and followed her "like a shadow" wherever she went. He eventually reported her absences to the mistress of the house. Joanna, confident that she would be leaving soon "smiled at his malice". She said that the Tuesday following "the housekeeper came out into the dairy where I was and, with tears flowing from her eyes, informed me that there was a maid come in my place and that I was to go tomorrow, it being the gentleman's custom never to allow servants any warning. The reason for my being turned away was through the false insinuations of the footman who, finding all his vile purposes baffled, persuaded my master I was going mad."

She claimed the housekeeper was heard to say: "My God! What is my master about? He has this day discharged the best servant in the house."

It is more likely true that she was sacked because she showed signs of instability. Whatever the truth, she was very bitter about it. It gave her great satisfaction to report, years later, that the master himself went mad and was sent to Bedlam leaving his young wife and four small children destitute.

He refused to give her a reference, which made finding a new job difficult. She stayed with some friends at Fairmile, near Ottery St. Mary, for a few days and then went on to West Devon to visit her sister. It would have taken her at least half a day to walk to Exeter and, lost in prayer, a divine message came that as soon as she reached Exeter she was to go to a huckster's shop and ask for some cakes, and she would be directed what to do next.

Weary and footsore, Joanna eventually arrived in Exeter and went to buy cakes. She said the mistress of the shop recognised her and asked if she was Mr. Southcott's daughter of Gittisham. Relieved to find a friendly face, Joanna said she was and that she was looking for a job and asked if she knew of anyone needing a servant. At that moment a customer came in, who told her that William Wills, the upholsterer of Woodford House, Exeter, needed a young woman to serve customers and do domestic chores. Joanna immediately went to the house and offered her services and was accepted. She stayed with the Wills family for five years. It was an important period of her life, for not only did she acquire upholstering skills, but she became hardened and more assertive.

At first all went well. She was treated as a member of the family and William Wills was impressed by her ability to learn quickly and her helpful nature. But it soon became clear that it was not only her skills that impressed him. Despite hopeful beginnings, "a scene of misery eventually broke out there". Although Wills was a Methodist minister, he started pestering her. She says she didn't encourage him but adds that she also felt sorry for him, having found out that his wife "had been caught with many men in adultery". The impression one gets is that Joanna quite liked Wills, who was an important figure in Exeter, and was flattered by his attentions. She may have succumbed to him but, if not, seemed to delight in his professed love.

Joanna describes Mrs. Wills as a "lewd woman whose heart was roving after every man she could make the object of her prey". She said the woman "defiled her husband's bed, wounded her husband's heart and broke the hearts of many married women by seducing their husbands". She painted as bad a picture of her as she possibly could - maybe in order to justify her own feelings towards Wills.

For some perverse reason, she compiled a list of all the men she believed Mrs. Wills had been caught in adultery with, and justified this with the excuse that it was done in God's name to teach Mrs. Wills the error of her ways.

One day Wills broke down and blurted out his feelings. At first she was shocked. "No tongue," wrote Joanna, "can paint my horror to hear of love from a married man. I asked him how he could talk of love for another whilst he had a wife of his own. He said his love was not sinful. It was only a religious love which no man that had a wife such as he had, could help. And now, to see a maid so mild and heavenly, endowed with every virtue, no religious man could help it."

She told him that "he should not venture into temptation's road and if his heart continued to love me I would leave his house". At which he threw himself at her feet and vowed he would keep his feelings to himself if only she would stay. But still he came to her when she was alone, and told her it could not be a sin to love her, because the more he prayed against it the more his heart was inflamed.

She could have solved the problem easily by leaving, but was comfortable there and jobs were hard to come by. She had also established position and power in the household. Mr. Wills allowed her privileges well above her station. Perhaps she even hoped Mrs. Wills would be conveniently dispensed with and she would replace her.

William Wills was a Leader of a group of John Wesley's followers who met at Exeter. He introduced her to the Methodist Church, which was to play an important part in her life. The Methodists still considered themselves members of the Church of England and so Joanna had no qualms about attending their Sunday evening meetings, although she says she never missed morning and afternoon service at the Cathedral.

This was her first involvement with a married man and her strange attitude towards him and her unnatural interest in Mrs. Wills' alleged love life, was unbecoming. Joanna maintained that the only reason for not leaving was because she believed it her Christian duty to reclaim her wayward mistress, and she was ordered to stay, adding she was "sometimes jealous it was the wrong spirit that ordered me" - meaning she was seriously concerned she might be acting under Satan's influence.

As was her custom, she prayed for a sign. When Wills' horse escaped from the stables she decided that, if God really wished her to leave the house, the runaway would be found within a week. A week slipped by and there was no news of the horse, so she thankfully decided God intended her to stay.

Initially it seemed this was the right thing to do, for William Wills stopped pursuing her and she said Mrs. Wills even went to a Methodist Church Meeting and confessed her sins.

Then life in this unsavoury household took a turn for the worse. A Methodist preacher, Mr. Hugh Saunderson, came to lodge there. He was already a notorious figure in the Methodist Church. In 1768 he had been John Wesley's constant companion and was highly regarded by him.

Wesley advised one of his own followers: "If you love me, hear Mr. Saunderson preach. He has tasted the pure love of God." Saunderson had such a powerful effect upon his congregation that when he preached the churches were always packed. Wesley said he was a remarkable man with a divine gift for stirring people.

Not all Methodists had the same high opinion of him. One told Saunderson: "Your youth, your natural propensity to gaiety and sprightliness, your unmarried state and the pride of your own heart, will insensibly incline you to little fopperies in gesture and dress and little niceties about yourself, which will hurt your own soul and lessen your usefulness."

Even Wesley, recognising he had been influenced by Saunderson's youth and charm, admitted: "If you can guard Brother Saunderson against pride and the applause of well meaning people, he will be a happy man and a useful labourer."

Then his true character emerged. During a trip to Ireland Wesley wrote a cautious letter to him, warning him to "avoid familiarity with women. This is deadly poison to them and to you. You cannot be too wary in this respect."

In 1774 he was arrested in Edinburgh and charged with stealing one hundred pounds from the wife of a former Methodist called George Sunderland and "upwards of thirty pounds a month and had, besides, terrified her into madness." Wesley was also arrested while walking to his lodging in the city and charged with aiding and abetting. Saunderson was acquitted but there were rumours that he had been having an affair with Sunderland's wife. The case attracted adverse publicity and cast a smear on the Methodist movement. By 1777 Wesley had grown wise and expelled him from the Methodist Church. Saunderson went on to Edinburgh and caused a schism amongst Methodists there and then arrived in Exeter intent on doing more damage. In his Diaries, John Wesley comments wryly on the time he visited Exeter in 1782. "Here Saunderson has pitched his standard and declared open war. Part of the Society have joined and the rest go quietly to make their calling and election sure."

 Wesley visited the city for the last time in August 1789 and went to the Society's permanent meeting place, Musgrave's Alley Chapel. "Here the scene is much changed. Many of the people are scattered and the rest faint and dead enough. The preaching house is swiftly running to ruin, the rain running through the room and five or six tenants living in the house were noisy enough, having no one to control them."

The thoroughly wicked and devastatingly charming Hugh Saunderson subsequently came to lodge at the Wills' household. Joanna was both fascinated and repulsed by him. He was the nearest she had ever come to anyone famous and she describes him with repressed excitement.

"He used to terrify all the people and was often telling what wondrous miracles he had wrought by prayer and that he had, at one meeting, made the whole Society lie stiff upon the floor until he got the evil spirits out of them."

At one Methodist meeting conducted by Saunderson, "a religious man shrieked out in such a manner as though he had sent an evil spirit over him. But I cannot say he ever had power over me. Only I used to think the room was full of spirits when he was in prayer. And he was so haunted by night he never could sleep in a room by himself. But the excuse he made was his wife's ghost came every night to trouble him and therefore he had wakers, or someone to sleep in the room with him. Before I saw his wretched conduct, this threw my mind into confusion about him and made me earnest in prayer that I might know by what spirit he did all these miracles."

She once remarked with awe: "Were I to go through all Saunderson's wonders and miracles that he told of, and all the wretched deeds that he did, I might fill many sheets of paper."

To impress her once, Saunderson told her there was never a man so highly favoured by God as he was, and he would not think God to make him anything if he would not make him greater than any man upon earth and give him power over all men.

Joanna replied guardedly: "I am happy for the Lord to have given you that power and favoured you above all men on earth but, if it is not, your end will be fated in Hell."

Saunderson laughed arrogantly and said: "Yes. And I will take care to get a good, warm corner there."

This remark convinced her he was the Devil himself. "The servants of the house were afraid of him, for they heard of the death of a man at Plymouth that had reproved Saunderson's conduct. When Saunderson heard he was dead, he boasted he had fasted and prayed for three days and three nights that God would take vengeance on the man and send him to eternity. But I had no fears of that sort. For it heightened my hatred and malice towards him."

The entire Wills household - servants, family and Joanna - were spellbound. No one would speak against him and for the first time Joanna saw the effect a person claiming supernatural powers could have upon the ignorant and the gullible. Genuinely shocked by his wickedness, she was at the same time fascinated by his power and dallied with the thought that she too might one day be able to influence people in the same way. Saunderson told her he was Mrs. Wills' lover and had made passes at the daughters too. She said she was horrified by his behaviour, especially after he had accepted Wills' hospitality.

She said she first tried to enlist the help of the Methodists to get rid of him and, finding this useless, decided to leave and stay with her brother at Sidmouth. But the affairs of the household continued to absorb her and she couldn't resist writing Mrs. Wills long letters of rebuke, which were duly ignored.

Unable to leave well alone, and perhaps regretting relinquishing her position in the household, she returned to the house early one morning to find Mrs. Wills was still in bed. Joanna waited for some time until eventually the lady came down in a dreadful fury and shouted: "You impudent wretch. What do you here, before I am up? What hast thou told thy master?   Thou hast told him all thou knowest and thou want to cut my throat."

In the middle of all this William Wills arrived home and his weeping wife said Joanna had insulted her. Wills accused Joanna of hypocrisy and told her: "You are as bad as her." Joanna was upset that Wills now seemed to prefer his sinful wife to her own sweet, saintly self, especially as she said she knew about bleaker deeds she hadn't even revealed.

She said his words cut her to the heart. Wills referred to his wife as "a virtuous, prudent woman" and said Joanna was wicked to cause trouble between them. Mrs. Wills asked for Saunderson to be sent for.

"When he came he looked like fury and swore by the eternal God he would punish me," said Joanna. "He called the Three-in-One-God to swear he had never touched me or kissed me in his life."

While William was out of the room, Joanna accused Saunderson and Mrs. Wills of adultery. One of the daughters, Polly, threatened to repeat her words to her father. The final outcome was that Joanna was told to leave on the grounds that she was a troublemaker. She later claimed that she alone in the household remained above criticism and the only reason she was dismissed was because she had exposed Mrs. Wills.

Joanna learned a lot from the wicked Saunderson which she used to her own advantage in later years. But nevertheless she was pleased to report that "that abominable, wicked preacher was driven in disgrace and infamy from Exeter and is now a vagabond living abroad."

Despite having now acquired a dubious reputation, she managed to find herself another job, 25 miles away, as servant to the Rev. Mr. Marshall, Rector of Musbury. But Wills would not give a reference. "Wills warned Mr. Marshall against me and he came home and told me to leave." Joanna complained that Marshall had accepted Wills' word against hers "because Wills was a man of substance in his parish" and blamed Marshall bitterly for the law suit that eventually followed. If he had listened to her, she would not have brought the case to court to save her reputation.

Like all her enemies, Marshall suffered for his lack of faith in her. She said he too mysteriously lost his senses and she had heard it was shocking the noise he made when he was out of his mind in the madhouse.

Joanna was intent on saving her good name. The rest of the Southcotts were ashamed of the scandal and she was anxious to restore their faith in her. As a result she became probably the first woman in England to sue her employer for sexual harrassment. "I saw his pretended love was temptations from the Devil and his disappointed malice. I thought so ungrateful a man could not exist."

The harrassment trial was at the Guildhall, Exeter, at the beginning of January 1784. Wills was defended by Exeter's leading lawyer, Mr. Fanshaw and Joanna's counsel was a Mr. Roberts.

Early on she accused Wills of swearing falsely and asked for Mr. Wills' son to be sent for, because she felt sure he would tell the truth. When Roberts asked why the son hadn't been brought as a witness, Fanshaw replied that he had brought as many witnesses as he thought proper. Roberts retorted: "You brought as many sir, as did not care what they swore to. Where is Mr. Wills' conscience gone now? His conscience has gone out of doors. He don't look after perjuring those that are out of his own house, but he won't perjure his own son. Then, what is his religion I wish to know?"

Fanshaw pleaded: "For God's sake, don't say a word about religion!" Roberts replied: "I will. You mocked her just now about her religion, and called her an enthusiast. Now I will mock his."

He went on to say that he could prove from the evidence that what Joanna had said was the truth and the witnesses had contradicted each other. "It is plain they have not spoken a true word."

When he asked Wills to allow his son to appear as a witness, he refused. Joanna described how Fanshaw leaned his arm on the table, threw down his head and covered his face with his hands. Roberts, on the other hand, fixed his eye "with courage and boldness" on the jury and went on to stress that Wills was a respectable man and Joanna merely a servant. Was it not therefore reasonable that he, as her master, might strike her in anger if she provoked him or refused to obey him? Joanna pricked up her ears at this change of tone. The suggestion appeared to be that, although it was wrong of Wills to behave in the way he had, it was excusable considering the difference in their stations.

Angry at the injustice of it all, she stood up and asked permission to conduct her own case because Roberts did not seem to be speaking with sufficient conviction on her behalf. She said that "every liberty was granted me in court, which is not common."

She asked to cross examine the witnesses and, permission granted, cleared her throat, raised her head and began to speak in public for the first time in her life - suddenly acquiring superhuman courage. Words poured forth as if she was possessed and the whole courthouse were amazed at the articulate speech and homely eloquence coming from her. She tore Wills' evidence to pieces and exposed him as a weak, immoral man who told lies after swearing on the Bible, a man who brought forth false witnesses, a man prepared to blacken the name of a simple, village woman.

The Jury were impressed and astonishment spread to the judge and spectators and even her own counsellor. After concluding her defence she retired exhausted and, hardly believing her own daring, she sat down on the oak bench and burst into tears. Roberts, with grudging admiration, told her not to distress herself.

The court was abuzz with speculation. It was remarked that it was a wonder proceedings had not been halted. The general feeling was that she would lose the case because of her audacity. Roberts commented quietly: "I don't think so!"

He was right! The Jury returned a verdict in Joanna's favour. Her good name was cleared and Wills' character ruined. He was ordered to pay damages and court costs and left the court swearing revenge. A month later he was in court again, accused of assaulting her and he was found guilty and fined £20.

He must have bitterly regretted ever having taken her into his home. She had managed to turn his smug, outwardly respectable little world upside down in a remarkably short time. He probably did act foolishly where Joanna was concerned, but he was fundamentally decent. When she spoke in court as "one possessed" Wills might have been forgiven for believing she spoke with such eloquence not because she was guided by God, but because she was possessed by the Devil. As a deeply religious man, he would have found it difficult to believe God would look kindly on a woman so intent on ruining a man's life.

Joanna, on the other hand, was elated. She had actually stood up in the City Court at the Guildhall and conducted her case powerfully and convincingly, and won. It was one of the high points of her life. She was to savour it for ever. She felt that now nothing was impossible and, the day after her triumph, she said she was ordered by an Inner Voice to write down a history of her life and have it "go into print for thousands shall be converted by it". However, she said she was not "pressed by the Spirit" until she was "visited" again in 1792.

Her success went to her head. Over the years, she became obsessed with a desire to hold another Trial - a Trial to decide whether she was guided by God or the Devil. She had fond visions of herself one day astonishing not just a country court but the whole world, with her eloquence and brilliance.

Chapter Three

Divine Guidance

Joanna thrived on the highs and lows of life. After her elation over her victory at the Guildhall, she hit a low and came down to earth with a bump. She wanted to consider herself a good woman but, even though she won her case gloriously, her character had been tarnished and her family felt that her involvement in the Wills case had cast a slur on the Southcott name. Only her sister, Susanna, showed her any compassion.

Joanna went through a period of serious depression. In the first half of 1784 she stayed with her childhood friend, Mrs. Woolland, of Heavitree, to give herself a chance to recuperate, and remained there for a year leading an aimless life because, she said, God forbade her to go to work, or work for the family in any way, or receive wages.

One day she was in Exeter shopping when she happened to pop into an upholsterer's shop, owned by Robert Taylor, a friend of William Wills. Taylor and his wife knew all about the court case and sordid incidents that had brought it about. Lucy Taylor had already formed an opinion that Joanna exercised a fatal sexual power over respectable married men and induced them to behave out of character.

They quickly worked out who she was and were fascinated. She appeared charming and unassuming and it seemed so unlikely that this pleasant, respectable looking woman was the one who had been involved in a scandal the likes of which Exeter had not seen for years. Robert Taylor asked her if she had once worked for Mr. Wills and Joanna replied that she had but now was staying with Mrs. Woolland, at Heavitree.

When he offered her a job and she accepted Lucy Taylor, listening at the back of the dark shop, could hardly believe her ears for she regarded Joanna as a scarlet woman.

"I did not want Mr. Taylor to hire her, because I had a great prejudice against her, because of what happened at the Wills's," she said. "I told Mr. Taylor he had hired a woman I would never like."

Taylor told his wife firmly: "We need such a person and I dare say you will like her in time."

Within a few days she was installed in the Taylor household as a part-time domestic servant and upholsterer. Initially, Lucy Taylor was very wary, having heard that Joanna was emotional and moody. And she watched suspiciously for signs of immoral behaviour.

"I did not notice anything strange in her manner, that she was deranged or anything," Lucy testified years later. "She worked for us for a year and seemed to be more in possession of her intellect than any person I had met with."

Joanna struck up a lasting friendship with the two Taylor children, Charles and Fanny, and Mrs. Taylor grew fond of her. She said she was impressed by the conscientious way Joanna got through her work, by her honesty and her dedication to God and the church. And she caused no trouble between husband and wife.

Then, we are told, she left to work for a Mr. Burrows in Exeter for a year before returning to the Taylors. Lucy was delighted to have her back. "She hadn't changed," she said. "She was the same person for honesty, sobriety and cheerful disposition."

After two years Mrs. Taylor *did* notice a worrying change in her. She became pale and thin. Her cheerfulness seemed forced and often she was withdrawn and inattentive to her duties. Lucy tried to find out what was wrong.

Joanna confided that she had been having strange dreams which frightened her. Some of these dreams were so detailed and vivid that Lucy was intrigued and encouraged her to tell her more. Joanna said she was inwardly troubled and needed to get away. Privately Lucy thought she was sulking because an additional servant had taken over some of Joanna's duties.

In 1792 a very severely depressed Joanna went to stay with her sister, Susanna. She was now 42 and claimed to still be a virgin. She was in a highly emotional state, prone to serious schizophrenic fantasies which terrified her but which she felt she had to prove true. She felt as though she had done nothing remarkable in her life so far, beyond a brief moment of fame when she had triumphed over learned men at court. As a young girl she had aspired to great heights. Now, it seemed, the years had slipped by and she had nothing to show for them.

Being an avid reader, she followed national events in the news-sheets and knew that France was agitating England and there were reports of bloodshed and horror. Mobs across the Channel were running riot, the

French King's palace had been stormed and the French Royal family held prisoner. French chateaux were being set alight by angry peasants and the aristocracy subjected to cruelty. Joanna had always been fascinated by the more lurid stories in the Bible and these incidents, happening across a narrow stretch of water, seemed to her a sign from God that the Day of Judgement was near.

The reports she read played on her mind. Night after night she woke in a cold sweat after being plagued by wild dreams. She dare not tell Lucy Taylor about them for fear she would think her insane. One night it seemed a voice spoke to her out of the darkness, as she lay in bed, telling her that "the Lord will terribly shake the earth". These words struck her as so dreadful she said they made her tremble.

In 1792 William Pitt, Prime Minster of England, declared in his budget speech: "There never was a time in the history of our country when from the situation in Europe we might reasonably expect fifteen years of peace." Joanna read this and became frantic because her voice told her the opposite - that there would be war and bloodshed as England had never seen before. She became convinced it was her divine mission to stop it.

Eventually what she identified as a "still, small voice" (Kings I, ch 19, v. 12) told her to "go, leave thy work and proceed to thy sister's house and write what I have revealed". So, equipped with paper, pens and ink, she went to stay with sister Susanna at Plymtree, 12 miles outside Exeter. Susanna was married with a brood of children and warmly welcomed her into her home. Joanna was lulled into a pleasant feeling of security. One evening they exchanged sisterly confidences and Joanna told Susanna about the voice that had spoken to her and the instructions she had been given.

Susanna was not only unimpressed - she was positively shocked! The Southcotts had suffered enough embarrassment. This sort of thing could only humiliate them more. So she told Joanna crisply: "If prophecies are to be given the Lord would not condescend to visit one of our family. For there is too much pride in the Southcotts." Then she confided: "I am always at war in my own heart, but I cannot conquer my pride. Therefore, I take after my father's side of the family."

Joanna admitted this applied to her too. "I never could conquer my own heart. This internal war will ever continue till we come out of ourselves."

She went on: "My own besetting sin is a resenting spirit. Our mother used to tell me I had a proud heart to be humbled and a hard head to be softened on account of my resenting spirit, which I never could conquer by nature, and my feelings are tender and quick."

Despite these confidences, Joanna insisted that no matter what Susanna thought, she believed her "still small voice" was from God. Susanna replied that she considered these to be blasphemous declarations and Joanna must be mad. She forbade her to write such rubbish in her household. Joanna went into more detail about her dreams and prophecies while Susanna briskly ticked off one claim after another.

"You say there will be a war. With whom shall we go to war? The French are too busy destroying themselves. As to the dearth of provisions you speak of, you are wrong. For corn will come down very low. I could not make 4s.6d a bushel of the best of the wheat this year. As to the distresses of the nations. You *are* wrong there! For England was never in a more flourishing state than it is at present."

Joanna replied: "Well, if it be of God, it will come to pass however unlikely or likely it may appear at present."

Explaining that she had been ordered to write all her prophecies down, she added: "I shall hurt no-one but myself by writing it. I am the fool. I must be the sufferer if it be not of God. If it be of God, I would not refuse for the world and am determined to err on the safest side."

But Susanna remained firm, saying: "I think **I** should err on the safest side and forbid you to do it in my house."

That night Joanna went to her room reflecting on their sisterly chat, thinking that maybe she had better put thoughts of prophecies and voices from her mind. She undressed and blew out the candle, before pulling back the covers ready to climb into bed. Then, she said, she sensed a strong presence in the room and asked cautiously, "What spirit is near?"

A voice whispered back: "Thy mother!" Hannah had been dead now for over twenty years! Joanna stood in the dark beside her bed, and trembled.

The voice continued: "If thou hast courage, I will appear." Joanna remained too frightened to speak. But the voice persisted: "This is a sign," it said and Joanna heard three hard knocks on the oak bedstead, at which she leapt into bed and buried her head under the bedclothes.

But the voice wouldn't go away. In a soft whisper, it spoke again: "Dear child, thou art afraid. Therefore I cannot appear, but I can converse with thee invisibly."

Before her mother's spirit left the room, Joanna found the courage to ask who had sent her and was relieved when she was told it was God. All that night, Joanna lay awake wrestling with her conscience. She half believed the visitation was part of a nightmare. And yet it had taken place before she had even got into bed. She remembered Susanna had said that "the Lord would not condescend to visit one of our family". The terrifying thought occurred to her that, if her sister was right, then her visitor might have been the Devil in disguise.

That night she went over her entire life, dwelling on events of little significance until she managed to read into them deep reasons for her own purpose in life. All the stories she had ever been told about her ancestors, came back to her. It finally dawned on her that God had "hedged up the way" so that she was able to go in one direction only, towards the work she was destined to do in His name.

Then the small inner voice called reassuringly: "Joanna! Joanna! The angels rejoiced at thy birth, for they had known that thou wouldst free them from the insults of the Devil!" This calmed her a little and suddenly all seemed clear. She worked out that she had been specifically chosen by God for a mission, which would eventually be revealed. Meanwhile, she was duty bound to obey God's instructions.

Told she must write a history of her life, she climbed out of bed and, through what was left of the night, wrote feverishly. Convinced now she was God's handmaiden, she felt it was vital to put down all she knew about herself, no matter how trivial, so that there would be no misunderstandings when her true nature was revealed to mankind.

She wrote as one possessed, incensed with a literary urge. The words seemed to seep through her fingers without much thought. It was, on reflection, a remarkable achievement for this sparsely-educated, middle-aged peasant woman to write 5,000 words by hand in one night. Perhaps it was madness that drove her on. Her writing is practically illegible, angular and difficult to decipher. Yet, when sense is made of the content, it comes as a surprise to realise that the words are literate, the predictions positive and the intentions clear.

She worked herself into a mad frenzy. All the odd, religious beliefs she had ever had converged, mingling with tales of the supernatural she had learned as a child. She was to become quite proud of her literary efforts and would have been upset to hear what Robert Southey, the poet, thought of them in his *"Letters from England"* some years later.

"The books she sends into the world are written partly in prose, partly in rhyme - all the verse and the greater part of the prose being delivered in the character of the Almighty. It is not possible to convey any adequate idea of this unparalleled and unimaginable nonsense by any other means than literal transcript. Her handwriting was illegibly so bad that at last she found it convenient to receive orders to throw away the pen and deliver her oracles orally. And the words flowed from her faster than her scribes can write them down.

"This may well be believed, for they are mere words and nothing else. A rhapsody of texts, vulgar dreams and vulgar interpretations, vulgar types and vulgar applications - the vilest string of words in the vilest doggerel verse. Her followers receive them as the dictates of immediate inspiration." He added with despair: "A herd, however, was ready to devour this garbage as the bread of life. Credulity and Vanity are foul breeders."

After her troubled night, she hid her notes under the mattress and fell into a deep sleep, emerging a few hours later refreshed and purposeful. She returned to Mrs. Taylor's house, confident that she had to warn people of the evils of the world and the dreadful things to come. She wasn't exactly sure what else her divine mission involved but was content to await further instructions.

At first she told no one about her revelations for fear she would be accused of madness. Then, towards the end of 1792, she happened to mention to Lucy Taylor that troublesome times were approaching and, though flour and grain were cheap, everything would rapidly become dearer than "was ever known in the memory of man". She advised Mr. Taylor to lay up a store of goods, to protect himself and his household from these bad times.

Robert Taylor took her advice, thinking that if she proved right he would be fortunate and if wrong, then he would still have his stock of goods. As she predicted, prices shot up and Taylor profited handsomely. Impressed, he remarked, "Why, Joanna, you are a prophetess!"

It then struck Joanna that it was *exactly* what God intended her to be. She replied, "Why, so I am!" From then on she took to prophesying openly and no one accused her of madness. She even showed Lucy Taylor some of her divinely dictated verse:

"Let Taylor now judge as a man.
If he had got no gold in store,
And all his labour was stopt here,
That he a penny would not gain.
Would he not judge a fatal time,
To see his family in distress.
To beg for mercy from the rest."

Lucy Taylor became her keenest fan. She reported with admiration: "There was scarcely anything that happened to the nation, or the families of anyone with whom she was acquainted, that Joanna did not inform me would happen before it did and all were fulfilled as predicted."

For the next three years Joanna practised her new skills - learning by trial and error how to predict convincingly. She discovered that it was easy to say grimly to someone "Ill fortune will befall you in a day or two", and when that person lost a glove or some trinket, to point out triumphantly that that was the very misfortune she had predicted. On the other hand, if the person's husband or child happened to drop down dead then Joanna was able to say, "That was the misfortune I warned you about!"

Either way, the person would be impressed and Joanna would have gained another recruit. If she happened to remark casually that it was likely to rain before nightfall, and it did, then it was considered another one of her prophecies come true. The times it didn't rain were overlooked. Her reputation that she had a gift for telling the future spread. She was encouraged to practise her powers by people who flattered her or sought help on personal matters. She still considered herself a good woman, a white witch acting under God's guidance. Her grandmother had taught her to delve deep into any incident to find a hidden meaning. She looked for signs and reasons in everything she did.

Lucy Taylor was now more than a friend; she was a devotee. "I believe Joanna was visited by the Living God. I believe that she was so good, she would not have said all these things otherwise." Joanna was allowed more and more privileges in the house, and was given writing facilities and told to write down her predictions whenever she felt inclined. One day, as she was sweeping up in the shop, she came across an old letter seal bearing the monogram "**I C**" and decorated with two stars. Joanna couldn't resist slipping it into her pocket. She needed a valid reason to keep it and struggled to think of one. Then, after days and nights battling with her conscience, it occurred to her that "**I C**". might in fact be "**J C**" - Jesus Christ. As always, once Joanna had convinced herself of something it became to her gospel truth. It was easy to work out from there that God had intended her to find it for some future purpose. She called it *"The Seal of the Living God"* and hid it away in readiness for the day when God would reveal to her what must be done with it.

Joanna's
Seal
(actual size)

A sample of Joanna's handwriting.
From the Blockley collection

At first glance it looks illegible but, once deciphered, makes surprising sense. Dated January 1803, the words suggest she is intent on convincing herself, as well as others, that it is God and not the Devil influencing her.

"I Joanna Southcott, am clearly convinced my Calling is of God and my writings are indicted by His Spirit; as it is impossible for any Spirit but an all-wise God that is wondrous in working, wondrous in Power, wondrous in Wisdom, wondrous in Truth, Could have brought round such Mysteries so full of Truth as are in my Writings - so I am clear and know in whom I have believed, that all my Writings came from the Spirit of the Most High God. Joanna Southcott."

Chapter Four

Signs of Insanity

The burning issue now was how to achieve recognition. She wanted the approval of an official body. To be acknowledged not merely as a soothsayer - for there were plenty of them in Devon - but as a divinely chosen messenger of God. A sort of female John the Baptist was what she had in mind. The Methodist Movement seemed an obvious route to recognition. She had been attending their meetings regularly, as well as going to the Cathedral, and had been told by her "still small voice" that "something would happen there to convince people of her claims". She felt that the emotional atmosphere of the meetings would be sympathetic to what she had to say.

On the day Joanna decided to make her stand, the class meeting was led by a "saintly character" called John Eastlake. Joanna admitted she was nervous as she stood up to face the meeting. "I thought they might judge me simple and I was much confused while I was speaking."

She didn't make a good impression. The meeting listened to her uneasily and some of the members were unpleasant. It was not what she had hoped for. She was told, in no uncertain terms, that she was mad. Consequently she had one of her brain storms and fled to her sister Susanna in Plymtree. It was a bad time for her. "I was assaulted by the Powers of Darkness for ten days," she wrote. But, under Susanna's care, she eventually regained her wits, if not her confidence.

An old friend, Mrs. Minifie, sent a message begging her to come. Her husband had deserted her, leaving her with many debts, and she was ill with worry. Joanna went immediately and found her friend very distressed, so decided to stay, for Mrs. Minifie's problems took her mind off her own.

One night she dreamt that Mrs. Minifie's house was ablaze. The impression was so strong, she said, that it jerked her awake. Sitting up in the dark, she listened for sounds of alarm and, because her dream was still so fresh in her mind, thought she must still be dreaming. Then she smelled smoke and went to investigate and was met with tongues of flames creeping up the staircase. She said it was her own quick action in raising the alarm that saved Mrs. Minifie and the rest of the household from being burnt alive.

Reflecting upon the incident afterwards, she decided it was a divine warning that messages given to her should *always* be regarded as important and acted upon immediately. Silence was sinful! She resolved that, no matter how unsure she was of her powers, the peril was great to others if she did not obey divine instructions. She also got it into her head that it was imperative to the whole world that she should be accepted as God's chosen messenger. At this time this was all she claimed to be. To be recognised officially became an obsession which she later extended to include the notion - amongst others - that she was Christ's reincarnation in female form.

This revelation gave her the courage to approach the Methodists again. She knew all the members in Exeter, because of her association with her ex employer, William Wills. In 1793 she confided to the Rev. Mr. Leach that she had been warned of the horror to come. He listened gravely, then told her: "Not one thing you have mentioned will come to pass. You have the war in your favour, which is all that will come true of your prophecies, and the war will be over in a quarter of a year. It is all from the Devil to disturb your mind. Satan hath a design to sift you as wheat. Besides, the Lord would never have revealed it to *you.* There are a thousand in Exeter I could point to to whom the Lord would have revealed all this before he would to you."

In a dream she had one night she said her room suddenly became lit by twelve candles, making it seem like daylight. She was so frightened she hid under the blankets. Her interpretation of the dream was that her writings had to be judged by twelve men and, when they met for that purpose, the candle of the Lord would burn brightly among them.

She sent a message to Leach telling him that the Day of Wrath was at hand and the truth of what she said was to be judged by twelve men. Leach offered to arrange for the twelve to gather together the following Monday morning. But Joanna said God told her that the reason Leach had agreed to do this was "in order to convince me of my folly" and Joanna didn't want to be convinced she was wrong. So she declined.

The Methodists were concerned about her and went to a lot of trouble to help her. John Eastlake asked her to visit him at his home. When she got there, Leach and several other Methodists were waiting. She was given a chance to explain her beliefs and this time they listened patiently.

Then Leach told her: "If it be God, we shall see more of it. If of yourself, your head is wiser than mine."

He considered the issue for a week and finally sent word he did not want to become further involved. "I cannot give warning of something I do not believe."

Mrs. Symond, of Exeter, offered her a room and freedom to do as she pleased in return for light domestic duties. During her stay with her, she approached Mr. Henry Tanner, another Methodist minister, and told him about her visitations. He had a saintly reputation and therefore his good opinion was worth having. She claimed he was sympathetic. His daughter insisted later this was not true and in fact her father had tried to convince Joanna that her revelations were satanic. She said Joanna became annoyed when Tanner refused to accept papers from her and told her she was a deluded woman.

Nobody of any importance was prepared to take her seriously so, frustrated, she returned to live with the Taylor family. Then God apparently told her: "I will direct you to a man whose talents are greater than thine."

Joanna was in the habit of attending services at the magnificent St. Peter's Cathedral, Exeter. Although grand, it was not formidable. Joanna enjoyed the homely atmosphere. It gave her a sense of security. So, several times a day, most days of the week, she went there. One Sunday during Advent, in 1793, she heard the Rev. Mr. Joseph Pomeroy preach. He was in fact Vicar of St. Kew Church, Cornwall, but frequently came to Exeter to visit his parents. On that particular day he had been invited to the service as a guest speaker.

Pomeroy was about the same age as Joanna, in his late forties. He was handsome and distinguished-looking and, consequently, a popular speaker, especially with the ladies. Because of his eloquence and charming manner he was often invited to preach further afield than his own parish. So, on that fateful Sunday, he stood in the pulpit in Exeter Cathedral and launched himself into his sermon with warm enthusiasm, warning the congregation that the Great Assize would begin sooner than people realised and each and everyone of them should brace themselves to face their Maker.

The harmless-looking little country woman sitting on a hard bench at the front of the congregation was to have a chilling and disruptive influence on his respectable existence. He probably didn't even notice her, although her sharp eyes were fixed constantly on him, drinking in every word he uttered. If he'd had any inkling of the trouble that lay in store for him, he would probably have taken flight there and then. But, in blissful ignorance, he dug himself deeper and deeper into Joanna's plans - so letting himself in for 20 years of ruthless persecution - by expanding on his theme about the Great Assize.

For Joanna it was love at first sight. Here was a man who echoed all her beliefs, talking about her favourite subject. As she sat spellbound, hypnotised by his pleasant manner, the still small voice "sent by God" advised her that "If Leach gives up, go to this preacher."

Joanna walked out of the Cathedral in a state of high elation. Pomeroy's sermon had stimulated her own enthusiasm and belief in herself. For days he filled her thoughts like a lover. She was so in awe of him she hadn't dared approach him at the service, but eventually wrote him a wordy letter, explaining in detail her visitation from God and the orders He had given her. Mrs. Taylor delivered it to him at his lodgings.

Joseph Pomeroy, happily married with a family, would have considered his matrimonial state fair protection against admiring spinster ladies. So he read Joanna's letter in good faith and decided it was a cry for help and it was his duty as a minister of God, to go to her. He promptly called at the Taylor's house and Lucy Taylor ushered him into the parlour. Before she called Joanna, he took the opportunity to ask if she thought Joanna was in possession of a sound mind and understanding. Mrs. Taylor loyally vowed she was.

He then asked about her character in general, saying he had heard she told lies. Mrs. Taylor was indignant, saying: "Indeed she does not. She prophesies nothing but the truth."

Pomeroy went on grilling her about Joanna's background and circumstances. Finally Joanna was called into the room and Lucy Taylor left them alone to talk. At this stage Pomeroy was genuinely concerned about the plump pretty woman who stood before him, neatly dressed and quietly composed. He couldn't at first reconcile her to the writer of the passionate letter he had received, so he had to ask incredulously: "Was it *you* who sent the letter?" She said it was and, as she began to speak, he said he realised he was in the presence of a powerful and strong-willed woman with singular beliefs.

He listened patiently as she poured out her heart to him, telling him about her divine communications which no-one in authority would acknowledge. He gave the impression of being sympathetic, and so Joanna spoke without reserve. What she wanted him to do was assure her that her instructions came from God and not the Devil, as Leach had suggested. She still harboured a fear that she might be wrong about them originating from a divine source. Pomeroy was a sensitive man who sensed her longing and was too soft-hearted to disillusion her utterly. As a compromise, he told her kindly that he saw nothing in what her voices told her, that seemed likely to have come from the Devil. Privately he hoped that, by humouring her in this way, he would at least avoid making her condition worse than he evidently thought it was. Joanna claimed he told her: "If you are called by God, you ought to warn the public before the road falls, as it will be no use afterwards."

Joanna left the room satisfied. Lucy Taylor showed Pomeroy out but, before leaving, he turned to her with real concern and warned her: "She will be out of her mind soon. I should not wonder if it was in a few weeks. If there is anything I can do for the poor woman, you must not hesitate to call me and I will come at once."

He returned home, perhaps feeling that he had conducted the interview rather well and had offered just the right amount of comfort and understanding to one of God's poor, deluded creatures.

But he was wrong! Joanna did *not* go out of her mind within weeks. She merely withdrew within herself for two or three months, brooding about the meeting and reading things into it that would have horrified Pomeroy had he only known. Secret longings stirred within her for the first time since Noah Bishop. Despite her years, she was like a shy young girl wanting to be wooed.

Her inner voice kept telling her that he was the man she must pin her hopes to, but she was frightened of rejection. If he scorned her, she would lose all confidence in herself. So she kept putting it off and then finally wrote to him, begging for a visit and reminding him he had promised to come if she needed him.

Unwittingly, he came. This time Joanna was prepared. She dressed in a neat, becoming dress and Lucy Taylor was told to remain in the room throughout the interview. Chairs were arranged so that Lucy could sit in a position where she would hear clearly and act as witness. Joanna had rehearsed exactly what she wanted to tell Pomeroy and, as soon as he had arrived and settled down, she rattled off all the dreadful things she had been warned would happen, as a lead-up to Judgement Day. Before Pomeroy had a chance to comment, she swiftly brought out her papers and read to him from her own writings, explaining these had been dictated to her by God.

She didn't *sound* like a mad woman and she chose her words so carefully and was so articulate that Pomeroy didn't know how to react. He said afterwards that, although she gave the impression of being totally sane, the content of her speech could well have been the ramblings of a deluded woman. So he shifted uneasily in his chair and struggled to think of something kind to say. He had no wish to hurt her feelings, for at this stage he still regarded her with compassion. But when she told him confidentially that not only had God spoken to her directly but had also told her she was the very Bride of Christ mentioned in the Scriptures, he was shocked. His horror mounted as she went on to discuss Judas's betrayal of Jesus in what he considered was a blasphemous manner, and could no longer contain himself.

"Joanna," he said grimly, "You have advanced things that make me shudder and I do not know, but that this borders on blasphemy."

Joanna replied resentfully, "I was ordered by God to tell you. I know what blasphemy is, but I was ordered to tell you these things."

She felt betrayed. This was the man God had told her to turn to and now he was behaving like the rest. Pomeroy sensed her disappointment and could not bring himself to be too hard on her, so said as a show of sympathy: "I know it is important to you to be told that all your writings come from the Spirit of God. But I feel I cannot do so. Yet, a greater part of them, I am sure, do."

Joanna was not sure if he was supporting her or rebuking her and decided it was safer to remain silent. After a long pause, Pomeroy said, choosing his words carefully but aware he probably wasn't making absolutely clear to her what his true attitude was. "I do believe that *one* word of yours at least is from the Spirit of the Devil."

Still she remained embarrassingly quiet, her head bowed. Pomeroy felt he could say no more without disturbing the woman alarmingly, so he took his leave. Joanna remained where she was, as if transfixed. Giving her one last pitying glance, Pomeroy said: "I shall always be happy to see you, Joanna, and to receive anything from you."

This conversation was repeated by Lucy Taylor at one of Joanna's Trials - organised by her followers at her own request - at Neckinger, London, in the Autumn of 1804. Mrs. Taylor was basically an honest woman and, although she intended her evidence to totally support Joanna, it was given under oath and she felt morally obliged to tell the "jury" every little detail. This was why she didn't pretend that Pomeroy was impressed, but couldn't resist loyally adding that, on this second visit, "he didn't say a word about her being out of her mind".

Afterwards Joanna made her own notes about the meeting and said that Pomeroy reasoned with her on the danger of her actions, if she was not called of God. She said that, finding he could not convince her, he asked why her writings had not been proved. If a jury of clergy examined her writings, would she accept their verdict?

"You will otherwise wait till you bring the sword, the plague and the famine upon us," he said.

The suggestion appealed to her, though she admitted she suspected he had "disguised his real sentiments and had thus promised to examine my writings to convince me of my folly".

But by now she was besotted with him and her suspicions of his true motives didn't put her off. Indeed, she even thought more highly of him as a result. Heaven, she wrote, could not have guided her to a wiser or better minister. "He that can conquer his own passions is a greater hero than he who doth take a city. He must be a good man who can so condescend to convince a fool of her folly." God seemed to agree with her and told her so:

> "So thou see'st plain that he did mean
> To stay thy written hand.
> To please a fool, he'd anger rule,
> Till he could all command.
> That is to see the mystery,
> And thus convince the whole.
> It was to lay thy follies by,
> Made him thy cause uphold."

She was now earning a reasonable living upholstering, not just for the Taylors but doing outside work too, but reckoned she was very lonely, with few friends. Apart from the Taylors, there were Mrs. Minifie and Mrs. Woolland whom she'd known from childhood. Unlike Lucy Taylor, these two women were sceptical about her claims to be a holy woman.

After reading Joanna's writings, Mrs. Minifie said with amusement that she could never imagine God condescending to consider such trivialities when He had much more important matters to contend with.

Upholstery work enabled her to save money, but her father's health was not good and she was irritated that she was expected to contribute so much towards his support. The rest of the Southcott family were uneasy about her depressing prophecies, feeling she was wishing ill luck on them. When her brother John, became seriously ill in 1794 she said God had revealed to her that he wouldn't die, but "his life would be of a short duration". In fact he died in 1797.

On Christmas Day, 1795, she was told by her divine guide to write King George III's name on a piece of paper and seal it up "with half the nations that was loyal to him". Then she was told to go and look at the Moon.

"I sealed the paper up at eleven and then went to look at the Moon and saw a good mist over the earth and in the heavens and there were no stars to be seen, but only a halo round the Moon." It struck her as an eerie sight and she called Mrs. Woolland and Mrs. Minifie to come and see. They politely declined saying it was too cold to venture outside. So Joanna stayed out by herself, indulging in fanciful thoughts, about the Moon and its connections with madness. She said she thought she saw a "shadow of a man dart across the moon" and, interpreting it as a vital sign regarding the King, went indoors to make a note of it.

She now conversed daily with her divine spirit and made notes of what she was told. The pile of writings got so thick, she was obliged to place them in a box and God advised her to seal all her prophecies up. At the end of 1795 she approached "six men of dissenting class" and asked for their opinion - spending a full hour trying to convince them of her beliefs. They listened to her patiently, but said they needed to examine the prophecies before making up their minds. Reluctantly she handed the prophecies over to them, making them promise not to break the seals unless she and her friends were present. They agreed but the next evening broke open the seals and examined the papers. They found the contents shocking and declared them the work of the Devil.

Joanna clung to the hope that at least Pomeroy would have faith in her. She had been writing to him regularly and in May 1796 gave him a sealed letter, explaining: "As you doubt by what Spirit I am led, be pleased to keep this until the end of the year. Then you will judge of its truth." The letter contained a prediction that Bishop William Buller, of Exeter - a man who that Spring seemed in the best of health - would not live until Christmas. The poor man died on December 12.

He was an important man in Exeter, having been elected Bishop in December 1792. He might have had the good fortune to have escaped Joanna's notice had it not been for her father William who one day arrived unexpectedly at the Woolland's house in Heavitree, excitedly claiming he had been given a lift into town by none other than the Bishop of Exeter himself.

"We all laughed at him," reported Joanna. William was getting senile and was inclined to tell wild stories. Nobody took him seriously. He admitted sheepishly that he didn't actually go IN the Bishop's coach, but rode BEHIND it with the footman.

"The Bishop had been for an airing," explained Joanna. "And his carriage overtook my father. He ordered the coachman to stop as he saw my father going towards Exeter, and enquired how far he was going." William explained he was on his way to Heavitree to see his daughter. Dusty from his long walk from Gittisham, he must have looked weary for the Bishop took pity on him and ordered his footman to help William get up behind the gleaming carriage. William asked the footman who the great gentleman was, so that he could thank him properly when he alighted.

Mr. Woolland's humble opinion was that William had had his leg pulled by someone and remarked: "It seems improbable that the Bishop would have condescended in that manner, to have stopped his coach to take up a poor man, although the Bishop is said to be a most noble character."

Joanna, far from humble, decided the incident was a sign from God and wrote one of her wild letters to the Bishop. It was ignored. This did not discourage her and she continued to pester him with letters. Then in 1794 a sinister sign came to her which she interpreted as a warning that Buller had not long to live. This sign was inspired by Mr. Woolland, who bought a flock of sheep but was not sure whether they were with lamb or not and decided the best way to find out was to kill one of the sheep. He was annoyed when it didn't have a lamb inside it. He threatened: "If there is not milk gathered in either of the others, then all my flock shall go to the butchers."

Joanna considered the sense of such drastic action and was then told by God that He would do as Woolland had done and cut down one of the Clergy to find out what evil was lurking in his flock of ministers.

> "But if I find my shepherds dry,
> And no true milk in them doth lie,
> Then sure, like Woolland, I'll go on,
> Till all my flock be dead and gone."

Poor Bishop Buller was the man Joanna decided was to be made an example of. Within two years, he was dead at the comparatively young age of 61. He was buried with honour in the Cathedral. His widow, Ann, died "of a broken heart" three years later, aged 63. William Buller had been hale and hearty and Pomeroy was shocked, not only by his death but by the fact that Joanna had predicted it. He put her to test again in January 1797 by asking her to predict events in England and Italy for the following year. To his astonishment, when he broke open the seals at the beginning of 1798 the two predictions she had made were correct. He began to doubt his judgement of her and wondered uneasily if Joanna was sane after all. Could there be some truth in her claims?

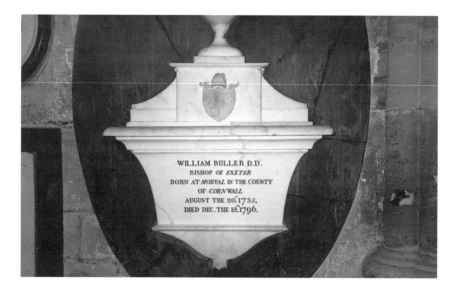

Plaque on wall at St. Peter's Cathedral, Exeter, in memory of William Buller, Bishop of Exeter, who died in 1796, within a year of Joanna putting a curse on him because he refused to take her seriously.

By the beginning of 1797 Joanna was living most of the time at Heavitree with the Woollands. She made cushions for them in return for bed and board. Her father was now very senile and an embarrassment to her. He had no savings and looked to his children for support, regularly calling at the Woollands to beg Joanna for money. Whenever he managed to extract money from her, he spent it irresponsibly. She said she gave him "many pounds" and sometimes had to borrow from Mrs. Woolland.

Mrs. Woolland felt sorry for him and often gave him meat to take home as well as money. He was so touched by her kindness, he told her one day that his "cup runneth over", which irritated Joanna who said witheringly he had become "a child of old age who had lost all prudence in the management of money". She lived in fear of ending up like her father, having to beg for food, and had become miserly, putting away every spare penny she had for her old age. She proudly noted that, through Lent one year, she had fasted for six days, taking no nourishment except a basin of broth with bread in it.

She had now progressed from making little, domestic prophecies which impressed the likes of Mrs. Taylor, to forecasting important world events, such as the war which was raging in Europe. "One night," she wrote, "I dreamt I saw men in the air who pitched their horses upon the earth. The horses fought furious and the men fought furious and so frightened me that I awoke and thought the French would land."

Lord Malmesbury, the most highly regarded diplomat in England at the time, went on a much publicised tour to Paris and was expected to return with a formula for peace in Europe. One of Joanna's sealed envelopes predicted his mission would fail. Malmesbury returned to England unsuccessful and her friends were impressed at her foresight.

In the same year, it seemed unlikely France's ill-equipped army could possibly conquer Italy. Joanna had given Pomeroy a written prediction that Italy would be invaded and taken. Within a short time the French replaced their General in Italy with a smart young officer named Napoleon Bonaparte, who soon made her words come true. She included with these predictions a general warning to England "lest they disagree and lay violent hands upon one another".

She may have had uncanny foresight or she may have just made some lucky guesses. Many of her other predictions were wrong, but these went unnoticed. She began to consider herself invincible. A man she had made cushions for complained they were a foot short of what he had ordered. She told him this was deliberate, to indicate that the next harvest would be cut short. Her exasperated employer tried to persuade her to remake the cushions to the required length and told her he couldn't afford to consider such nonsense, but Joanna refused to remake the cushions without God's permission. Nothing the poor man said could induce Joanna to change her mind.

In 1797 she wrote to "a second Dignitary of Exeter Cathedral" explaining her beliefs. On May 29 the same dignitary stood in the pulpit of the Cathedral and referred to her letter in harsh terms. Joanna said his words "pierced" her heart. "I marvelled that a gentleman to whom I had appealed should decline to see me to convince me of my wrong, but should do so publicly." She ran home to cry bitterly. Then she remembered God had warned her that the Dignitaries of the Church would treat her letters with contempt.

"Thus both will thee deceive,
  But shall they laugh there unto shame,
  For what thou dost believe?
  If they agree to laugh at thee,
  Their laughter I shall turn.
  And in the end thou'lt find these men
  Like thee, will sorely mourn."

She feared lonely old age. Unmarried working women of her age were much pitied in those days. Joanna didn't enjoy the stigma of being unmarried and considered herself to be socially at a disadvantage. She made some mild attempts to protest at people's attitude towards spinsters. Before her death, in 1814, she remarked that: "It is no reproach for a woman never to have been married."

But at 48 she was still attractive and at heart the same haughty girl of her youth who had considered herself a cut above the rest. If Pomeroy had been free she would have jumped at the chance to marry him, but no simple shopkeeper would have done for Joanna even then. So she faced the fact that she would have to fend for herself. Her savings grew as she deprived herself of comforts and food. She became more and more obsessed with the thought that time was short and soon Christ would return to judge the "quick and the dead".

Everywhere she looked, she thought she saw signs. The French Revolution had stirred the minds of intelligent people and set men arguing about the *Book of Revelation*. Eminent doctors of divinity discussed the issue through exchanges in letters in the newspapers. Joanna read as many newspapers as she could lay hands upon and, after considering carefully the opinions dealing with the Day of Judgement, told her followers and anyone else prepared to listen:

"The purpose of my prophecies is to warn the world that Christ's second coming is nigh."

Of course, she was not the only person in England expecting a second coming of Christ. Many others preached the same thing with equal conviction. Joanna's proclamation seemed not much different from the rest. Small wonder no one took her seriously.

Joanna had unwittingly become a feminist. She had survived so far by herself. She saw no reason why any woman should not do so and felt that women should be treated with more respect and their abilities in all fields - not just housekeeping and mothering - should be properly appreciated.

Then she thought: "If women were called upon to save the world, they would probably do a better job of it than a man."

Her inner voice explained that David, in the Old Testament, had been allowed many wives. So she invited all her women friends to become Brides of Christ. Mrs. Taylor and Mrs. Minifie and probably Mrs. Woolland, all went through a simple initiation ceremony bonding themselves to Christ, as nuns do when they take their vows. Then it occurred to her that she was the true and faithful bride of Christ. There had to be a *chosen* Bride and it had to be *her*. The others were merely symbolic. The idea began to germinate that she might be destined to become the divine mother of His Holy Child, the Second Messiah.

She surrounded herself with devoted women who stayed with her constantly and took it in turns to wait upon her. But Joanna, being a complex character, was at odds with herself. Part of her wanted to be tough and independent, while another part of her yearned for masculine protection, even though her women friends nursed and soothed her and acted as sounding boards for her outrageous ideas. She ate and slept with them, often in the same bed, on the most intimate terms.

Few men were allowed into this tight feminine world, for she enjoyed the power she had over women. Yet she was still in love with Pomeroy and pestered him relentlessly. Of all people, she wanted *him* to accept her. He was the man she had decided had been specifically chosen by God to convince the Church that she, as the Bride of the Lamb of God, was the "woman clothed with the sun" mentioned in *Revelation*, who had been placed on this earth at this particular time to prepare sinners for Judgement Day.

Pomeroy filled her thoughts and she worried about his rejection of her. He *had* to believe in her. He *had* to believe her inner voice was from God and not from the Devil, who she feared and dreaded. He *had* to recognise she was as good as the Virgin Mary. She couldn't bear his harsh assessment of her, that she was a poor, deluded woman at the mercy of Satan, and she became more and more determined to *make* him accept that she spoke under divine guidance.

Pleadingly she wrote to him: "Nothing will awaken the Ministers, till you are awakened to awaken them."

Chapter Five

Sojourn in Bristol

Joanna had achieved fame or, at least, notoriety. It wasn't quite what she coveted and was restricted to her small corner of England, where local people looked upon her as a sort of witch and came to her for spells and charms. On several occasions she was involved in distinctly witchlike practices.

For instance, there is the story of the Richards family, who had a smallholding just outside Exeter. They had been mysteriously losing one or two of their cattle every day and were convinced it was the result of witchcraft. They approached Joanna for help and she told them to write on pieces of parchment the magic words "Holiness to the Lord" and to put the pieces inside their horses' bridles. It apparently worked, for they soon stopped losing their cattle.

Then Mrs. Richards developed a bad headache which nothing seemed to shift, and her husband suggested she should try wearing one of the pieces of parchment under her cap. The pain vanished and the family became believers and joined Joanna's ranks. In similar ways she managed to build a strong following.

But to her own family she was an embarrassment. They felt that her witchlike reputation brought shame to the Southcotts and would have little to do with her. Joanna didn't like being disowned by her family. Even Susanna no longer replied to her letters and, despite an admiring circle of women friends, she felt isolated.

The only member of her family she had any influence over was her brother Joseph, five years her junior. Even as a child, Joseph was nervous of her and, as an adult, she terrified him. Yet he was the only Southcott ever to succumb to her powers.

She turned his little world upside down on more than one occasion with her blatant interference. Eventually the only way to stop her, it seemed, was to join her ranks, although deep down he believed her to be mad and unpredictable. As a young man, he remarked: "Joanna is not visited by the Spirit of Prophecy, but is misled either by a deranged mind or some evil spirit."

Joseph was a weak young man, given to exaggeration. Once he tried to impress his family by saying he had landed a glamorous job in the West Indies. Joanna saw through him at once. "I don't believe you," she told him contemptuously. "God has said you will go to Bristol soon and settle down there."

It was unnerving when, within weeks, he was offered a job in the Customs Office in Bristol. Although wary that it was part of one of Joanna's devious schemes for him, it was too good an offer to turn down. At least by going to Bristol he was putting a comfortable distance between himself and Joanna. Once there, with his wife and family, he made no attempt to contact her and rather hoped she would conveniently disappear from his life. But Joanna needed at least one member of her family to become part of her Mission, and knew Joseph was the only one she had any hope of recruiting. So she gave him half a year to settle down and then, in 1798, went to Bristol unannounced staying the night in lodgings.

Next morning, in the market place, she just happened to bump into Joseph's young wife who appeared to be unaware of the strained relationship between them and was happy to supply Joanna with all the family news. She explained that Joseph had given up the Customs job and was renting a smallholding, a mile out of the city, from a wealthy woman called Mrs. Edgar. He had planted apple trees and fruit bushes and was planning to make a comfortable living selling cider in the winter and fruit in the summer. So far, she said, everything seemed to be going according to plan. If Joanna wanted to see Joseph, he was coming into town that afternoon with produce to sell.

Joanna sensed that if they tried to meet by arrangement, he would snub her. So she deviously suggested her sister-in-law should tell him a "stranger" wanted to talk to him and was waiting for him in a nearby tea-house. It would be a merry surprise, she said. Joseph's young wife loved the idea of playing a prank on her husband and agreed. So when Joseph walked into the crowded tea-house, he was taken aback to see his sister sitting there. But, as Joanna had known full well, he was not the sort to make a scene and he greeted her politely. To his own amazement he even found himself inviting her to stay with him "for a few days".

Which was exactly what Joanna had in mind, except a few days was not sufficient time to gain control of him. She in fact stayed for over six months, by the end of which she had reduced him to a dithering wreck.

During her long visit, she became friendly with a Mr. and Mrs. Brown, who ran a book shop in Bristol. They had once lived in Honiton and knew the Southcott family well. They may have been the same Brown family she went to work for when she was 18, a short time before her mother died. Certainly they knew all about Joanna and her strange powers and wasted no time telling the rest of Bristol about her. News of her reached Mrs Edgar's son, who was a very curious young man and couldn't resist going to find out about her for himself.

When he called, Joanna was out and it was Joseph who answered the door. He was behind with the rent and at first thought that this was the reason for the visit. Already flustered, he became even more confused and embarrassed when asked about his sister who, Mr. Edgar said, he had heard from Mr. Brown was a prophetess.

"No," denied Joseph. "Mr. Brown has got it wrong. He has mixed us up with another family in Getson."

By the time Joanna came home, Joseph had convinced himself she would be sure to find the incident amusing. She didn't, but listened grimly as he told her about Mr. Edgar's visit. She then flew into a rage and gave him a scathing lecture, comparing his denial of her with Peter's denial of Christ.

"If you are ashamed of my prophecies you could have said you had a sister whose head was filled with strange ideas, but you didn't believe in them," she said. "At least then he could have decided to judge for himself whether or not to believe in me."

Joseph was made to feel extremely uncomfortable. As a child, Joanna had often scolded him in this way. It seemed as if things hadn't changed at all, except this time his wife and children were there watching and Joanna was making him look small in front of them. Hoping she would let the matter drop, he apologised. But a mere apology was not enough to satisfy her. She wanted him totally under her thumb.

"If you had told the truth, Mr. Edgar would have respected you and remained your friend. But, now you have deceived him, Mr. Edgar will become your enemy," she warned grimly.

This sounded unpleasantly like one of Joanna's predictions and made Joseph uneasy. To qualify her argument she said that the gentlemen of Bristol had announced publicly that they would wager £300 - a vast sum then - to £1 that there would be a King on the French throne in 1799.

"If Mr. Edgar had had the chance to hear my prophecies, I would have told him there will be no King on the throne by 1799 and he would have gained £300. What's more, if I had the money I would wager £3,000."

Joseph's wife even took Joanna's side and said he was wrong to have denied her and should have let Mr. Edgar make up his own mind. Thoroughly humiliated, Joseph repeated his apology, but refused to believe Mr. Edgar would turn against him. "He is too much of a gentleman," he insisted.

"No," warned Joanna ominously. "Now you have provoked him, he will no longer have faith in you."

It seemed she would never stop, but finally ended the lecture with one daunting sentence: "Realise, Joseph, once and for all, that people who deny Joanna Southcott only bring down God's wrath upon them."

It was a dreadful interview and Joseph never fully recovered from it. Before Joanna's untimely visit he had had such high hopes. The rent for his land was £8 an acre and he had reckoned that, with hard work, it would not be long before he made a reasonable profit. The future had never looked so bright. Now, it seemed, Joanna had put a curse on him. He soon sank into deep depression and was unable to cope. His land became over-run with weeds, which choked the fruit bushes so that the crop was poor and he had nothing to sell at the market. Within a short time he was seriously behind with the rent and too much in debt ever to catch up.

However, in an enlightened moment he worked out that if he asked Mrs. Edgar to accept, in lieu of the rent he owed, the trees and bushes he had planted - total value £30 - this would make up the difference. It seemed such a reasonable proposition he couldn't visualise it being turned down. Joanna approved of the plan but shrewdly told him to quickly discuss it with Mrs. Edgar so that, if she refused he still would have time to dig up the trees and bushes and sell them.

But Joseph no longer had the nerve. "Mr. Edgar would be offended if I made such an offer," he said weakly. "He'd think I didn't trust him. I prefer to leave it to his honour, as a gentleman." Joanna prophesied darkly that Edgar would deceive him. "After you have given up the land you won't be able to claim the trees legally and you will be arrested for the rent you owe."

"He will make sure I will not be hurt," was all Joseph could say. He made no more effort to solve the matter, preferring to leave it all to providence.

By Christmas Joanna was bored with Bristol anyway. Joseph was in such a pathetic state he was almost no longer worth converting. So she left, with an ominous warning to him to prepare for hard times. As she predicted, Mr. Edgar refused to accept the trees and bushes in payment for the rent owed. No amount of pleading would soften him. "It is my mother's business and nothing to do with me," he insisted.

So Joseph was arrested and thrown into jail for debt. The Bristol Humane Society appealed to Mr. Edgar's Christian soul, but he remained unmoved. Joseph had to remain in prison until the debt was paid.

From prison, Joseph wrote to his family begging for help. Kind-hearted Susanna scraped together enough money to pay half the debt but Joanna refused to contribute, saying he deserved his punishment since he had refused to listen to her. Finally the Bristol Humane Society paid the balance and Joseph was released. Joanna wrote smugly to him: "And so my prophecies, which I warned you of, were fulfilled in time."

After such an experience, the last thing one would have expected was for Joseph to become one of Joanna's converts. But he was weak and gullible. As she became more famous he was impressed to see her mixing with respectable, educated people he considered socially and intellectually superior to her and certainly to himself. Yet they seemed to regard Joanna with awe. So he had a change of mind and ingratiatingly offered to make out copies of her writings for her. It was hard to find anyone prepared to do this laborious job and of course she accepted. Soon he was doing this chore regularly.

At her farcical Neckinger Trial, in December 1804, Joseph swore to God on oath that, as a child, Joanna had a mild and placid disposition. "I have never known her to be false or of want of charity and inattentive to God. She always possessed an even temper and a regular turn of mind."

He didn't mention her cruel displays of temper and the way she had once ruined his life in Bristol. But by then he was totally under her spell. Susanna and the rest of the Southcotts remained convinced that she was insane and an embarrassment to them all.

Having thus dealt smartly with her brother Joseph, she turned her attention to that other Joseph, the Rev. Mr. Pomeroy. But he was to prove a much more difficult nut to crack.

Chapter Six

Joanna Replaces Brothers

After Joanna left Bristol her father, William, became ill. He was not expected to live long and was being nursed by Susanna at her home in Plymtree. Joanna decided this would be worth capitalising on, so she prophesied very publicly that he would die soon. Unfortunately for her reputation as a prophetess, he made an ill-timed recovery.

She had to then admit to her followers that she had made a mistake. In October 1800 William became ill again and Joanna was this time so convinced he would die that she even named the exact day - *St. Swithin's Day*. But, as if to spite her, the old rascal recovered. Joanna's enemies were delighted and referred to it often whenever they wanted to cast aspersions on her prophetic powers.

Meanwhile, Joseph Pomeroy obsessively filled her thoughts. She had been plaguing him with lengthy letters and fresh prophecies, all the time pleading with him to proclaim her divinely guided. A gentle sense of justice persuaded Pomeroy that maybe she had the right to some consideration, so he promised he would ask some of his clerical friends to examine her position.

In 1799 Pomeroy's wife suddenly died and consequently his problems with Joanna briefly paled. As soon as Joanna heard the news, she got it into her head that Pomeroy's wife had deliberately been removed from this earth by God to leave Pomeroy free to marry her. God, she was convinced, had appointed them a joint spiritual purpose and it was therefore desirable for them to tackle it together as man and wife.

From the day she heard about Mrs. Pomeroy's death, Joanna embarked on a determined campaign to get Pomeroy to seriously consider her as his second wife. She tried to involve him more and more in her activities, and promised: "I will conceal nothing from you. I have written as I was commanded and trust to your goodness to weigh it deeply."

As he struggled to overcome his grief, she plagued him with letters. Practically every day, one was delivered and each upset him more. He took to flinging them wearily into the fire, unopened. Then, in December 1799, one arrived which he did happen to open.

"I must beg of you a favour," she wrote. "Take care of *all* my letters. For you will find them the Lord's doing. If I stay for two years in Exeter, as Mr. Taylor expects me to, by then I believe the letters will convince you it is from God and no enthusiasm of a disordered brain."

Pomeroy suddenly felt guilty. The letters she was asking him to take care of he had already burnt. His Christian soul told him it was morally wrong to destroy papers which were of the greatest importance to Joanna, no matter what he thought of them. Since the letters could not now be recovered, he decided that the best thing was to ignore the issue.

Within a few days another letter came telling him that if he wouldn't help her prove herself, then she would go abroad for two years and he would not see her for a long time. Of course, this threat delighted Pomeroy and for a brief spell he dared visualise a period free from persecution. But it was too good to be true! Another letter followed: "You may be surprised to hear from me so soon," she wrote. And then went on to say she had changed her mind about going abroad.

Pomeroy's kindly patience finally snapped and he wrote curtly to her, telling her she was deranged and all she ever wrote was blasphemy, a remark which genuinely upset Joanna. Displaying unaccustomed humility, she replied it was "kind and generous" of him to point out to her that he considered her writings blasphemy and "my soul shudders at the thought". But she didn't remain humble for long. Her astounding powers of self-delusion soon convinced her that it was Pomeroy, not herself, under Satanic influence. She dismissed his condemnation as of no importance.

It was now eight years since that fateful night at her sister Susanna's house, when her dead mother's ghost had paid her a visit. She had made no positive progress towards convincing the world of her importance, and had made no real converts in the church, certainly none of any influence. No one else was rushing to help her, and so she put into practice the theory that God helped those who helped themselves. Her consequent plan was wildly ambitious for someone as sparsely educated as she was. After carefully compiling a collection of her "divine communications" she decided to publish them herself.

First, though, she made one last effort to seek recognition by asking her friends to make copies of the communications, which she delivered to Pomeroy. Then she wrote to five influential clergymen in Exeter and told them they could go to Pomeroy's house to read her writings and judge them for themselves. If, after seven days, they could prove she was a fraud then she would not publish them. Her intention was to provoke the clergy into some sort of action, for the writings included the names of prominent people in the city.

The five ministers included Archdeacon Moore, of Exeter Cathedral, the Rev. Mr. Tucker, of Heavitree and the Rev. Denny of Exeter. She gave them up to New Year's Day 1801 to reply. When not one of them did, she drew out the £100 she had saved for her old age and took her money and her writings to an Exeter printer and asked him to print them in pamphlet form.

The printer, Thomas Brice, was amused to see this extraordinary little country woman brandishing her bundle of scrappy, hand-written papers at him. She told him earnestly about her divine mission and aroused a certain amount of sympathy with her story of how she was risking her life's savings. He decided she was not mad, but harmlessly eccentric and accepted her order.

Obligingly he corrected her spelling mistakes and adjusted the bad grammar, but insisted on leaving out all the proper names, recognising she had written libellous things about some very respectable people in Exeter. He said he had no wish to be prosecuted for printing slander. He also objected to the words "the heads of the nation, not the King but those around him, are buying the judgement of the Lord on our land". This was too strong for comfort, he told her. Joanna, however, insisted on him printing dotted lines in their place to show that her words had been censored.

When she protested about the omissions, he told her diplomatically that he was full of admiration for her initiative and for having the courage of her convictions, and that he recognised she had a shrewd instinct for survival which he felt was akin to his own, but added he was a businessman and therefore obliged to put his own interests first.

"However perfect your convictions may be that what you have written is of God, and however strong your resolution to hazard all consequences, I have received no supernatural instructions and therefore feel not the spirit of martyrdom in me," he told her dryly. In the end, Joanna had to accept his conditions.

Despite this difference of opinion, he put a lot of effort into her project and charged her the minimum. In February, 1801, her first book was printed. To describe it as a book is generous. It was a humble, ninepenny pamphlet of 48 crudely bound pages covered in wobbly print. The title was *"The Strange Effects of Faith"*. In it she described her spiritual experiences, her struggle to gain recognition and her faith in herself.

Copies sold for ninepence each. *Part 2* was sixpence to subscribers and eightpence to non-subscribers. Subsequent editions varied from ninepence to one shilling and threepence. The cost of printing her first book was over £40. To break even, she would have had to sell more than a thousand copies. Even so, the price charged (of which she took a percentage) scandalised her enemies and they accused her of writing shocking material purely for financial gain.

She complained that: "I now stand £100 worse than I should have had I never took pen to hand."

On the first page she challenged the church, the clergy and the establishment. "If any twelve ministers who are good and worthy men will prove these writings come from the Devil, I will refrain from further printing. If they cannot, I shall go on."

A thousand copies were printed. In March, the rest of her savings were used to print a second booklet of similar length. By then her money had all gone and she needed to print the third section. She asked her sister, Susanna, for a loan but Susanna was not prepared to waste her money.

Joanna became thoroughly bitten by the publishing bug. It gave her a big thrill to see her name and her writings in print. Determined to go on, she approached a money-lender who was prepared to lend her money but charged, she said, "usurious interest". Joanna put up with it, feeling that, if she dropped dead that year, the publishing of her three little pieces of writing made her whole life worthwhile.

In modern terms, the scrappy, ragged-edged booklets became the most unlikely of best sellers. They were circulated round the country to various booksellers and by subscription, capturing the imagination of a public terrified by events taking place across the Channel and desperate for a spiritual solution to a troubled Europe. By January the following year, she somehow found the money to print four more booklets. Readers clamoured for them. Within a few months Joanna had achieved the recognition she wanted and had become a best-selling author into the bargain.

Up to now, she had been living in extreme poverty. She wrote that "the manner of my situation in Exeter was so mean and low, that I worked early and late to support myself and to go on with my writings, that I often experienced hunger and want. But I was told in 1801 that that was the last year I should ever know poverty and I bless the Lord from my inmost soul, for He has blessed me in my basket and in my store."

It was an age when religious fanatics abounded. Mystics sprouted up in the most unlikely of places and were never short of followers eager to be convinced. Many of them were fake mystics with astounding eccentricities who claimed to have incredible powers, and ruthlessly took advantage of simple minds. A sad fact was that the most gullible were usually the poorest and simplest, and therefore in dire need of spiritual comfort and guidance and eager to be told that the next world was better than the present one. So the mood of the times played an essential part in influencing the growth of Joanna's movement.

A young naval officer called Richard Brothers, who emerged as a man of note a few years before Joanna published her books, unwittingly became almost directly responsible for the rest of England taking any notice of her. A brief account of him is necessary at this point, because Joanna eventually stole from him not only his theories and beliefs and proclaimed them her own, but also took his disciples.

Richard Brothers had served under Admiral Keppel and Admiral Rodney and, during his time spent in France, had been distressed by the dreadful scenes he had witnessed. While still stunned, he came under the influence of a creed in Avignon, France, known as the New Israel. This fanatical group preached that the Bible taught that a King would one day rule the world from Jerusalem. The members were primarily Catholics and the young Richard was a devout Protestant and so, though he was drawn to their beliefs, he was wary of the Catholicism. Frightening hallucinations began to haunt him and affected his efficiency as an officer, so he was asked to leave the navy and promised a pension.

He returned to England hoping to regain his sanity. A London family, impressed by his naval background and educated accent, offered him lodgings. Although clearly deranged, he seemed harmless compared with the rough-neck lodgers they were accustomed to. He paid his rent regularly and so they left him in peace. Despite his eccentric manners, his neighbours generally were of the opinion he was good and inoffensive, and his landlady said she had never met a more pious and generous man.

For a year, Richard Brothers rarely left his room. He locked himself up with his Bible, studying it avidly and constantly drifting into a twilight world of weird dreams and trances chiefly concerned with the Day of Judgement. All times of the day and night he saw the most fantastic visions. He took to wailing and crying, which upset his landlady who began to have a change of mind.

He dreamt of a cynical and powerfully triumphant Satan striding down the streets of London, followed by rivers of blood, and he prayed to God to save the city from doom. His stories frightened his neighbours and many of them were scared to go to bed at night for fear Satan would take them unawares, for some of his prophecies came chillingly true! He said that the King of Sweden and Louis XVI would die violently. They did!

In between bouts of madness he was able to think clearly and worked out some brilliantly conceived mathematical calculations based on evidence from the Bible. He reckoned that the world would last only seven thousand years, by going back through all the biblical begats. He read in chapter 3, verse 8 of the second Epistle of St. Peter that a thousand years was the equivalent of only one day to God. God is described in *Genesis* as having made the world in a week, or seven thousand years in earthly terms.

So Brothers reckoned that the world was still in the process of being developed. According to the evidence in the Scriptures, the world was nearly 6,000 years, or six heavenly days, old. However, on the assumption that every working week ends with a Sabbath, Brothers' reasoning was that the six thousand years of the earth's existence would end with a *Millennium of Peace*. The early English Bible, he noted, stated that the world was created in 4004 BC. Therefore, the *Millennium of Peace* would begin in the year 2004 AD.

But Brothers was not satisfied with his own clever reckoning, which alone was sufficient to impress. Jewish years were lunar years and only lasted 354 days. This meant that the *Millennium of Peace* could begin literally any day.

After spending so much time working on this mind-shattering theory, Brothers' savings ran out and his landlady sued him for £33 rent. By now he was completely out of touch with worldly affairs and incapable of raising money. He was flung into Newgate Prison, which he didn't mind one bit. Worldly comforts meant nothing to him. He felt thoroughly at home in prison. He had a roof over his head and basic food to eat and was relieved of the burden of possessions or of making earthly decisions. In his element, he found himself a bare, cold corner and settled down happily to his fantastic calculations.

He went on to work out that the time had come for the Jews to regain Palestine and that God would send a glorious Redeemer to rule the world from the new Jerusalem. Finally, he came to the daunting conclusion that the man God had chosen to be that Redeemer was none other than Richard Brothers himself. Even as this stupendous revelation hit him, wrapped up in spiritual matters as he was and cloistered in the misery of a poorhouse, the state of world affairs filtered through to him. The French Revolution was three years old by then and the British Prime Minister, William Pitt,

Richard Brothers
engraving by William Sharp

William Sharp engraved this handsome likeness of Richard Brothers in 1795 when he believed the man was a true prophet and the Second Messiah the world was awaiting. After Brothers was certified mad, Sharp threatened to destroy all prints of him. But Joanna saw a chance to score over her rival and suggested that instead Brothers' name should simply be defaced on each print.

was refusing to interfere in French politics. But the new, French Revolutionary Government looked like becoming a threat to England. The English people were terrified of an invasion by the French and Brothers became aware of his new responsibilities as Redeemer. In 1792 - the year Joanna had her first divine visitation - Richard Brothers pulled himself together and left Newgate intent on saving England from disaster.

He was concerned for his country and did everything he thought practical to turn the tide of war. "I knew that the King would enter war, unless I could persuade him to remain at peace," he wrote. "I wrote to the King and I wrote to the Queen and the Minister of State. I beseeched them not to join this war. I explained to them that the Revolution in France proceeded from the Judgement of God. Therefore all attempts to preserve the Monarchy would be opposing God."

These letters were followed up with one to the Speaker of the House of Commons, asking if he could be allowed to address the House on the issue and was hurt when his letter was returned with a contemptuous note, dismissing his request as unthinkable. Brothers returned to the poorhouse at Newgate, where he felt safe. He was receiving clear messages from God, which he wrote down meticulously. He received his back-dated pension from the Navy and with this windfall was able to pay for the publishing of more books.

In one he wrote: "The Lord commands me to say to you, George III, King of England that, immediately on my being revealed to the Hebrews as their Prince, and to all nations as their Governor, your crown must be delivered up to me, so that your power and authority may cease."

He predicted that the King would involve himself and his entire family in misery and death unless all thought of war was abandoned. George III was going through his own private mental breakdown and so might well have considered these words perfectly reasonable, but other members of the Royal Family were shocked.

Brothers ordered every new disciple to state why they were convinced by him. Thousands obeyed him. Pamphlets testifying for him were published by the dozen, but these were countered with articles in the press such as "Lying Prophet Unmasked" and "Brothers' Forecasts Contested". Satirists had a field day writing parodies and caricaturists made him look ridiculous with obscene cartoons.

Richard Brothers' books also drew widespread interest from the intelligent and rational. Men and women of note were amongst these, the most surprising being William Sharp, the talented engraver famous throughout Europe for his work, who lived at 50 Titchfield Street, London.

Sharp was a member of the Imperial Academy of Vienna and the Royal Academy of Munich. At one time he was examined by the Privy Council as a suspect Radicalist but they decided that "this bold, handsome, jocular man looked as if he liked the good things of life too well to become a conspirator and the Council concluded that the Altar and the Throne had not much to fear from him".

He engraved a portrait of Richard Brothers which he ceremoniously unveiled on May 14, 1795. Under the picture was the inscription: "Fully believing this man whom God has appointed, I engrave his portrait. Wm. Sharp." He even made a second plate, convinced that one would not be enough to produce second copies when the *Final Millennium* began.

Another admirer was Thomas Philip Foley, M.A., Fellow of Jesus College, Cambridge. He came from a wealthy, influential Worcestershire family and was a nephew of Lord Foley. Thomas Foley lived a pampered life. Being a youngest son, not a great deal was expected of him except that he should be entertaining and pleasant. He was popular at Cambridge because of his good looks and private income, but also because he was outrageous and flamboyant. He took his MA in 1782, became a fellow of Jesus College and then his family offered him the Old Swinford Parish, near Stourbridge, West Midlands, which he accepted and looked forward to a pleasant, easy life.

He soon achieved a reputation for irreverent frivolity unbecoming to a man in his position. He scandalised his parishioners by conducting a funeral service with a surplice tossed over his hunting pink, and his fellow dons were appalled when he delivered lectures without a cap and gown, but dressed like a Regency buck. After reading Brothers' book, he was transformed to a certain extent, although he remained eccentric all his life.

Thomas Webster, of Falcon Court, High Street, Borough, was also a clergyman and lecturer in two City churches. He had published evangelical sermons, but a talk with Brothers convinced him that living prophets were more important than prophets in the Bible. When he first met Brothers he was young, less than twenty. He began to see visions himself and fell into a trance while conducting a funeral, and published a description of what he saw, with coloured illustrations.

During a visit to London, he was once waylaid by cut-throats and knocked down. He later became Rector of St. Botolphs, Cambridge and then Vicar of Oakington Parish Church, Cambridge. He married late in life and died in 1840, aged 60.

The Rev. Stanhope Bruce, Vicar of Inglesham, and his son, Colonel Basil Bruce, also became followers. "For six years," the Rev. Bruce noted in 1801, "I have fully believed through the writings of Brothers, that I should live to see the glory burst on an astonished world and it has been no small comfort to me to be blessed with a wife whose sentiments are in unity with my own."

George Turner, a rich Leeds trader, had been going about his daily business when a voice urged him to read one of Brothers' books. He borrowed one and as he read it, the divine voice revealed to him: "This is the Word of the Lord" and from that moment on he accepted that Brothers' ravings were the ultimate truth. As he grew older, he went steadily round the bend himself and spent the last few years of his life in an asylum, believing himself an instrument of God.

Peter Morrison, a wealthy cotton merchant of 12 Old Street, Liverpool, and Bartholomew Prescott, of Manchester, were also converts. Nathaniel Brassey Halhed, the distinguished M.P for Lymington, was so convinced that Brothers was a man with genuine vision that, on March 4, 1795, he raised a question in the House of Commons about Brothers' prophecies and asked for them to be considered seriously. He astonished the House by speaking on the subject, and in Brothers' defence, for three solid hours. Within a few years, all these men had transferred their loyalty and devotion to Joanna.

At the time Brothers was the most talked about man in England. Joanna Southcott, who took a deep interest in the national news, without doubt would have heard about him. Despite his madness, his movement grew to unexpected proportions. The Government became uneasy for, although they felt that Brothers was only a harmless crank, it was possible that with such a following the Revolutionists might make use of him politically.

On March 4, 1795, Brothers was arrested for treason and "maliciously publishing fantastical prophecies with intent to cause disturbances". The Privy Council adjourned the case for a report on his mental condition. He was certified insane by two doctors and the charges withdrawn. On May 4, 1795, he was sent to the Fisher Madhouse, Islington and remained there for eleven years until, on the death of William Pitt in 1806, his friends secured an order for his release from the new Government.

A problem was that, as a result of Richard Brothers being suddenly locked away, his predictions which so many people found convincing were left hanging in the air without a leader to fulfil them. On July 1 he should have been marching triumphantly into Constantinople at the head of an Israeli army. On November 9, he should have been crowned Redeemer of the World, in the new Jerusalem. On both occasions he was unfortunately detained in an English madhouse.

But he was not being idle. His mind was working overtime as he produced more prophecies of a preposterous nature, prophecies so bizarre, so clearly from the mind of a madman that respect from his followers diminished. In 1798 he published a list of what he demanded from every nation, in order to rebuild Jerusalem. Every King and Emperor, from the Czar of Russia to the King of Siam, was included on the list. From the King of England he wanted 90,000 sacks of flour and 60,000 iron shovels. The King of Denmark was ordered to supply 300 shiploads of timber and a suitable quantity of hammers, saws and axes and from the Emperor of Turkey he required 3,000 camels.

In 1801 he published an impressive description of his new Jerusalem which contained 200 pages of the exact dimension of every street, square, college, palace, cathedral, school and entertainment house planned, which he intended to build as soon as he was released from the madhouse. He created a fantastic picture of his own important flag - a golden sun on a background of bright green. He visualised himself marching in triumph, like a golden god at the head of a magnificent holy army. Even the most loyal of his believers were unable to take him seriously. He had become crazily overwhelmed with power and dreamt of ruling the world. In the end he was no more than a demented fool of a figure. Believers held a meeting to discuss him and concluded that he had "once been a true prophet" but that he had erred through pride.

But his theory about the imminent millennium had made too much of an impact and few were prepared to abandon it. It was decided, therefore, that most of what he wrote and said were the words of a lunatic but, despite his madness, God had revealed to him the truth of the *Final Millennium*. In this instance alone, it was agreed, he was sane.

Brothers had excited people's imaginations and made them question why there were no longer prophets to guide them as there had been in Biblical days. His followers desperately needed a replacement for him and Joanna's timely emergence seemed providential. It was an ideal moment for her to launch herself on an eagerly awaiting world. The time was ripe for a new prophet or prophetess to replace the one the people of England had just been deprived of.

Richard Brothers
an engraving by "Monk", 1795

This 1795 engraving of Brothers makes him look fanatical, unlike the handsome likeness William Sharp engraved of him in the same year.

Chapter Seven

The Box of Prophecies

It was the eccentric Thomas Foley who first took notice of Joanna, after Brothers had been in the madhouse for six years and his disciples were looking for a replacement. "Extraordinary accounts of Mrs. Southcott are in circulation," wrote Foley, giving her the title of Mrs, though she was unmarried, as a mark of respect. He placed an order for her books at once.

"I read them with attention, comparing them to the Scriptures, and I found them so consistent therewith and so agreeable in common sense, I was wonderfully struck. In my opinion, there is a greater body of spiritual light given to the world in these writings than was ever given since the Bible was written. There were, however, mysteries in them and I wrote to her for an explanation."

Brothers' other disillusioned disciples were equally excited by her. They wrote flattering letters, praising her and telling her all the things she had for years dearly wanted to hear from Pomeroy. "By reading her first three books," wrote the distinguished engraver, William Sharp, from his home in Titchfield Street, London, "I was convinced that her visitation was not of human wisdom."

Joanna was suddenly fashionable. She could scarcely believe that, after nine years of indifference, she was now being given the credence she felt she deserved. Her new converts sent her money to print more books. She didn't need much more encouragement than that and published every scrap of writing she had ever written, including letters to and from friends, family and enemies. She wrote back to her admirers and, despite her awful handwriting, the likes of Foley and Sharp were excited by her accounts of her dreams and her communications with God.

On October 10, 1801 she described in a letter to Stanhope Bruce how she dreamt she was lifted up and carried through the air, more than the height of the hedges above ground. "I was carried for miles and every field was ploughed and rolled and marked in squares like a pavement of roadstones. Every field was white and there were no green fields to be seen and every hedge and tree pruned bare. I was brought to a landing place where there was a house and two roads, one high and one low, and there was a tumult of people disputing my writings."

Joseph Pomeroy asked her: "Why do you suffer things to go forwards and backwards concerning your father's death?" Having been wrong twice about the day she said her father would die, it was a sensitive subject. To distract him, she wrote of mysterious reasons divinely assigned, but Pomeroy insisted she made herself plainer. Joanna then said that some gentlemen from London were to come to examine her writings. Pomeroy didn't believe her and asked to meet them. In a letter to him, she boasted that people were going to be astonished by her:

> "The more they see, the more they'll gaze,
> The more, like Adam, stand amazed.
> Till, like the Jews, they will begin
> To wonder where all her learning come."

Not all her letters were concerned with such lofty matters. On October 11, 1801, she wrote to Colonel Basil Bruce about an unpleasant incident involving a Mr. Purnell, a friend of her landlady, who argued constantly about her books, saying they were "enough to distract the head of anyone who read them". A quarrel between Mr. Purnell and a Southcottian called Mr. Clive, resulted in Purnell being struck in the face with the bridle of Clive's horse. Purnell retaliated by striking him on the back of the head with a heavy stick. The blow was fatal.

Joanna had been sleeping in a spare room while her bedstead was being repaired. On September 28, the day after the incident, she decided to sleep in her own room instead, on the floorboards. That night her landlady came to tell her to vacate the spare room, because it was needed for Mr. Purnell who had fled to her for safety after the ugly scene with Mr. Clive, and was surprised to find Joanna had already done so. Joanna capitalised by saying God had told her the spare room would be needed.

Flattered by the attention she was receiving from London, she tried to impress her new believers. A strong draw seemed to be her sealed writings. So she decided to emphasise the importance of them:

> "To see the Mysteries all appear,
> And then the wonder you'll see clear,

For the rockets all will burn
Just as the candles they will see,
And hung together on the line,
You'll see the mystery at the time.
For in a wonder all will gaze,
And in a wonder stand amazed.
To see the box of seals brought in.
And here's a mystery deep for Man,
And then some books to send to thee.
And with thy fifth book sealed must be,
And all will find the Book of Life,
And the Sixth Thousand end in the strife,
And every mystery will make clear,
When my Command is all done here."

She sometimes got confused about the identity of her new friends, and sent a letter by mistake to a Mr. Cadbury when it should have gone to a Mr. Bryson. Instead of forwarding the letter, Cadbury opened it and read it, and then wrote an angry reply, telling Joanna her writings were from the Devil and she was "in need of a physic".

"Whatever some men may think," she wrote to him, indignantly, "the same Spirit which inspired men to write the Bible has inspired me. How far I want a physic I cannot say - but whatever Spirit directs me hath more wisdom and knowledge than all men upon earth. Was every man a wonder for wisdom, they could not bring round such a mystery and make it appear in a straight line at last, as my writings are. So it is a Spirit wondrous in Wisdom, wondrous in Working, wondrous in Counsel, wondrous in Truth and wondrous you will find the end."

On November 5 it was traditional to light bonfires and send gunpowder rockets into the sky to mark the unsuccessful conspiracy in 1605 to blow up James I and Parliament at Westminster. It was considered a good excuse to get drunk and be merry. In a letter to Stanhope Bruce, on October 17, 1801, she used the celebrations to illustrate how men will behave in different ways when Judgement Day eventually arrives.

"November is a sure and certain sign,
How it will end with all the human kind,
The foot at first resembled that of hell.
Where the informal fiend does ever dwell.
The arts of man resemble all mankind,

That to such a master do their spirits bind,
And in the manner they have kept the day,
So in like manner all will pass away.
While lukewarm Christians they will little care,
And say, if we're in Christ, what shall we fear?
What further hopes have we for to believe?
If we're in Christ, what more can we receive?
But those that do profess to know My Name,
And by their conduct do deny the same,
Them of high treason I will sure condemn,
And lay it heavier on such sons of men,
For once my anger does begin to smoke,
Then sure such souls shall sink beneath my yoke.
Now from this type a warning I do give,
However every man now begin to live."

There were seven important new converts: 42-year-old Rev. Thomas P.Foley; Rev. Stanhope Bruce; Thomas Webster, only 20 years old but about to be ordained; 51-year-old William Sharp, the talented engraver; George Turner, a Leeds merchant; John Wilson of 113 Long Acre, London, and Peter Morrison, of Liverpool. She called them her "Seven Stars".

She wrote invitations to twelve people to come to Exeter to examine her writings but inexplicably received answers from thirteen. It would have been a simple task to track down the extra visitor, but she preferred to make a mystery of it. The last person to reply and accept, was John Wilson, the Kent coachbuilder and a disciple of Brothers.

Joanna had prepared twelve hand-written sets of sealed writings. Now, faced with a thirteenth visitor, she made up another set and sent them to Mr. Wilson with a note explaining the situation but warning him that one of the thirteen would die. "For that seal discovers the twelve - but one will fall, if *you* do stand!"

Amongst those chosen was Colonel Basil Bruce, son of the Rev. Stanhope Bruce, who she had a grudge against. On December 26, ten days after Joanna wrote of her sinister warning to Wilson, Basil Bruce - a healthy man in his early forties - inexplicably dropped dead. Joanna's new followers were stunned by his death but, far from discouraging them, it seemed to strengthen their faith in her. She followed this triumph almost immediately by darkly prophesying that another of his children would die shortly. Within weeks Bruce's *own* son died.

Out of the original twelve, Bruce had been the only one amongst them to express doubt. When she first wrote to him, he sent a reply saying: "I joyfully accept the arduous station to which it hath pleased God to call me."

But Basil, being a cautious man, was loth to waste good money buying a coach fare to Exeter, without first checking she was a *bona fide* prophetess. He took the precaution of writing to the Rev. Joseph Pomeroy to ask for his opinion of Joanna and, of course, Pomeroy replied immediately warning him that she was a demented blasphemer and a trouble-maker.

As a result, he abandoned his journey. Joanna was furious and later said his death was a manifold judgement of his lack of faith. Poor Mr. Bruce! Perhaps he would have survived if he had had a less suspicious nature. In her notes, Joanna claims Basil Bruce died at the exact hour as her own father. This is contradicted elsewhere, where she names the date of William's death as January 21, 1802.

Thomas Foley wrote his own account of what happened when they went to visit her. "At the end of 1801 I went to Exeter with the Rev. Stanhope Bruce, the Rev. Thomas Webster, Mr. William Sharp and Mr. John Wilson. We met a gentleman from Leeds called George Turner and another from Liverpool called Peter Morrison, which made us seven. Also supposed to be present was the Bishop of Exeter, the Archdeacon and three local clergy to complete the number.

"The Bishop told us he considered her mad and refused to come. The other clergy declined also. Therefore the full investigation of her writings had to be put off."

Foley and the other six men, however, were not disappointed for Joanna allowed them to read the prophecies anyway and Foley said their faith was confirmed.

For some reason the three deaths mentioned - that of Basil Bruce, his son and her own father - merged into one in her mind and seemed to assume spiritual significance. She also needed to pacify the Bruce family, having recently deeply distressed Basil's father, the Rev. Stanhope Bruce. He had confided to Joanna that he too had had a strange visitation from a heavenly spirit and gave her a written account of his experience. Without asking, Joanna published it. Stanhope Bruce was embarrassed and protested but she briskly swept aside his objections telling him she was only acting on God's orders.

In a letter to Thomas Foley, she commented: "It was not in the power of the Rev. Stanhope Bruce to prevent publishing them. He wrote to me that he wished them not to be put into print, as he feared that the world would mock him. But you see, the Lord hath wise ends in the way he taketh away."

Her rascally old father William eventually did die, on January 21, 1802. This time she didn't dare predict it, since her enemies gloated on the fact that she had been wrong twice on this issue. For years William had been a source of shame and embarrassment to her. He had been living in lodgings and an unscrupulous old woman was paid to look after him. Joanna was too busy to see him often, although she said she frequently sent money which she could ill afford.

She said she visited him once each summer to make sure his lodgings were clean and even scrubbed the floor herself. His room as she described it, sounded like a hovel of a place.

"The window glass was broken, but the landlady would not mend it," complained Joanna. "So it was stopped up with rags, which I pulled out to dry the floors."

This final illness of William's irked her more than she cared to admit. She almost suspected him of shamming and that he would never die but would go on being a burden to her forever.

The Devil tempted her, she said, by saying: "Thou fool. It is an easy matter for thee to go in and choke thy Father, and then all thy prophecies will appear true."

She said this suggestion appalled her because she was at heart a dutiful and devoted daughter and she thrust the awful thought from her mind.

"My heart grew more in love for my father than ever," she insisted.

During his last days, William was in a miserable state. The women attending him later told Joanna that they heard him talking to the Devil, who said he had come to take him away. William screamed he wouldn't go. "How can you think to have me when you know I have an interest in Christ?"

He continued to argue hotly with the Devil who, he said, he could see clearly although other occupants of the room couldn't. Those by his bedside said they could tell by William's answers he was terrified that the Devil would take him and, as a result, he had a convulsive fit.

When Joanna arrived William was insensible and unable to recognise anyone. She held his hand and he asked her hopefully, "Father?   Be you my father?"

Joanna replied patiently: "No, my dear father. **You** are **my** father."

William asked weakly who she was. She told him and she said he then recognised her and clasped her hand, telling her: "My dear, if *thou* art come, then Christ is coming."

Joanna stayed up with him all night and he died at half past four that morning, January 21. She said she was tired after her long journey and after keeping vigil beside her father for so many hours. Feeling drained, next morning she looked out of the window and saw the day was foul with black skies and heavy rain. Her spirits fell and she was too depressed to go to her father's burial.

"I was ill from my journey," she wrote defensively. "God ordered me not to go. Let the dead bury the dead, were the words spoken to me."

So that cold winter morning, with the rain dismally falling in grey sheets, she stayed in her warm bed nursing an aching head. The only ones to turn up at William's lodging house, to accompany his body to the churchyard, were Susanna and the old woman paid to look after him. Susanna was tearful and full of remorse, feeling she could have done more for her father in his last days and it had been wrong to allow him to be looked after by strangers.

She waited at the house for Joanna to arrive and was disappointed when she didn't turn up. William's body was brought downstairs and, as soon as it was taken out of the room, Susanna said she heard the most beautiful, heavenly music and singing. Pleasantly surprised, she cheered up a little and thanked the woman of the house for the singers, thinking that perhaps she had been a bit harsh in classing her as unscrupulous and grasping. The woman replied that there were no singers and, since by now the music had vanished, Susanna thought no more about it.

Braving the bleak weather, the two women walked behind the coffin to the churchyard. Susanna avoided speaking to her companion, having reaffirmed her opinion that she hadn't taken proper care of William. They trudged along the muddy lane in strained silence and, as they neared the churchyard, Susanna said she heard again the heavenly music and "it seemed to ascend higher and higher till it ascended out of my hearing".

By the time they arrived at the graveside, Susanna became faint with emotion as her father's body was lowered into the hole, which was flooded with water. "Water flounced almost over the coffin, which they told me could not be avoided as the churchyard lay so damp."

The grimness of the occasion was too much for her and she broke down in tears and sobbed. Onlookers were "astonished to see her in such agonies at the funeral of so helpless an old man" Joanna remarked later. But the truth was that Susanna was feeling ashamed at the way they had all neglected him.

When she returned to the house, Joanna was waiting. Susanna was now angry with her sister, for she'd heard the old woman remark that soon after William died, Joanna had thanked God that he had taken him out of a miserable world. Susanna accused Joanna of being hard and unfeeling.

Joanna replied calmly: "How can you wish to see him live in such misery, when he told us how miserable he was with the people he lodged with?"

Susanna said if she had known his end was near, she would have tried to alter his misery. Now, she said, her conscience reproached her. Joanna, dry-eyed and resolute, replied firmly: "I have nothing to reproach my conscience with. For I have done for my father the utmost and supported him to the last penny." As ever, Joanna was inspired to write a verse about the quarrel.

> "Repentance strong in some will come,
>   And like my sister say,
>   If we had known the day at hand,
>   We'd have done a different way.
>   No, here my heart doth burn,
>   My conscience I can clear.
>   He did entreat to come,
>   And dwell with me, I plain do see,
>   But him I did refuse."

After this, relations between the two sisters cooled and from then on they rarely saw each other. On January 27 she wrote to Thomas Foley giving him an alternative version of William's death, more becoming to the father of a divine prophetess. The petty family squabbles were, of course, left out. She enclosed a curious symbolic gift - a pair of gloves as a token of love. It was a sign, she said, that as the gloves are for the hand, so it was that the hand of the Lord was in her father's death. She explained how, when she had heard William was dying yet again, she hastily hired a horse "the worst that I have ever rode". When she arrived at her father's bedside, she thought he could not live till the close of day.

"But it came strongly to me that he would live till midnight, or cock crowing. I was to be particular to mark what hour he died. He had convulsive fits from eight at night till cock crowing. As soon as the cock crowed, my father's arms fell down, having been fighting before. At this we were all astonished. At half past four his breath stopped and he was gone."

Joanna decided, despite the vicious storm that had raged all night and continued next day, to return home the following morning, probably to escape the unpleasant atmosphere after her quarrel with Susanna. The roads were bad, the sky heavy and there was a hard wind to struggle against.

"The wind frightened the horse so that I thought he would have thrown me," she noted.

One mile from Exeter, a whirlwind rose and the horse rose on his back legs. Fearing for her life, Joanna dismounted and sent the horse off and walked the rest of the way. She finally reached home exhausted. Waiting for her were more glowing letters from her new admirers and she was able to put William's death and the quarrel with Susanna, to the back of her mind while she assessed her new position. As well as letters, believers were sending money, which she used to pay her publishing bills. Financially as well as spiritually, Joanna was coming up in the world. The £100 she had risked at the beginning of 1801 was producing handsome dividends.

On November 28 that year a parcel came from William Sharp crammed with expensive gifts. Still a very poor woman, she was overwhelmed. For a few days she struggled with her conscience, wondering whether to keep them or not. She desperately wanted to. She had rarely possessed anything pretty or expensive. By December 1 she had persuaded herself that God would have wanted her to keep them and so wrote a gushing thank-you note to Sharp.

"I received your box and presents. On opening the box I was surprised to see the valuable gifts. I found the thoughts of my heart true - you are still conferring your favours on me and though I am sorry my friends should put themselves to such an expense as they do for me, yet the presents are of such a nature that I am compelled to look at them with pleasure and delight, and accept them."

The seven disciples had returned to their homes singing her praises, and thoroughly satisfied with their new prophetess. Before they left Exeter most of the sealed papers were placed in a box which was entrusted to Sharp.

"I had a large case made," he recorded, "which enclosed the whole box, for the cords around it were sealed with seven seals and I put two between the box and the case, that the seals might not be broken." William Sharp took the sealed box with him on the coach to London, to keep in the safety of his large house in Titchfield Street.

Sharp and Foley felt Joanna would be better promoted in London and they asked her to come to London to live - assuring her that she would be taken care of financially. Joanna liked the idea and made plans to leave Exeter, being shrewd enough to recognise that a "prophet is not known in his own country" and, in order to safeguard her own future, it would be necessary to uproot herself and join her new friends.

But, first of all, she had some unfinished business to attend to in Exeter, the ungrateful city she considered had spurned her.

William Sharp
distinguished engraver and
First Custodian of Joanna's Box

In 1801 Joanna's writings and prophecies were placed in a Box which was entrusted to William Sharp, who took it with him on a coach from Exeter to London to keep in the safety of his house at 50, Titchfield Street.

"I had a large case made which enclosed the whole box, for the cords around it were sealed with seven seals and I put two between the box and the case, that the seals might not be broken."

Chapter Eight

Feuds with Pomeroy

Meanwhile the Rev. Mr. Joseph Pomeroy was enjoying a welcome break from Joanna's tiresome letters. She had been so busy corresponding with her new admirers that Pomeroy had temporarily taken second place on her list of priorities. But once her "Seven Stars" left Exeter, she again turned her attention to him. It irked her that so many respectable people now thought so much of her, yet so great was his contempt he was refusing even to accept her letters. For Pomeroy now held the opinion that Joanna was not only mentally unhinged, but cleverly calculating.

He told one of her most enthusiastic friends, Mr. Jones, that he considered Joanna Southcott had a "great deal of shrewd sense" and was not so innocent as she made out to be. Joanna asked Jones to deliver a letter to Pomeroy at his home in Cornwall. On his way he bumped into him in a narrow court in Bodmin and so, to save himself a journey, handed the letter to him at once. Pomeroy asked suspiciously: "Is it from that mad woman of Exeter?"

He spoke so loudly that Jones said his voice echoed in the narrow alley and people stopped curiously to hear what the fuss was about. "He said she was as mad as a March Hare," reported Jones. "I replied that there were many people of respect who supported her. He said that they were all mad. I did not like to say any more, for fear of a mob, so I apologised for upsetting him."

Pomeroy told him: "I know you do not mean to offend me. If I thought that, I would not speak to you." He refused to take the letter and went on his way. Jones said he arranged for the letter to be delivered by messenger and, about six weeks later, it was returned to him, having been opened.

By January, 1802, Pomeroy's reasons for not trusting Joanna took on more sinister dimensions. She had given permission to her "Seven Stars" to print all her letters in a new book to be published in London, and which they had agreed to pay for. When the book reached Exeter, Pomeroy's name was on almost every page.

He felt he didn't deserve this after all the kindness he had shown her, and regarded it as a public humiliation. Practically all his colleagues and friends thought her mad and here was he portrayed as one of her devoted followers. He felt sure they would laugh at him and he would be ridiculed throughout Exeter and the rest of the country.

The clergy of Exeter used to meet socially at Moll's Coffee House, in Cathedral Close, in the centre of the city. Pomeroy, desperately embarrassed, avoided the place because he was scared of being made fun of. In a bid to clear his name, he asked Joanna to sign a document stating that he considered her writings were from the Devil. She warned him of "fatal consequences" and so he agreed that his name should remain in the book but only on page three, included with a list of other ministers. He then told her she was "murdering his character, setting his house on fire and killing him". In the end, to his surprise, she signed the document, which he promptly took to the local newspaper and had inserted as an advertisement to clear his name.

"The Rev. Mr. Pomeroy and I have been at war ever since," she wrote to Bruce. "He says he can go into no company without being called a prophet and upbraided for supporting me. He said he was worried out of the Coffee House."

Angry at him for allowing the letter she had signed to be printed in the newspaper, Joanna wrote a letter of her own, and sent it to the Coffee House. It was cleverly pious and made Pomeroy look foolish and herself vastly superior.

"A prevalent report is amongst you in the Coffee House, that the Rev. Mr. Pomeroy has strengthened my hand in prophecies. He was so far from strengthening my hand that he told me in 1796, that if God had not spoken, I was writing blasphemy. In this manner he has continued ever since, reasoning with me concerning the danger I was in if my calling was not from God, which he could not see. To convert him, I put letters into his hands informing him of what would follow before it came to pass. And this truth he only disputed what might be my own fore-knowledge. Therefore he never strengthened my hand in one word of prophecies in his life.

"Had my writings not been of God, Mr. Pomeroy's wisdom and persuasion would have stopped my hand years ago. But my calling is from on high. So Mr. Pomeroy would have had to have more than the most high, if he was to overthrow it. For what is of man will come to nothing. But what is of God no man can overthrow.

"The world, the flesh and the Devil have tried against me but the power of God hath overcome all. Had Mr. Pomeroy acted contrary to what he has done, he would have acted contrary to the Gospel of Christ. For it is written in the Gospel that every Minister is a copy after Christ and can send no one empty away. But they must give their advice as Christ's ministers, according to the best of their judgement.

"And this Mr. Pomeroy has always done, though not believing my calling to be from God. But this respect to me proves the truth of our Saviour's words. If ministers pay no regard to the Gospel, how can the heavens? I am sorry the world has blamed Mr. Pomeroy. Is Christ's minister to be mocked and disregarded for paying respect to the laws of God and Man?"

Joanna then had a thousand handbills printed and distributed all over the city, displayed on every tree, post and wall space she could find. "To prevent any misrepresentation of the Rev. Mr. Pomeroy's opinion of me or my writings, I think it necessary to thus publicly announce that he used every argument of reason and religion to convince me that my pretensions to prophecy were false, that I was influenced by a deranged state of mind or the evil spirit, and that my writings were full of blasphemy. To contradict whatever may have been to the contrary, I fully make this public declaration."

Pomeroy came rushing round to Joanna's lodgings in a blind rage. He said he would rather she had set fire to his house, than humiliate him in such a way. Joanna replied demurely that God had ordered her to do it. "The Devil ordered you to," thundered Pomeroy. "I believe you were born for my ruin."

Pomeroy was beside himself with despair. Every street he turned into in the city, the offending piece of paper was there to mock him, hanging menacingly from a nail in a prominent place, like a warning corpse on a gibbet. It seemed there was no way he could defend himself. Joanna remained unrepentant. She said that God had told her the entire episode represented the fall of Man, who blamed Woman but did worse himself.

Pomeroy's close friends got together to decide how this evil woman could be dealt with. An official complaint was lodged with the Mayor of Exeter, Alderman Flood, and he sent for Joanna to attend the Guildhall to explain her behaviour to himself and other officials. It turned out not quite as Pomeroy's friends had intended. Instead of ticking her off, the Mayor and his councillors showed an undue amount of vulgar curiosity. They had heard of her reputation and were dying to find out for themselves what all the fuss was about.

They were rather disappointed to find that the woman they had been led to believe was quite remarkable, arrived looking unglamorous and homely.

In appearance, she certainly didn't live up to her reputation. However, the Mayor, who prided himself on being fair, found her inoffensive and harmless. He gave her a warm welcome and explained about the complaints he had had about the handbills she had posted all over the city. "I have been told that they hover on blasphemy," he said gently, not wishing to alarm her.

"My reason for printing the bills," replied Joanna, "was merely to clear my name, which has been tarnished as a result of an advertisement Mr. Pomeroy placed in the newspaper."

Mayor Flood was very understanding and said he felt she was justified considering the circumstances. He tentatively asked if she would demonstrate her amazing powers, by telling him what was going to happen during the next 12 months, but she said God would not allow her to trust anyone but close friends with her prophecies. So, once again she left the Guildhall in triumph, having impressed the Mayor and the other important gentlemen of her apparent sincerity, and the handbills remained in position until the wind or Pomeroy chose to tear them down.

Meanwhile her London friends proceeded to print every letter they could find, that Pomeroy had ever sent to Joanna. They took to writing to him regularly, pestering him almost as much as Joanna had done, and he was made to feel even more devastated. All the letters they wrote to him, they kept copies of and published. If they were lucky enough to get the occasional reply from him, that was published too. His name was mentioned over three hundred times in her publications until, in 1813, she finally instructed her people to write to him no more, since by then she had given up hope of ever winning him over.

At first he would write, begging them to stop using his name. Of course, these letters were printed, so he stopped. The affair caught the imagination of the newspapers and the public, and all the pamphlets that had the slightest reference to the quarrel between Joanna and Pomeroy, were instantly sold out. There was no way he could win. Appealing to their Christian souls was pointless because they had been told by Joanna to say they were acting on God's instructions.

He gathered any papers of hers left in his possession and, as he had done once before, flung them into the fire, cursing the day he had met her. When he received a letter from her, reminding him that it was God's will to safeguard her letters and papers she had put in his keeping, he replied that he had burnt them because they were written under the influence of the Devil.

Joanna was unreasonably upset, although she knew he had done this before. "Oh, the agonies of my soul, when he sent word that he had burned them," she moaned and then denounced him as a second Jehoiakim who, amongst other evil deeds, burnt the prophet's roll.

Regarding his reference to the Devil, she said bitterly: "Have I, by directions of the Devil, gone to your house when I had rather have gone ten miles another way than put my foot within your doors? For my heart always trembled, my legs always shook, whenever I was ordered to go to you. But you and I must shine as stars forever, if we don't make shipwreck of our faith with a good conscience."

News of the animosity between Pomeroy and Joanna reached London illuminaries, who discussed the affair with amusement. Robert Southey, the poet and travel writer and brother-in-law to Samuel Taylor Coleridge, took a keen interest in the affair and thought it amusing enough to comment on in his book, *"Letters from England"*.

"In an unhappy hour did Pomeroy burn those papers. Day after day, long letters were dispatched to him, sometimes from Joanna and sometimes from her followers, filled with exhortation, invective, texts of Scripture and denunciations of the Law in this world and the Devil in the next. And all these letters the prophetess prints, for this very sufficient reason - that all her believers purchase them. Mr. Pomeroy sometimes treats them with contempt, at other times he appeals to their compassion and, if they have any bowels of Christian charity, to let him rest and no longer add to the inconceivable and irreparable injuries which they have clearly occasioned him.

"If he is silent, they go on printing copies of all they write. When he is worried into replying, his answers do serve to swell Joanna's books. In this manner, this poor man is persecuted by a crazy prophetess and her four and twenty crazy elders who seem determined not to desist till, one way or other, they will have made him as ripe for Bedlam as they are themselves."

Southey left no one in any doubt about his opinion of her. "She is old and vulgar and illiterate. In all the innumerable volumes which she has sent into the world, there are not three connected sentences in sequence and the language alike violate common sense and common syntax."

He referred to a statement Joanna had once made, that "if Adam had refused listening to a foolish and ignorant woman at first, then man might refuse listening to a foolish woman at last." Southey conceded this was as good an argument as any to win over otherwise intelligent people.

He wrote that Joanna's pamphlets were half a yard high. "Had the heretics of old been half as voluminous and half as dull, St. Epiphanius would never have persevered through his task." He pointed out that her prophecies mostly concerned the weather and were of the sort that popular English almanacs contained, and threats concerning the fate of Europe and the successes of the French which were, at the time, the speculations of every newspaper and every politician in the country.

Southey noted in a letter to J. Neville White: "Had she been sent to Bedlam ten years ago, how many hundred persons would have been preserved from this infectious and disgraceful insanity!"

Pomeroy withdrew from public life as much as possible, although he still preached in his own church at St. Kew and at the Cathedral in Exeter. She had ruined his life and destroyed everything he held dear. He now believed she was not only insane, but calculating, ambitious and wicked and he was not alone in his views. No one in Exeter, of any note, took Joanna seriously. Most now believed she would do anything to achieve her own evil ends and there was a general feeling of unease about who her next target would be.

When a rumour spread that she had prophesied the city would be savagely destroyed by an immense fire which would lick up half the buildings, including the Guildhall, there was a mad panic to get out of the city and into the countryside.

So, after offending so many, Joanna finally decided she had had enough of her home town and made plans to join her new friends in London. It was arranged she should stay with Mrs. Basil Bruce, widow of the Colonel who had died after a serious lack of faith.

Her seven new disciples were now under the illusion that they had been divinely appointed to promote Joanna, and so were anxious to have their valuable prodigy under their direct control, feeling that if God was giving out important revelations through this simple woman, there was an urgent need to harness her gifts.

Foley and Sharp forwarded her the ten shillings for her coach fare and, on May 2, 1802, to the intense relief of most of Exeter, she was seen boarding the stagecoach to London with all her personal belongings - which seemed to suggest she was going for good.

Because roads had improved so much, it was possible to set off, by coach, early in the morning and arrive in London by nightfall. Joanna had never been further from Exeter than Bristol, so it was quite an adventure for her.

She was full of confidence that she was doing the right thing, for God had told her that her days of poverty were over for good. At 52 years old, it seemed, her life was about to begin all over again.

Chapter Nine

New Life in London

For the next few years Joanna was treated like a High Priestess. Pampered and lavished with love and devotion, she was fed, clothed and housed and inundated with gifts and money and grew fat on her fortune. With all this rich living, by the time William Sharp engraved her portrait on copper in 1812 (see cover), she had grown positively plump with large jowls, an ample bosom and sloping shoulders. Her eyes are shrewd and alert and there is a middle-aged Mona Lisa smile lurking round the corners of her thin lips.

From beneath an expensive, fashionable, floppy-brimmed bonnet tied with a wide ribbon escapes a mass of tight curls and, round her thick neck, she wears a large, soft-laced collar. She poses formidably behind a Bible, opened at Isaiah I, which rests on top of a pile of thick books level with her midriff. The general impression is of a smugly satisfied, but amiable matron of humble stock, who has done rather well for herself. Prints of the picture were distributed to her followers nation-wide, so that they would know what she looked like.

Her new friends were as cautious about her as she was of them. They were trying her out, testing her to see if she lived up to their high expectations. Foley, in particular, was uneasy. According to a Cambridge university friend, Henry Gunning, he was eating out one evening with a party of sophisticates who idly started talking about Joanna, voting her an impostor who needed to be taught a lesson. When they planned a prank to show her up in her true colours, Foley was too cowardly to admit that up to now he had taken her seriously, and went along with it.

Next morning the group called on Joanna and pretended to be in need of spiritual advice. She coolly invited them in and then pointed out that one of the people who had dined out with them the previous night, was absent. Their attitude changed when she told them that he had become ill after returning home from the party and would soon be dead. They hastened to his house and found him critically ill. Foley was staggered and his belief in Joanna was strengthened, perhaps out of fear of what might happen to him should he doubt her ever again. He said he sat beside his friend's bed, deeply grieved, and "scarcely left him during the few days he lived".

Although all her earthly needs were being taken care of, Joanna was not idle. From the luxury of Mrs. Bruce's house in Jermyn Street, she dictated to her disciples - at least one or two of them was always in attendance. In the space of a month, between them they wrote almost a thousand letters, according to Thomas Foley, scribbling uncomplainingly until their arms ached. Letters were sent to the "Lords Spiritual and Temporal and all the gentlemen of the House of Commons". Of these, some were received with amusement. A few people were converted. About a hundred were returned with contempt by those who believed Joanna demented and dangerous.

Her disciples drove her on relentlessly, as if she was a superwoman, until her highly-strung nature could take no more and she became exhausted and broke down. It was decided a spell of fresh, country air would do her good and in June that year she was sent to Market Deeping, Lincolnshire, to stay with the Rev. Stanhope Bruce's daughter. Away from the noise and bustle of London, Joanna calmed down and even found the energy to win another convert, the Rev. John Mossop.

News came that John Wilson was seriously ill and so she cut short her holiday and, on June 20, 1802, returned to London. She was met by her grim-faced disciples and taken to 113, Long Acre, Kentish Town, where John Wilson lay on his bed, doubled up in agony. Dr. William Roundell Wetherall, one of Joanna's believers, shook his head at her to indicate there was no hope. Joanna said she would pray for him for two days.

"In less than 24 hours," Wilson gratefully recorded, "I was delivered from excruciating pain." Everyone said it was a miracle, but Joanna modestly shrugged it off as merely "an answer to prayer".

Her list of converts was growing and her reputation had spread throughout London and had now reached the provinces. It was the influential and established converts she most valued, for she was now rubbing shoulders with the elite of London's intellectuals. William Sharp, for instance, was probably the most talented engraver of his day and his close friend was William Blake, engraver as well as painter, poet and mystic.

Sharp encouraged Blake to embrace Joanna's cause. He was certainly intrigued by her, being a highly sensitive and mystical person himself, instinctively drawn to psychic phenomena. But he was also blessed with common sense and once shrewdly said that "true superstition is ignorant honesty and that is beloved of god and man". As far as he could judge, Joanna was all talk and no action. She had performed no miracles nor accomplished anything superhuman, but had merely made a few lucky guesses about bad harvests and people dying suddenly. Before he was prepared to succumb to her, he needed more positive proof of her powers, but meanwhile found himself "obliged to regard her as an ordinary mortal".

Another close friend of the two of them was John Flaxman, the famous sculptor, who once remarked that Sharp had tried to make a convert of Blake but "such men as Blake are not fond of playing second fiddle. Hence Blake, himself a seer of visions and a dreamer of dreams, would not do homage to a rival claimant of the privilege of prophecy".

William Owen Pugh, a Welsh lexicographer who was one of Joanna's two dozen special advisers, also tried to influence Blake but had no more success. John Pye, landscape artist and talented engraver and a founder of the Artists' Benevolent Society, was another useful believer. In 1803 he made for her two exquisite glass communion chalices, intricately engraved, which are now in the Royal Albert Museum, Exeter.

An impressive member of Joanna's inner circle of devotees was Colonel William Tooke Harwood. His uncle was William Tooke, of Purley, a wealthy man obsessed with politics. Having no children of his own, he took a fatherly interest in a young politician called John Horne and promised to make him his heir if he adopted his name. John Horne Tooke never succeeded in politics and his main claim to fame was as a brilliant conversationalist. He used to give dazzling dinners at his Wimbledon home, his guests being among some of the most interesting men and women of the age.

William Hazlitt, the English essayist, said admiringly of John Horne Tooke: "His intellect was like a bow of polished steel, from which he shot sharp-pointed poisoned arrows at his friends in private and at his enemies in public" and that at Wimbledon "he sat like a king at his own table and gave law to his guests - and to the world". Joanna would not have been considered eligible to attend one of these elite gatherings - although she would have dearly loved to - but it is certain she would have frequently been a main topic of conversation.

Another dazzling member of the circle was William Godwin, political writer and novelist married to fellow writer, Mary Wollstonecraft. Their daughter, Mary, married Percy Bysshe Shelley and wrote *Frankenstein*.

A man Joanna admired and set her sights on, was Bermondsey philanthropist, Elias Carpenter, wealthy owner of a papermill on the river. Catherine ran a night school in the mill and for two hours each evening taught the basic skills of reading, writing and sums. The class of about fifty consisted mostly of his own workers and their families. A sermon was preached by the local preacher once a week, when the workers were reminded constantly of how well off they were.

Elias Carpenter was a hard man to win. He had already considered Brothers' preachings and rejected them because he recognised early that he was insane. He had heard of Joanna and reckoned she was of the same mould. Joanna asked him to visit her. Being a broad-minded man always willing to give new ideas a fair hearing, he went to see her and she read him some of her divine communications. He listened quietly and said he was very moved and the readings were "beautiful".

On July 14, 1802, he invited Joanna and some of her friends to his Bermondsey home to convince him further. He said he felt a "command to descend from the tree of worldly pursuits and advocate the cause of which she was an instrument". He told his wife: "I believe she has teachings from the Lord, to instruct us how He will prepare the inhabitants of the earth for the latter-day glory."

Only a few months before meeting Joanna, Carpenter had rescued a young, retarded lad called Joseph Prescott from a miserable existence in a London workhouse and given him a job at his mill on Jacob's island, in Bermondsey. Having some artistic ability, he painted the visions he saw. Carpenter was so impressed, he eventually took him into his own home to live.

Joseph Prescott was "uncultivated" but able to read a little. Carpenter paid him eighteen shillings a week to work at his mill, which gave him a chance to study the lad closely.

"His growth was checked each week and I tried to improve it by making him work in the garden and have plenty of air and exercise. This, with good living, soon altered his appearance. His temper was good, his mind cheerful, but volatile and giddy to excess. Yet, while with me, free from any known vice.

"He was very ingenious, apt to learn and, having musical instruments about the house, from seeing others perform he learned to play the flute. When I first took him in he was about fourteen years old, but so small he appeared not to exceed ten."

Prescott drew pictures of visions which further convinced Carpenter of Joanna's authenticity. He described how he saw a dove fly through a window, place itself before Joanna and vanish. He said he heard a voice say: "That is the Spirit of God, which influences Joanna Southcott." Flattered by the lad's pictures of her, Joanna even took some of them on her trips and showed them proudly to her followers.

After three years, the relationship between Carpenter and Joanna fell apart. His opinion of her changed radically and he lost faith and, as a result, became another target of her wild persecutions, figuring in her letters and other publications almost as much as Pomeroy himself.

Surrounded, as she was, by the constant cloying attentions of her devotees, Joanna often retired early to her room at Mrs. Bruce's house, with a glass of watered wine to strengthen her. In the bliss of her own company, she felt more receptive to divine attempts to contact her.

On August 2, 1802, she said God commanded her to "go to a house alone and dispute with the Powers of Darkness for seven days". She compared it to the time Christ was told by God to spend forty days in the Wilderness. Her friends didn't like the idea of her spending seven days alone - particularly as they couldn't help noticing she was already in a highly emotional state. But she insisted, sensing she was about to have one of her brainstorms and wanting to hide herself away. Before, it had always been easy to run to her sister Susanna for comfort. But Susanna was too far away and they had lost contact anyway. She didn't want her influential friends to think her mad, like Brothers.

The seven days she spent alone had a profound effect upon her. She said she physically battled with the Devil, who took on the form of a black pig with his mouth tied. She skinned his face with her nails, till she drew blood, sank her teeth into his flesh and bit off his finger. She said his blood tasted sweet.

Satan brought a friend called Appollyon with him and between them they made up an ingenious story: "It is written," they said with demonic glee, "Be still, and know that I am God." Satan maintained that this sort of immobile worship didn't suit him because he was a lively, cheerful spirit, full of mirth and gaiety, which God could not tolerate and therefore he was cast out of Heaven.

Appollyon claimed this was no great evil. "Thou knowest," he said in his own defence, "it is written of God, he is consuming fire and who can dwell in everlasting burnings? Our backs are not brass nor our sinews iron, to dwell with God in Heaven."

He went on to explain that the Heaven that men mistakenly desire, is in its nature the very hell of which they are so much afraid and this was sufficient proof of the truth of it all. The Devil invited all men to make themselves happy and lead a gay, agreeable life to suit his own cheerful disposition, whereas religion enjoined self-denial, penitence and all things contrary to man's natural inclinations.

Then Satan explained to Joanna about her so called divine spirit. He said that an evil spirit had loved her from her youth up and he found there was no other access to her heart, than by means of religion. Being himself able to foresee future events, he imparted this knowledge to her in the character of a good spirit.

This evil spirit had apparently lived in the body of a neighbour, called Mr. Follard, who told her that if she would not have him for a husband, he would die for her sake - which he promptly did, and then possessed her body. But Satan said he now wanted Joanna as his own mistress, and he threatened that, unless she broke her seals and destroyed her writings, he would tear her to pieces. The dispute became heated and Joanna "talked Satan out of patience". He complained that she gave him ten words for one and allowed him no time to speak. All men, he said, were tired of her tongue already and now she had tired the Devil himself.

He abused all women, saying no man could tame a woman's tongue - the sands of an hour-glass did not run faster - and it was better to dispute with a thousand men than one woman.

Then he became really nasty: "You infamous bitch! Thou has been flattering God that he may stand thy friend. Such low cunning arts I despise. Thou wheening devil! Stop thy damned eternal tongue. Thou runnest so fast all the devils in Hell cannot keep up with thee. God hath done something to choose a bitch of a woman that will down-argue the Devil and scarce give him room to speak."

To which Joanna replied, "If the woman is not ashamed of herself, the Devil cannot shame her."

After a week, she returned to Mrs. Bruce's house, thoroughly debilitated, and told her she was going to be very ill, but she was not to worry because eventually she would recover. Mrs. Bruce put her to bed and for forty days, Joanna said she refused food and drank nothing but watered wine. Her seven disciples watched her anxiously, afraid their new-found prophetess would be snatched from them. Only Sharp maintained faith, pointing out that Joanna had predicted her own recovery, so all must be well.

She was often alone in Mrs. Bruce's house. On September 21, 1802, Joanna awoke in terrible pain and was told by God to get out of bed and drink a glass of wine. She had a good stock of wine, which William Sharp had sent her. The wine relieved her pain "with a comfortable warmth" and she returned to her bed. Soon Ann Field, the wife of her bookseller, came to check on her, letting herself in with her own key.

Joanna became ill again and said she was seized with "a choking which seemed to rise from my stomach". This was accompanied by hysterical laughing fits, which lasted more than an hour. Though it was late, a doctor was sent for who prescribed some medicine and she recovered slightly but "by midnight was in a delirium". She said some strange power "invisibly forced" her out of bed and she lay senseless on the floor. Mrs. Field got her into bed again. Sluggish and incapable, Joanna was "forced" out of it again. Her friends said they were alarmed to see her so deathlike "without the least appearance of sense". She was incoherent and showed all the signs of being hopelessly drunk.

After a few weeks she recovered and there is an extraordinary account of a prank she and Ann Field once played on William Sharp. Not the sort of prank one would expect a divine prophetess to be party to.

William Sharp and a friend were expected one afternoon - not having been told she had recovered from her illness. Ann Field suggested playfully they should surprise him by making a dummy roughly the shape of Joanna's body and placing it under the bedclothes. The idea was that when William Sharp arrived, with a friend who had voiced the opinion that Joanna would not recover from her illness, Joanna would pretend to be still desperately ill so that William's friend could claim to have been right! Joanna first asked God to approve the joke and she said He agreed the idea was harmless. So, having had the prank condoned from the very highest level, the two giggling women made a dummy dressed in Joanna's night-clothes, and placed it in the bed she had just risen from. Then Joanna hid herself in another room and waited gleefully for the visitors to arrive.

The joke inevitably misfired. William Sharp walked into the room, saw the dummy lying there and said that he was sure "her health is perfectly restored and she is merely asleep". At this point, Joanna burst laughing into the room to share the joke. William Sharp's friend was offended and turned sulkily away saying she thought the joke presumptuous "with intent to cause fear". She was probably right.

As soon as she was strong enough, Joanna wrote about her confrontation with the Devil, in her own scrawly, impossible-to-read handwriting. Then she wrote a second book, on the same subject, which she dictated to William Sharp. Both books were published together.

It was about this time that Joanna took to using the seal which she had found years ago, while working in Mr. and Mrs. Taylor's upholstery shop in Exeter. She was fascinated by the seal and always carried it with her, using it to seal her letters and communications from God. After her fight with Satan and her consequent illness, her mind became hot and active. She remembered that the Apocalypse mentioned sealed people as well as sealed writings. She had always suspected that the seal had been deliberately placed in the Taylors' shop for her to find, and one day its special purpose would be revealed.

Elias Carpenter brought her a whole ream of new paper from his mill, as a gift. She looked at it for a while and then, in a burst of inspiration, dramatically took the paper from him, cut it into squares and drew circles on each square. Inside each circle she wrote the words:

"THE SEALED OF THE LORD, THE ELECT AND PRECIOUS. MAN'S REDEMPTION TO INHERIT THE TREE OF LIFE, TO BE MADE HEIRS OF GOD AND JOINT HEIRS OF JESUS CHRIST."

Carpenter asked her to explain. She told him that, since it appeared the Devil had the earth in his evil grip, no delivery could be hoped for until a sufficient number of people renounced him. "This is a petition believers must sign. that the earth may be the Lord's and that we may be delivered from Satan," she told him.

He asked if he could be the first to be sealed. He signed his own name below the petition and Joanna signed hers beneath his. Then she carefully folded it, envelope fashion, melted a blob of wax onto the folds and finally pressed her precious Seal on the soft wax. In this way, Elias Carpenter became the first of thousands who were eventually sealed by Joanna Southcott, in order to become one of the elite "sealed servants of the Lord".

Joanna was delighted with her own brilliance. One of her favourite phrases became "Sign for Satan's destruction". It became a sort of certificate to prove, in material terms, that the sealed person had officially renounced Satan - rather like signing a Temperance Oath. Soldiers fighting in the battle of Waterloo carried Joanna's seals close to their breasts, as a protection from the horrors of war.

To the poor and ignorant, it was a visible passport to heaven and they clamoured for the privilege of being sealed by her. To carry one of her seals in their pockets gave them a feeling of security, no matter how poor and miserable they were, for it guaranteed them a comfortable life after death, despite the abysmal state of the present world. Less ignorant people used the seals as lucky charms to ward off bad luck. Her enemies spitefully accused her of selling the seals for half-a-crown each and making money from them.

"Some say I have half-a-guinea for every seal. Others say five guineas. I answer I never took a penny for sealing and neither have my friends. I have ordered the thing to go out without money and without price."

It was true she had no need to sell them. There was enough money coming in in gifts. However, once the seals had been handed over to a person, there was nothing to stop them being sold or bartered. These seals were the subject of amused gossip. One practical advantage was that it was a way of counting the number of followers Joanna had. By the end of her first year in London, she had distributed a thousand. Four years later - by the end of 1807 - she reckoned she had sealed nearly 14,000. This is a good indication of how rapid her climb to fame was, since she decided to publish her first book with her own paltry savings.

She had every reason to feel fulfilled. Everything seemed to be going as planned. But every night she tossed and turned, unable to sleep. Nagging at the back of her mind was the thought of Pomeroy's accusation that she was deluded and guided by Satan. Still in love with him, she hankered after his approval.

She was plagued by vivid dreams. In 1802, she described how she dreamt she felt an arm round her neck, although she knew she was in bed by herself. She turned and saw a beautiful youth in blue clothes, spring out of bed. She followed him. He went into Mrs. Bruce's dining room, where there were six blind men. Another man had perfect sight and he told her that the six men would remain blind until her writings were proved.

However calculating Joanna appeared to be, however cruel and spiteful, to a certain extent she retained the pious spirit of her youth. She wanted to be regarded as good and pure, like her legendary Great Aunt Sarah, and desperately needed to be sure in her own mind that her divine voice was from God and not the Devil. No matter how many new believers joined her ranks, no matter how much she was flattered and pampered, she yearned for total reassurance from an authoritative figure that she was divinely guided. Her great wish was that one day Pomeroy would come to her and gently tell her that he had seen the light and truly believed she was one of God's messengers.

Fits of depression returned each day with a vengeance. During these bouts of despair, she struggled to convince herself she had not deluded thousands with her lies. At the back of her mind there was a nagging fear that she was being influenced by the Devil in a way that was too devious

One of Joanna's sealed
"proclamations of faith"

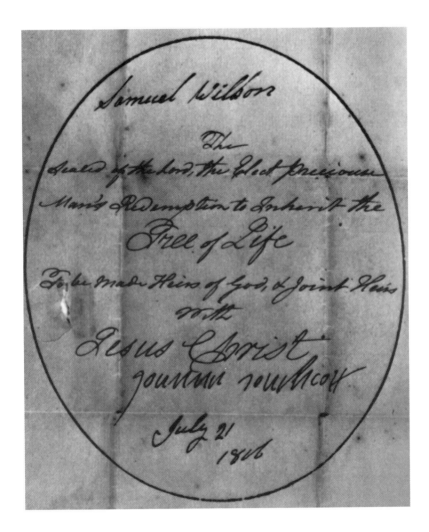

Joanna was able to count how many followers she had by the number of people she officially "sealed". This typical example, dated July 21, 1806, is made out to a Samuel Wilson. According to the poet, Lord Byron, these sealed proclamations often sold for a guinea each and were considered by many to be "Passports to Heaven".

for her to figure out. There was also the degrading feeling that she was virtually a "kept woman", depending on others to give her money. All her life she had worked hard. As an upholsteress she had been able to go to bed each night, knowing that her sore and bleeding fingers were proof that she had earned her keep that day. Now her hands were smooth from lack of physical work. It seemed unnatural for a farmer's daughter to be living the life of a lady, even though she did claim genteel origins. Her father's words came back to her: "I am ashamed to see you, a farmer's daughter, dressed like this."

Overcome with self-loathing, she took to beating herself severely. She would lash at her own legs with a leather strap, to atone for her vanity. Often she drew blood and she woke up with huge black bruises on her thighs. The women who attended her couldn't help noticing. But they didn't condemn her for these self-inflicted wounds, but accepted unquestioningly that it was the sort of behaviour only to be expected from a holy woman.

She began to take pride in the extent of her bruises, for they were visible proof to herself of how much she was prepared to suffer for God. She would sometimes claw at her own body with her finger nails, and in the morning claim she had been in a fierce tussle with the Devil.

As always, she emerged from her depressions with demonic confidence. As her brain cooled, thoughts of Satan fled. She would seem refreshed and inspired with new faith in herself.

Now that Richard Brothers had been abandoned by most of his followers in preference for Joanna, they looked to her for an opinion of him. Was he to be condemned as a madman or upheld as a prophet? He was still in the Fisher madhouse at Islington, still scribbling away crazily each day. Aware she had to tread carefully where he was concerned, since most of her new followers half believed in him, she decided to examine all his writings. On July 10, 1802, she noted cautiously that "we were all seated in Mr. Beecraft's parlour, busily reading Mr. Brothers' prophecies". This is a contradiction of a later statement, in April 1806, when she wrote: "I have never read Mr. Brothers' books in my life."

Brothers was a potential danger to her and, if he was ever taken seriously again, she was aware she could well lose all her new followers. She knew she had to be assertive in her views and at the same time firm and convincing. At first she said guardedly: "I was never told what of his books was right and what was wrong. I cannot decide upon them."

Then, realising this sounded feeble, she announced more certainly that: "Brothers' writings are fully of blasphemy that shocked me and I marvelled how it was said in my writings that the Lord had ever visited him at all." His prophecies, she said, were erroneous and he himself "deranged in his senses".

The truth was Joanna was jealous of Brothers, particularly of the special relationship he claimed he had with God and which in her madness she believed was hers exclusively. Her divine voice, however, guessed what she was thinking and reassured her: "I love none but thee."

One of Brothers' believers who she particularly coveted was Nathaniel Brassey Halhed, the distinguished MP for Lymington. She made a conscious effort to steal him from her rival by devious means, and was rewarded on November 10, 1802, when he accepted his seal and acknowledged his faith in her.

After giving him a few weeks to adjust to his new beliefs, Joanna sent him a cautious note: "I am now ordered to write you, as your faith for a long time has been to believe in Mr. Brothers and me as being both directed by God."

She told him that, since Brothers' last publication, it was clear he had abandoned the pathways of God and "his book must shame everyone that is endowed with reason and religion". She continued: "One would scarce believe a man in his right senses would write such a book. It must mortify his friends and give his enemies triumph over him."

It was vital not to upset those who had once sincerely committed themselves to Brothers. She had to choose her words carefully. Eventually, she felt it wise to give a verdict on Brothers which would satisfy everyone.

"After prophesying in God's name, and many of his prophecies coming true, God suffered a lying spirit to deceive him because some looked upon him as the Saviour who would redeem Israel."

In other words, Brothers had been one of God's prophets but the Devil had clouded his judgement and seduced him with promises of power and grandeur. It sounded remarkably like the very description many people, including most of all Pomeroy, might have used to describe Joanna.

Even though he was in a lunatic asylum, stories of Joanna penetrated Brothers' madness. The thought of a female usurper did not make him at all happy. On November 8, 1802, he published his final book, entitled "*A Dissertation on the Fall of Eve*". In it he concentrated on the *Book of Revelation* and stated that "it was God Himself that ordained the trial of obedience in our first parents". Joanna attacked these words, saying they were blasphemy. "He makes God the author of temptation," she said.

On being told that Joanna claimed the woman mentioned in *Revelation xii* was herself. Brothers remarked that the reference "is only to those resembling in faith that modest, identical woman and not any wild, impudent, misguided, seditious fanatic".

Joanna reacted to this like the true feminist she had become. "Being in prison," she wrote with contempt, "the powers of darkness worked hard upon him to load him with pride and envy against me." She then published a communication from God, which she said was the divine answer to Brothers' book. It was, she explained, "the answer of the Lord to prove that the last book printed in the name of Richard Brothers was written under the influence of the Devil".

Joanna was confident she had finally triumphed when, in the summer of 1806, William Sharp said he was going to destroy all the prints he had made of Brothers' likeness. She felt she could afford to appear generous and protested that such an action would be cruel, and suggested that instead Brothers' name should simply be defaced and with it the legend "Prince of the Hebrews".

Sharp agreed, and Joanna immediately sent for one of the prints. "I painted his name over in three red streaks and blotted out his name with red paint, knowing it was the Blood of Christ that must cleanse us from all sin and bring in the redemption of Man." She told her seven disciples about a dream she had, concerning two wagons driving along a country lane. One of them became stuck in a bog. The driver of the other wagon, seeing the plight his friend was in, decided to take another track.

This dream, she explained, was a message to herself that Brothers' way was impractical and she therefore should follow another course in order to achieve much the same as Brothers had intended to. She was fired by a burning ambition not just to become famous, but to become great and she expressed these feelings in verse.

> "How high on wondrous works, my name is brought.
> I, now forgetful of my wanted state,
> Talk with the rich - am courted by the great!
> From lisping childhood I Thy slave have been,
> Brought thousands to believe Thee, rich and poor.
> But, spare me! I'll bring some thousands more."

Chapter 10

High House Trial

Meanwhile, at Old Swinford, near Stourbridge, West Midlands, Thomas Foley was leading the rather dull life of a country pastor - a sharp contrast to London. He wasn't really cut out for the job, being a man who thrived on constant excitement. If it wasn't there he was inclined to manufacture it.

Joanna was shrewd enough to understand that, having embraced her Cause, he was eager for action and so she wrote asking him to help her increase her list of Sealed Believers by getting his parishioners to sign a seemingly harmless piece of paper proclaiming: "Christ's Glorious and Peaceable Kingdom to be established and come upon earth, and His Will be done upon Earth as it is done in Heaven, and Satan's kingdom to be destroyed in the prayer and desire of Joanna Southcott".

Foley was childishly thrilled, for the words seemed to clarify the whole purpose of the mission and give him a specific aim. He also saw it as an opportunity to tell his own parishioners of his enlightened views on Joanna Southcott.

Dizzily inspired, as only he could be, he gave her a glowing reference. "From a minute and diligent enquiry into the Inspired Writings and Character of Joanna Southcott and from other irresistible proofs laid before me, I do declare it is my firm and decided opinion that she is empowered by God to seal up the people in His Name - according to the Seventh Chapter of the *Revelation*."

He made a list of twenty-four influential local people he wanted to convert and sat up all night making copies of the two statements, Joanna's and his own, to send to them. These were delivered next day, Sunday, October 11, 1802, by his servant, George. Amongst those listed were eight members of the clergy and two members of the nobility, Lord Lyttleton and Lord Dudley. While he waited hopefully for replies, he decided to start a diary and that evening made his first entry, noting that it had been "a fine day after a night of rain".

By the Wednesday, he wrote in his diary, he had had no replies and so he sent his sexton, Mr. Harford, to circulate 200 printed leaflets about Joanna. Old Swinford was a sleepy little village. Villagers had already accepted that their vicar was mildly eccentric and didn't seem to mind.

However, the leaflets woke them up to the fact that he had now seriously taken leave of his senses. A close friend, the Rev. Pattinson, came to see him and there was some "pointed" conversation between them about Joanna's authenticity. "He could by no means convince me, nor could I convince him," wrote Foley.

That afternoon a curt note arrived from his own sister, returning the papers he had sent her and commenting stiffly that it was utterly beyond her comprehension and she firmly declined signing.

The weather was depressing, which didn't help. It rained dismally and each day in his diary he gloomily noted that "nothing happened". The monotony was broken by occasional letters or visitors curious to find out for themselves whether the Vicar of Old Swinford really had gone mad after flooding the neighbourhood with cranky literature about a crazy fanatic who appeared to have bewitched him.

Just as he was beginning to despair at his lack of success, a letter arrived from Joanna summoning him to London. With relief, he set off by coach and took up residence in his uncle Lord Foley's town house, High House, Paddington. Joanna wanted him and other disciples to write letters to important people and make dozens of copies of them and her divine communications.

Foley thoroughly enjoyed mixing with stimulating people such as William Sharp, John Wilson and Thomas Webster and, of course, Joanna. Not a day went by without him visiting her at her lodgings at Mrs. Bruce's house.

Joanna was still uneasy about accusations that she was really an instrument of the Devil and longed for respectability. It wasn't just a matter of personal pride. The very idea that the Devil might be controlling her without her realising it was upsetting.

She decided the most sensible way to tackle the situation was to have a public enquiry into her character, to which established members of the Church, the Government and Members of the House of Commons and the Royal Family, would be invited. They would be given the opportunity to cross examine her and decide for themselves whether or not she was evil.

A date was chosen - January 12, 1803 - and, during December, 1802, a huge publicity campaign was launched. Twenty pounds was spent on an advertisement in *The Star* newspaper inviting anyone who wished to attend. In answer to those who suggested this was blasphemy, Joanna loftily replied that God had ordered her to place the advertisement.

> "The Star of Judah shall arise,
> And I shall open many eyes.
> For now her Trial will come on.
> Judges & Jury bold may stand,
> Because the Victory they will gain,
> I've blunted the edge of every man."

Joanna had been having success upon success with her books. They were selling like hotcakes! Despite two periods of mental instability, she felt she was riding on a wave of good fortune and a properly conducted enquiry, to confirm she was an instrument of God, would be the climax to it all.

On December 10, Foley wrote to King George III inviting him to Joanna's Trial. There was no reply! He remained optimistic, predicting that "all would come in an honest way to investigate". On December 12, his eighteen-month old son, Richard, was baptised and Joanna was Godmother. She gave him one of her Seals as a christening gift. William Sharp was the second Godfather but didn't turn up for the service and so Elias Carpenter stood proxy for him. Later everyone returned to High House - including Joanna - for a celebration meal. William Sharp eventually arrived late, but in time to hear Joanna read some of the wordy communications.

On December 22, Foley wrote again to King George III, saying Joanna was ready to prove herself before any learned men or ministers that His Majesty might be pleased to appoint. The letter was again ignored. Poor King George! Little did he realise that, by ignoring Joanna, such horrors lay in store for him. Those that offended her were usually cursed, in God's name, and being of royal blood was no guarantee of immunity.

Joanna was disappointed when Nathaniel Halhed, MP for Lymington, turned down her invitation, particularly as he was one of Richard Brothers' supporters. He cautiously wrote to say he preferred to await the directions of the Lord himself.

God had said it was all right for her seven disciples to seal people too, and so they were each ordered to acquire a personal seal. Foley's portrayed a lion and he proudly noted in his diary that he went to collect it. On Christmas Day, 1802, Joanna went with Thomas and Elizabeth Foley to the parish church and later they all enjoyed a merry dinner at High House with Charles Taylor, son of Joanna's close friend from Exeter, Lucy Taylor, and a special favourite of hers.

On December 31, New Year's Eve, encouraging news arrived that several of the Bishops had sent for Joanna's books, and hopes were raised that they were coming round to Joanna's way of thinking. There was also "a very pretty letter" from a young man called Richard Law, begging Joanna to allow him to be present at the Trial. Charmed by his flattering prose and smooth manner, Joanna invited him to be one of her Jurymen.

Installed in the luxury of his uncle's house with his wife, Elizabeth, and their son, Richard, Thomas Foley wrote in his diary that he was looking forward to Joanna's Trial with "satisfaction and joy" and hoping it would bring him deep personal fulfilment. He had decided that High House was the most suitable venue for the Trial, since several hundreds were expected to come. So, on the Monday, he went shopping to buy new crockery for the event.

On January 6, he wrote to Pomeroy again urging him to participate and Pomeroy stiffly declined. Mrs. Lucy Taylor and her daughter Fanny, Mrs. Beecraft from Market Deeping, and George Turner from Leeds, arrived. "The whole day was a bustle, to make our beloved friends comfortable and happy," wrote Foley, who was hugely enjoying the event.

Foley's forty-fifth birthday fell on the Sunday and, to make it particularly memorable, he formally asked Joanna to take up residence there, proudly noting that "Joanna came to HER house - High House, Paddington". As a flamboyant gesture, that evening he presented her with the Great Key of the house. Joanna, realising it wasn't his to give, tactfully returned it for him to "look after for her". Guests at his birthday dinner included Stanhope Bruce, George Turner, William Sharp, John Wilson, Charles Abbott, Elias Field (her book-seller), Dr. Wetherall (Joanna's doctor), Richard Law, William Jowett, Lucy Taylor, Fanny Taylor, Peter Morrison and Charles Taylor, Mrs. Beecraft, Mr. Dix and Elizabeth Foley and Joanna.

In a curious preliminary ritual the party, solemnly carrying Joanna's Box of Sealed Writings, trooped to the dark vaults below stairs. The writings were to remain there until the day of the Trial when, at 11am they were to be taken from the cellars into the Great Room of the house. During the ceremony, Foley said, an excessively high wind raged through the house, which he seemed to think was significant.

January 12 finally dawned, frosty but fine with bright sunshine. Foley was as excited as a schoolboy. Everyone had some part to play in the planned rituals for, at various times, Joanna had given out copies of her prophecies and there were many bundles of papers all sealed up with different seals. These were the writings that were to be examined. The group of believers resident at High House now numbered eighteen.

Forty-nine people assembled in the kitchen that morning with not a single non-believer amongst them. Joanna was not there! She had staged her entry for later on. All the women were dressed in white wedding dresses, to indicate that they were all brides of Christ. The judges were to be Stanhope Bruce, Thomas Foley, Elias Carpenter, William Jowett, Peter Morrison, William Sharp, Charles Taylor, George Turner, Dr. William Roundell Wetherall, and John Wilson. The chief judge should have been Joseph Pomeroy. In his absence, his place was symbolically taken by Foley's baby son Richard.

After some initial shyness, the group got themselves awkwardly organised. The men segregated themselves from the women and then followed Foley out of the kitchen and down to the cellar, where the box containing the parcels of sealed prophecies had been placed three days earlier. After a short interval, the women joined them. They all stood solemnly regarding the writings. There was some sense in this bizarre ritual. The bundles of writings represented the body of Christ (or Word of God) which had been buried in the vaults for three days and three nights. A symbolic Resurrection was enacted. The *Box,* draped with an ornate cover, was carried up into the Great Room, followed first by the judges and jurymen and then by the women. The writings were placed upon a table around which everyone seated themselves.

Then the double doors were dramatically flung open and Joanna made a spectacular entry, her stocky form clothed in virgin-white from head to toe like a young bride. She carried Foley's baby son in her arms, whose chubby hands clutched a cake decorated with a starry crown. His mother, Elizabeth followed, watching anxiously in case he disgraced her by dropping the cake, which had unwittingly been sent by one of Foley's lady admirers. He pointed out that it was made of "the type of good fruit now to be brought forward and given to men".

It was a moving moment for the assembly and Foley said Joanna was "much affected". She delivered an animated speech, referring to the infant and her own writings and comparing them to the Birth, the Burial and the Resurrection. Foley described her speech as forceful and said the company was "much roused".

Happy that her words had produced the desired effect, Joanna ordered the *Box of Writings* to be opened. As this was about to be done, proceedings were dramatically halted by a message from a servant to say that there were two female non-believers waiting in the hall who wished to join the assembly. They had called on impulse and were not dressed in white, which Joanna had ordered was to be worn that day by all women present. Foley said that, after this had been explained to them, they were offered appropriate dresses to change into but, somewhat embarrassed, they declined and hurriedly departed. Peter Morrison pointed out triumphantly that only the previous day he had predicted someone would come without a wedding dress and go away again. Many present remembered and congratulated him. Some years later Joanna was to jealously reprimand him for predicting in his own right.

Charles Taylor had the honour of taking the cover off the *Box*. The cords were cut and the seals broken and then, after reading a wordy communication from God to them all, Joanna ordered everyone to kiss Baby Richard. Foley was beside himself with fatherly pride and wrote: "The conduct of the little boy was most remarkable and extraordinary, as he received the kisses of all present with evident marks of delight and satisfaction, that appeared to most of those present almost equal to a miracle."

Attention was then directed upon the sealed papers. Joanna read some of her writings and the judges made copies of them. There was a distinct lack of discipline as papers were passed haphazardly to and fro across the table, examined and copied and handed back.

Eventually, the papers became so mixed up Joanna couldn't lay her hands on the ones she wanted and so "could not refer to those interesting parts she wished to". Utter shambles resulted as the whole proceedings went to pot and many began to suspect uneasily that they were participating in some ridiculous farce. Foley admitted sadly that, "some confusion and embarrassment took place, which soon after occasioned the assembly to break up. Many who expected to see this day great signs and wonders, were evidently much disappointed and probably what had happened appeared to them as idle tales and they believed them not."

During the first few days of the trial, the weather was nasty and a savage wind howled constantly. It seemed to affect Joanna for she came down on the third day to breakfast, looking ill. After taking some medicine and a little wine she seemed to recover. The third and fourth days were spent copying letters and communications. Nobody complained and Foley, though rather weary like everyone else, remained hopeful that there would be an astounding and uplifting climax.

Foley wrote loyally that:"Joanna Southcott is now so clear that her calling is of God that she is ready to meet any diviners or any of the Learned and if they deny her, then they deny their Bibles."

The next two days passed much the same. There was some light discussion about the wisdom of a new ruling that, at Exeter Cathedral, worshippers would be allowed to dispense with the custom of kneeling painfully on the cold marble slabs and merely turn to the altar when praying.

The final day arrived! Everyone assembled in the Great Room at half-past eleven in the morning, vaguely anticipating a miracle. Prayers were said and all present agreed that Joanna was *definitely* divine. She entered the room in apparent good spirits, looking extremely solid and unethereal, and shook everyone by the hand while Foley read aloud.

Foley was sure something spectacular would happen now. His dearest wish was that she would go into a trance, during which God would take the opportunity to reveal through her his ultimate plans. But no such luck! She stood up and gave an animated speech, challenging anyone who believed she was under the influence of the Devil, to come forward and give their reasons. No one stirred, so Joanna spoke on monotonously for another hour, explaining at length what she had explained each day throughout the week.

She then read her proclamation: (see page 52)

"I, Joanna Southcott, am clearly convinced that my calling is of God and my writings are indicted by His Spirit as it is impossible for any Spirit but an All-Wise God, that is wondrous in working, wondrous in power, wondrous in wisdom, wondrous in Truth, could have brought round such mysteries so full of Truth as are in my writings - so I am clear and know in whom I have believed, that all my writings came from the Spirit of the Most High God."

This speech marked the end of the Trial. It was a real anti-climax and a flat sense of disappointment prevailed. But if Foley felt let down it did not show when he noted in his diary: "The Trial ended on 18th January, 1803, and Satan was cast out and the woman was freed. Thank God! Thank God! Thank God!"

He added more formally: "The prophecies of Joanna Southcott have been closely examined for seven days. The examination of her writings was made public to everyone who wished to come. None were refused admittance. As unbelievers were invited by repeated letters, so now let every mouth be stopped and every tongue silent and know that the end is near at hand, that Satan's power will be destroyed and Christ's Kingdom near."

Even so, there *was* dissatisfaction amongst the believers and that evening strong opinions were freely expressed. Even Foley joined the dissenters and next day there were rumours he had withdrawn from Joanna's Mission.

But if he *was* disillusioned Joanna must have had a firm talk with him, for the next day he wrote defensively in his diary: "Never was a more false and wicked report given out than saying that I had withdrawn from the Cause of Joanna Southcott, which I now believe we have a proof positive and demonstrative. It is the Cause of the Most High God - in which Cause I hope ever to live and die."

Despite provoking ridicule, a bonus of the Trial was that, because it created valuable publicity which made the public curious, sales of books rocketed. On January 22, 1803, less than a week after the last day of the Trial, Foley advertised that Joanna's prophecies could be bought at Elias Field's bookshop, 3, Broad Court, Long Acre, London, and at Symon's bookshop, Gandy Lane, Exeter. The books were also available on subscription from William Sharp and Elias Carpenter at Paddington. The results of the Trial were published in the form of a handbill entitled *"Examination of Prophecies"*. It bore the names of the twenty-three people who signed the document of testimony of the truth of Joanna's writings.

A celebrated preacher called Rowland Hill held one of these bills over his pulpit and exclaimed scornfully: "Here are three and twenty mad fools."

The expense of entertaining so many during the Trial had been a drain on Thomas Foley's limited private income. On February 18 he was forced to borrow two guineas from Joanna towards the housekeeping. Next day he was able to pay Elias Field ten shillings and sixpence for four of Joanna's books and a week later paid out five shillings and a penny to William Sharp for some letters and spent seven shillings on purchasing "a ring of Joanna's hair", which he believed was remarkably good value.

He later made a careful list of nearly a hundred people invited to the High House trial. Those that returned their letters "with contempt" he marked with an incriminating cross. Included were Lord Northwick, the Duke of Kent, William Pitt, the Earl of Derby, Earl Grosvenor, Lord

Palmerston, Lord Scarsdale, the Duke of Devonshire, the Duke of Rutland, Earl Darnley, Lord Douglas and the Duke of Bridgewater.

Those that ignored the invitations were asked to return them and when these people remained aloof, their names were placed in what Foley described as The Dead Letter Office, to be dealt with later as Joanna saw fit. King George III's name was amongst these.

Details of the rituals which had taken place in Lord Foley's London home soon leaked out. Lord Foley was horrified when he heard of what his nephew had been getting up to and, deciding it was an abuse of his generosity, cut Thomas out of his will.

Even Joanna was unable to pretend that the trial had been anything but a fiasco, for she was the laughing stock of London and the Press wallowed in her humiliation. But she nonetheless convinced herself that she had merely been premature in hoping for success and she should now concentrate on building up her following. She received divine instructions to preach further afield - which was very convenient since just at that moment there was nothing she wanted more than to get right out of London, away from all the scorn.

In June she embarked on a tour, first going to Bristol to spend time with her brother, Joseph, who had become a convert. From there she went to Exeter. Her fame had reached her home town and citizens came out in droves to be sealed by her. Flushed with this success she went to stay with Foley and his wife at Old Swinford and in this lovely village, Joanna remained for three months, enjoying the rest of the summer. She dictated to Foley a short book, entitled "*Spiritual Communications on the Prayers of the Church of England*" and he said he was thrilled to be allowed the privilege of taking dictation from her.

But she wasn't totally relaxed! Although Elizabeth and Thomas made sure she was comfortable they were just a little bit too earnest. Her slightest remark was considered incredibly meaningful by the impressionable Foley. It was such an effort, forever acting the part of the divinely-inspired prophetess. So she tried to get away from them, by taking long coach rides in the country. In this way she became familiar with the charming village of Blockley, Gloucestershire. She yearned for her own country retreat for those awful times when her mind became "agitated" and she needed to hide herself away. Blockley enchanted her. It was peaceful and quaint and reminded her of Gittisham. She didn't feel at ease at Old Swinford, despite Foley's eager kindness.

She was inwardly lonely and looking for affection, which she found on a trip to Blockley, where George Troup, a page to the Prince Regent, introduced her to his cousin, John Smith, six years her junior and charming, educated and refined. He was steward to the Earl of Darnley and very much a gentleman. He owned a perfumery in Princes Street, Cavendish Square - Smith and Nephew. The nephew part of the partnership, Samuel, inherited the business when his uncle died in 1829. The firm supplied the Prince Regent and other members of the Royal Court with exotic perfumes. John Smith owned Rock Cottage in Blockley, Gloucestershire, a lovely old house nestling in the rockface just outside the village. Joanna came to regard it as her country retreat, although she never actually owned it. But part of it was reserved exclusively for her and from 1803 onwards she went there regularly to hide from the prying eyes of the world.

It had to be a secret arrangement. Although John Smith and Joanna were virtually living together, it would not have been good for Joanna's image for this to become generally known - particularly amongst her own believers. There were stories already circulating that she was pregnant, although she still claimed to be a virgin. William Blake wrote a fragment of verse about her - because he was a bit of a mystic himself people later presumed that he was writing prophetically about Joanna's alleged immaculate pregnancy in 1814. It was entitled "*On the Virginity of the Virgin Mary and Joanna Southcott*".

> "Whate'er is done to her, she cannot know.
> And if you'll ask her she will swear it so.
> Whether 'tis good or evil, none's to blame.
> No one can take the pride, no one the shame."

The poet, despite his strange surrealistic poems and paintings, was shrewd enough to see through Joanna. He was part of a group of witty, mainstream intellectuals who made it their business to know all that was going on, so any suggestion that Joanna was pregnant, or rumoured to be, would have reached him and he'd have been amused enough to write the above odd lines.

Both John Smith and George Troup were devoted disciples but John Smith also became Joanna's lover. There is strong evidence that during this period she bore him a child, whom she called Sarah after the Great Aunt she admired so much. Sarah was born in 1803, a short time before Joanna took to staying regularly at Rock Cottage.

Joanna's peaceful stay with the Foleys was interrupted by unpleasant news. A London convert, a rough, red-necked Irish soap-boiler called

William Blake
engraving by Louis Schiavonetti 1808

William Blake, gifted mystic as well as brilliant artist and poet, was urged by his friend and fellow artist, William Sharp, to consider joining Joanna Southcott's ranks. He declined, saying she was all talk and no action having, as far as he could see, performed no miracles nor accomplished anything superhuman.

Michael Carney, had come home one day with two fine cauliflowers which he ordered his wife to cook for his supper. Then he went off to the alehouse to raise his spirits after a hard day's work. Mrs. Carney was a gentle, timid soul. Both she and her husband had been sealed together by Joanna. That evening poor Mrs. Carney forgot to cook the cauliflowers and, when her husband came home drunk, he was outraged to find there was no supper waiting for him.

He picked up a wooden chair and brought it down on her skull, knocking her unconscious and then, in a panic, smashed open the box where she kept her private things, hoping to find the precious Seal, vaguely believing that if he destroyed it he would somehow escape detection. His wife died within hours and he was arrested and charged with murder and sentenced to death. His wife's father and his own children gave evidence against him and he was hanged at the Old Bailey.

It was bad publicity for Joanna. Not only had one of her converts been murdered, but another was the proved murderer. It came too soon after her High House Trial and put her in an even worse light. She decided to turn her back on it all and in October left Old Swinford and headed for Yorkshire to stay in Halifax with William Jowett, who had been one of her judges at her trial.

This visit excited attention. On October 29, 1803 an article appeared in the *Halifax Journal*, which Joanna said gave a false impression of her. Jowett wrote to the newspaper pointing out errors, but the editor refused to publish the reply unless it was paid for as an advertisement, which Jowett refused to do.

However, Jowett made an excellent job of promoting the visit. Yorkshire folk warm naturally to new religious movements, sages, soothsayers, miracle-makers and witches. They have a celebrated witch of their own - Old Mother Shipton - who in Henry VIII's time prophesied the era of aeroplanes, submarines and electricity and Judgement Day.

People flocked to Halifax from surrounding villages to hear Joanna preach. John Wesley had recently forbidden women to preach in Methodist Churches, because he said it was unseemly and women belonged in the home administering religious comfort to members of their immediate family. Consequently women preachers were a rare treat. On the first day Joanna preached, an audience of fifteen hundred turned up to hear her, and hundreds were sealed and returned home happy that a place had been reserved for them in Heaven.

Joanna found it an ordeal to stand on a platform and address a large audience. She was most at ease with small groups. She said that sometimes she was unable "to know how to speak to the people at all, yet I have a feeling in my heart that I can by no means refrain from speaking."

At Stockton-on-Tees Methodists accused her of fraudulently publishing prophecies after the event. She replied that all her books containing prophecies were entered at Stationer's Hall on the date named on them, to safeguard her from such accusations.

Fom Stockton she went to Leeds to stay with Turner for six months, travelling from her lodging to nearby towns to preach. These gatherings were always well advertised and so huge crowds flocked to hear her. Leeds, she felt, was a model of the kind of Christianity she hoped would prevail throughout her own movement.

"I wish you could all be united together in love as they are in Leeds," she wrote to a friend. "I never hear of no discord between them, and they have thousands to attend them in many places and yet they are united together in brotherly love."

On January 2, 1804, she wrote to Lucy Taylor, telling her how busy she was. "I have not time to send a long letter, as I have been every day this week signing and sealing upwards of 2,000 in a few days." In order to deal with them, she said she had to take on another 300 assistants. "We are all working furiously to make up the number of seals required."

At one gathering in Leeds she talked about how Satan was to blame for the wickedness of the world. A man stood up and mildly disagreed with her, laying the responsibility on Adam and Eve. Joanna told him stiffly that she had been told personally by God that the culprit was Satan. The man refused to accept her word and Joanna told him to quit the room as he was a friend of the Devil and not of hers. She told him curtly that she wished to spend the day with her friends only, who had come long distances to see her.

When the man refused to budge, Joanna asked those present to raise their hands if they were against him. She reported with satisfaction that every hand in the room shot up. The man was put out of the room and proclaimed an enemy to the human race and "the Devil's friend". The bewildered man protested that all he had wanted was to express a humble opinion.

Another story was circulating about two men who set out for Leeds intent on confronting Joanna. "A sudden stroke of death befelled them on their way," wrote Joanna with satisfaction. "An angel served a death warrant on them because of their insolence."

She stayed eight miles out of the city and said she received visitors day and night. One Sunday a country lady invited her to her home to talk to her staff. Joanna described in a letter to Elias Carpenter how the staff were so excited they assembled "before they had even finished their dinners". Several hundred crowded into the large kitchen and Joanna had to climb onto the scrubbed pine table to address them. While she was speaking, a clergyman came to say there were several thousands out doors pleading for her to talk in the courtyard. She promptly climbed from the table and walked outside, standing on the steps so that everyone would have a good view. She said they listened to her with great respect, after which she had tea with the lady of the house before going to her next meeting.

If Leeds folk were fascinated by her, the local press was scornful. *The Leeds Mercury* reported her visit. "In announcing the arrival of distinguished personages, we have to mention that Johanna Southcote, the celebrated Prophetess of Exeter has, in pursuance of her mission, arrived in Leeds. Johanna's disciples are numerous both in Leeds and many other parts of the Kingdom and all of them believe in the marvellous prophecies of this Lady of Exeter as ever did good Catholics in the miracles wrought at the shrine of the Lady of Loretta."

The newspaper went on to explain that the object of Joanna's visit was to distribute celestial seals to the faithful, adding dryly "these seals, like the Agis of Minerva, will protect the possessor from all danger even at the cannon's mouth. We recommend the volunteers to lay a stock preparatory to the arrival of Bonaparte and his sharp-shooters."

Her reputation drew the crowds and made them stay to listen to her. Having done so, hundreds were disappointed when she failed to project herself well and live up to her reputation. She kept writing to Carpenter, telling him of the thousands that were flocking to see her, but in her heart knew that preaching in this way was not helping her Cause. But she did suss out that Yorkshire folk were tight and canny and needed assurance that they would prosper in the Promised Land.

"Don't think," she told them, "that trade and business will cease in our land after deliverance comes of the clouds that now hang over us. All kinds of trade will go on the same."

It was a great relief to many, who had no wish to relinquish lucrative businesses and property. One property owner asked for specific advice and got it: "God never directs any man's property what he shall do. In these things we are left to judge for ourselves and you must be the best judge whether you can sell the estate to an advantage to do you good. But as you ask my advice, I shall tell you what I should do myself, unless I was obliged to sell. I should not sell if it was land for, come what will, that will stand. But if it be in houses, or the greater value of it be in a house, I should sell it as soon as I could get its worth."

A wealthy Quaker called Daniel Roberts was worried about losing his lucrative coal mines. After consulting her divine guide, Joanna was able to assure him that "he had nothing to fear of losing his mines and, as for loss of family and friends, he would receive spiritual reward which would amply repay the loss."

A rumour was in circulation that, while she was in Stockton, she had had a passionate affair with a married man and had consequently become pregnant and had had a stillborn child. Joanna denied the reports but it was noticed she was not well, looking pale and sick and showing signs of exhaustion and tearfulness. It had been a tough few months. Preaching in fields and market places week after week to often hostile audiences, was debilitating. As doubts about herself crept in, one of her dark depressions took hold of her. Was she the mistress of the Devil, after all?

"I have feared this past week, that I had done wrong in sealing people if my prophecies come from a spirit that is not God."

Feeling heavily guilty, she consequently became emotionally ill. "I prayed for the Lord to take my life sooner than suffer me to seal His Name." God suggested a brilliant solution to her problems. "If this is not for thee, I will take thee by death before the year ends. But, if I preserve thy life, it is fatal to disobey."

Joanna's divine instructions were usually first conceived in her own mind and then later conveniently attributed to a divine command. It was as if she was tempting providence, making a bargain with God. If I'm doing wrong - you take my life. If I live - then I'm on the right track.

Although in good physical health, she was convinced the bargain was a fair test and she maintained stoutly: "I should rejoice at the summons of death to stop my hand and leave this world, if I am deceived and deceiving mankind." So she returned to London to prepare for what she persuaded herself and her believers was a real possibility of death.

She stopped issuing seals. Too many were capitalising on them, such as the enterprising Exeter tradesman, for instance, who mustered good business by advertising that all who feared God could sign in his shop a paper that would entitle them to a "Seal of Safety" - promising it would be as protective as the blood on the doorpost was to the children of Israel. If, as a sign of gratitude, they happened to buy some of his goods, then this was purely coincidental.

To combat such problems, she ordered a list of genuine believers to be drawn up. The names were written on special parchment paper from Elias

Carpenter's Bermondsey paper mill. She warned: "Let no man sign his name till he hath read the book and judged for himself. It will be more fatal to break the seals than it was for Adam to eat of the forbidden fruit."

Reluctant to lose those that were wavering, she added ominously: "Those that sign and draw back by destroying their seals of safety have only signed for their own destruction, having destroyed my protection against the powers of darkness." All those on the list were to be officially resealed on New Year's Day - only, of course, if Joanna survived. News of the test God had set her was broadcast to her believers, who braced themselves for the possibility of losing her.

On January 1, 1804, Joanna woke to find herself alive and well and she said her faith was joyfully restored to her. That evening, the new list of believers was brought to her and the names found worthy numbered eight thousand one hundred and forty four. "This is besides those that are blotted out, and some lists are not even gathered in yet," she noted with satisfaction.

It was encouraging to be left with so many after eliminating the unworthy ones. The clouds of self-doubt that had been troubling her for months dispersed, and Joanna emerged from her ordeal refreshed and jubilant.

She was such a mistress of self-delusion, she convinced herself that it had been a fair test of her authenticity and, as she celebrated with her usual glass of Madeira, she wrote contentedly: "The load fell off and a heavenly joy seized my soul."

Chapter 11

Three Women

Joanna's wealthy friends were demanding too much of her. They expected her to be visibly divinely inspired night and day and Joanna found it both irritating and exhausting to have them hanging on to every word she uttered, constantly on the alert for any gems of wisdom that might chance to fall from her lips. Frequently flustered and tired, the profound words she always intended saying came out as garbled nonsense.

She began to live in fear that someone would decide she was mad and that she would be condemned to the madhouse, as Brothers had been. Her inner voice talked incessantly inside her head. Sometimes there seemed to be two voices in there, discussing, arguing and agitating. It was as if she had no privacy inside or outside her own body.

She struggled to pull herself together and, in an attempt to appear positive, warned grimly that the "Terrors of the Apocalypse" were imminent. It would begin, she said, with the French sailing up the Thames and invading London and then the City would be "filled with the dead bodies of the enemy and of those that are enemies to me". William Sharp was told to pass the message on that "friends should settle their affairs as fast as they can, so that they will be able to leave at a week's warning. I will tell them where to go!"

The British Government was growing uneasy about Joanna. Her wild warnings were creating unrest in London and the provinces. The authorities decided, however, to leave well alone - for arresting Joanna would not necessarily rid the nation of her fanatical hangers-on. The real instigators of panic, Elias Carpenter for example, were arousing excited mobs in Joanna's name. Elias was twice arrested but charges were not pressed.

In a burst of enthusiasm Carpenter converted a loft to accommodate over a thousand people. A team worked under his supervision to turn it into a splendid chapel. At one end was a huge table covered with a white cloth. Three candlesticks were placed on it and between the candlesticks were decanters filled with wine. In the centre was a silver urn and two silver cups. To create a suitably mysterious effect, lamps and candles were hung in the rafters and beams.

The first spectacular meeting took place there on January 12, 1804. Elias Field, Joanna's bookseller, remarked that "an astonishing body of people met together in such a solemn purpose that has seldom been seen in any nation". Included were people from all over Europe, Roman Catholics, Dissenters, Quakers, Wesleysians and members of the Church of England.

Field said he found the service so moving that he was in tears when the congregation broke into song "all uniting in one common bond of love and friendship" regardless of their nationality or religion. For the first time the ceremony of the "Uplifting of Hands" took place which, in years to come, was to be a regular part of a Southcottian service. The hour and a half meeting was followed by communion and one German gentleman produced a thousand loaves made from the "finest Hertfordshire flour". This huge meeting, however, was unusual - the average attendance was about a hundred according to Thomas Foley's diary.

Joanna's formidable warning about the Apocalypse proved a damp squib. No terrors manifested and London continued as usual. But for her followers it was a nerve-wracking anti-climax. Hundreds had packed all their personal belongings and sold property and consequently many lost faith in her.

In April 1804 Joanna returned to London, miserable and lacking confidence and not at all happy at the prospect of lodging with the Bruce family again. Their loving company was oppressive. With them she felt like a caged phenomenon always expected to perform. They were wealthy, influential and interesting but nonetheless Joanna yearned for relief from their cloying attention.

Thomas and Elizabeth Foley, still her closest companions, were particularly clinging. Joanna described wearily a journey she made, accompanied by the Foleys, on May 8, 1804, to see Dr. Wetherall who lived on top of Highgate Hill. Since the weather was fine, Foley had enthusiastically decided it would do them good to walk.

"When we left the green fields for the high road," wrote Joanna, "my feet began to be painful. Mrs. Foley called to her husband to assist us as we were feeling faint and tired. He had gone before us to lead the way, but turned back and lent us the assistance of his arms and encouraged us by saying we were near the house."

However, he kept on saying this, even though they weren't, until Joanna became disillusioned. "My hopes began to fail and I could scarcely go no further," she complained. Eventually, at the top of the hill, Foley asked a youth for directions to Wetherall's house. After searching around the village, they eventually found it. Joanna said she felt so weak she could hardly speak. But, once there, her spirits were lifted when she was given a letter from a believer in Leeds, who had sent her gold and silver.

Elizabeth Foley was very sick on the return journey. The poor woman was pregnant at the time and a few months later she gave birth to a baby girl whom she named "Mary Joanna". The arduous walk must have been too much for her, because the baby was born weak and died after a few short weeks of life.

A wealthy invalid, Miss Jane Townley, entered Joanna's life at this point. She was to have a profound influence on the way events progressed. She had read Joanna's books and was so impressed by them she invited Joanna to visit her at her home at 17, Weston Place, St. Pancras, London. The two women took to each other and a rapport quickly built up which eventually grew into a strong bond. Jane and her companion-maid, Ann Underwood, were to become Joanna's closest friends and devoted disciples - to be regarded as a sort of Holy Trinity by Foley and Joanna's more emotive followers, after her death.

Jane was rich and attractive and suffered poor health. After recovering from one serious illness, she decided she had only been spared long enough to witness Christ's return to earth. A short time before hearing of Joanna, she said she was cured by a brilliant doctor. The nature of the illness is not specified but her own writings seem to suggest she was highly-strung and susceptible. Her close friend, the Bishop of London, described her as "fey". Near the end of 1802, she wrote about an experience she had which shows that, even before meeting Joanna, she was receptive to atmospheric conditions.

"I became suddenly enabled to look steadfastly at the sky," she wrote. "And all over London appeared streams of fire in the sky, of a blood-red colour. The sun appeared very white, but all around was black and parts of this blackness fell away from time to time, as if from the sun. This continued occasionally for several months. Always, after looking at the sun, I had a most beautiful vision of flowers - more beautiful than I ever saw in reality, as to the elegance of form and delicacy of colour."

Jane was younger than Joanna and had a refined quality about her which Joanna admired and envied. Her manner put her in mind of the idyllic image she had of her Great Aunt Sarah. Joanna was also impressed by Jane's influential friends - one of them being the Bishop of London. Jane had already written to him saying that when she first heard of Joanna's prophecies "I thought it was my duty to read them and judge them for myself".

Jane was convinced it was her duty to offer to share her home with Joanna. Joanna accepted gladly, for she saw a chance to escape from her loving oppressors. She had no fears about Jane, for she recognised in her two assets which she knew would be of great value to her - weakness of character and great wealth. Jane had nothing to spend her money on, except doctors and medicines, and clearly needed a purpose - a Cause. Why, thought our cunning prophetess, should this Cause not be Joanna Southcott?

Jane was gullible and easily influenced and Joanna realised at their first meeting how easy it would be to rule her completely. "I know the weakness of thy nature," she once wrote to her from Blockley.

Joanna devised a scheme to ensure her friend spent all her time, money and energy almost entirely on her. God, she said, had brought them together for a reason. Jane was to be a type of mother to Joanna, despite the fact that she was considerably younger. And, as a mother naturally would want to support the honour and happiness of her child, so would Jane want to "spend her time and money, like a mother, for my honour and glory".

So the pattern for this bizarre and intense relationship became established. The three women seemed to genuinely love each other. For the first time since she had left Exeter, Joanna felt able to speak frankly and the sheer relief from her previous feelings of oppression resulted in a severe nervous collapse and her two new friends whisked her off to Bristol, where they had a house in Trinity Street. They forbade anyone to visit her, although friends were allowed to write. They nursed her through a bad mental illness with the same devotion that her sister Susanna had once shown her.

Her brother, Joseph, still in Bristol, was now well under her spell and she sent her two friends to visit him on her behalf. Jane Townley wrote to the Bishop of London about the visit.

"On our arrival, I found Mrs. Southcott (Joseph's wife) had an infant born on 9 April and called John, who appeared to be dying of convulsions. They told me the child was suddenly seized with convulsive fits a little before one o' clock on Friday afternoon, when it laid in peace till after the clock struck five, when it expired in sleep."

Jane reported back to Joanna, who said she already knew all about it having prophesied the tragic event in 1794 when she had told her brother he would have a son who would suffer convulsions and die in the month of May. Joseph and his wife must surely have felt that Joanna's curse was continuing to plague them.

But Jane Townley was very impressed and wrote to the Bishop of London again telling him about the prophesy. The letter was returned without comment. The Bishop's patience was beginning to wear thin.

Joanna's mind then snapped completely, as it had been threatening to do for years, and she gave in to uncontrolled madness, going into regular passions of rage, beating herself savagely until she was raw and bleeding. Her friends had to pin her down in a chair with cushions on her lap to prevent her from harming herself.

Often suicidal, on June 13, 1804, she wrote: "The horror of the Devil was upon me. I felt I couldn't bear my existence. I desired Mrs. Underwood to take away every knife out of the room that, in my despairing moments, I might not lay violent hands upon myself. I fell on my knees in prayer and could not avoid crying aloud, but could not express with my tongue what I felt in my heart."

When there was no answer to her prayers, she told Ann Underwood that, since God was not giving her instructions, she could no longer help them and they must henceforth direct themselves. Ann Underwood, burst into tears and said helplessly: "We cannot direct ourselves and no more letters shall go out of the house, unless the Lord, in his unbounded love, mercy and goodness, will direct us through thee."

She ran sobbing to tell Jane Townley that God had withdrawn his love and was no longer communicating with Joanna and that "the Lord had hid his face from us". They knelt down to pray to God to fulfil his promises to them and continue to direct them through Joanna. But there was no relief. Joanna stayed in her room, insisting on wearing all-white to symbolise her purity, and spent her time walking up and down "in great agonies".

These incidents indicate just how highly charged emotions were between the three women. Joanna had such total power over the other two, she was able to reduce them to tears by her own hysterical behaviour. Her depressions became their depressions and, equally, her elations too. She ruled them completely.

After her death, a bewildered Jane Townley admitted: "I obeyed her in all things, as one must have obeyed the Duke of Wellington, as would an officer in his army, without taking into question the duty assigned to him.

Thus, as no responsibility rested on me, I had only to obey the commands given in her lifetime."

Blind obedience was not confined to her women friends. Thomas Foley said he relied on the prophetess "for directions how to act as I shall not take a step of my own in this momentous cause, without consulting her, having found every direction given me by the Spirit through her, to be the most true and correct".

Believers were told by Joanna to swear the following: "I do swear by Him that liveth I will obey in all things Thy strict command given to Thy Handmaiden, Joanna Southcott, and it is not all the Powers of Earth and Hell shall make me turn to the Right Hand or to the Left."

Joanna also stipulated that "if thou followest my direction thou will escape Satan's wiles". It is easy to understand why, having sworn this solemn oath, devout, gentle people such as Jane Townley, Ann Underwood and Thomas Foley, who lived in daily fear of God, were prepared to carry out the most bizarre instructions from her. Under such circumstances and with such absolute power over them, Joanna could have acted in any abominable way she wished (and probably did) and it would not have raised a single eyebrow amongst her believers. Her hysterical behaviour was accepted as beyond her control and part of the heavy burden she had to bear as God's servant.

Her seven disciples were kept informed of her strange behaviour. Ann wrote to Foley: "She sometimes stamps till the whole house shakes. When she emptied her glass once, she cried that the Lord would break all who fall from their faith like this and she flung it to the floor and it was dashed to pieces."

On another occasion, Jane came home from church and found Joanna standing in the middle of the room in an agitated state, having just finished reading a letter from Pomeroy. She clutched her stomach and was promptly sick. Instead of lying down on her bed she deliberately flung herself onto the floor, screaming that she did not know whether to pity or condemn Pomeroy and that her revenge would be to cut him to pieces. Finally they got her to bed, and she cursed the clergy as a whole and asked for a glass of wine, which she brought up at once. A basin was given to her for her to be sick in, but she picked it up and dashed it violently across the room. Later they brought her some lamb for her dinner, but as soon as she tried to swallow it it stuck in her throat and she spat it into another basin and said she could neither swallow the wine nor the lamb because of her fury and she dashed the second basin to the floor in another fit of anger. Then, smiling sweetly as if all this was perfectly normal, she told Jane she felt easier now she had broken both basins for so would the Lord, in his anger, break the clergy.

Between brainstorms, she appeared sane and rational and during lucid intervals dictated messages for Ann and Jane to post to Sharp and Foley. They were edited and printed as "Communications from Joanna Southcott" which ensured that at least her name was kept well in the public eye. Jane wrote to the Bishop of London telling him he should take Joanna seriously and enclosing a copy of one of Joanna's letters, which she seemed to think proved her point beyond question. Three thousand copies of the same letter were sent to the same number of clergy.

Until now, Joanna had been writing out all her communications herself "free from erasures and alterations but illegible to everyone but myself". To save herself work, she took to dictating to either Jane or Ann. Soon this became accepted practice. Joanna claimed that the three of them were in a state of such perfect harmony that it was the same as writing her messages out herself.

Unstinting in their devotion, nonetheless Ann Underwood and Jane Townley found Joanna exhausting. She expected them to be at her beck and call day and night and the divine communications she said she was receiving were coming now at a staggering rate. Jane Townley admitted in a letter she wrote to Mrs. Taylor in Exeter: "I find the task too hard for me."

Despite her mad spells, her output while in Bristol was impressive. She claimed that while there her visitations were stronger than she had ever before experienced. Her followers were concerned that she was taking the same grim path as their previous prodigy, Richard Brothers, but were comforted by the fact that, despite alarming reports they had been receiving from Jane Townley and Ann Underwood regarding seven months of mental anguish in Bristol, she had managed to write several startling books which had sold well. Therefore, they felt inclined to overlook her madness and keep faith.

To Joanna's intense irritation, Miss Townley acquired an ardent admirer - the young man, Richard Law, who Joanna had taken a shine to just before her High House Trial. A flaxdresser by trade, he professed to be passionately in love with Jane and for once Joanna was not the centre of attention. She was jealous and, when Jane received a proposal of marriage from the young man, flew into a rage and did her utmost to persuade Jane not to accept. Jane was too valuable a benefactor to risk losing to another.

He professed to be one of her followers but, in reality, Richard Law was a smooth young man who neither liked nor trusted Joanna. He correctly surmised that Jane was unworldly and gullible and "unskilled in the way of religion" and Joanna was a wicked exploiter taking advantage of her trusting nature. Jane's gentle rejection of him he found unbearable.

"You have drove me mad," he wrote to her bitterly. "You have made me run distracted and you have bewitched me out of my wits. Nevertheless, I may be fully restored again if you will consent to a reconciliation."

But Jane said she wanted to devote her life to God and Joanna, and refused to yield. He wrote again: "Inexorable Jane. What if Heaven should be barred to you as you have barred yourself from me?   Come, come! Don't puff yourself up about your virginity. Such foolish celibacy only means that many a brave and proper man goes wifeless and childless to the grave."

He argued imploringly that she was his "rightful partner" and there was still time to realise this and for the two of them to find happiness together. But by now Jane had committed herself to Christ and Joanna and firmly rejected Richard Law's proposal. Bitterly, he dubbed Joanna an old witch. After her death, he wrote to Jane Townley: "Though the witch is dead, her spells yet continue and are set with the most infernal art."

In her madness, Joanna convinced herself she was going to die and set about distributing gifts to the people she was fond of. On July 31, 1804, she wrote to Lucy Taylor, in Exeter: "As the hour of my departure draweth near, I wish to give to my near and dear friends something to keep in remembrance of me. I have sent a chambre muslin, as I know you don't like white gowns, and Miss Fanny told me you like them muslins and I hope you will be pleased with the colour, as it was the choice of everyone of us and they look neat for young and old.

"I have writ this in a separate letter for you, as I wish no one to know but yourself, that no envy nor jealousy may arrive in the hearts of the believers. It would cause jealousy and pain if it was known, for I find there is a great deal of jealousy at Exeter about our friendship, judging I love your family better than I do any in Exeter, and I should think myself ungrateful if I did not. Miss Townley thought it her duty to give a new suit of clothes to each of the jurymen at my new Trial and, as my brother was to be called as a witness, she made him a present the same and now Mr. Jones is to be called as a witness, Miss Townley desire he will receive a handsome dark blue broadcloth coat, waistcoat and breeches, of what he please, and send her the bill."

With the onset of winter, Joanna recovered. They left Bristol on

November 22, 1804 for Jane Townley's London home and a new campaign for another investigation into her powers was launched. It had become an obsession. Her disciples were convinced a proper, balanced investigation had to take place and a satisfactory and fair conclusion reached. Advertisements were placed in practically every newspaper in the country, appealing for 24 Bishops to judge her writings. They could, she said, bring her greatest enemies to speak against her. "Let my enemies be my judges. I will stand or fall by their judgement, for this I am ordered to do."

Sure that this time the challenge was so straightforward and no Bishop could reasonably refuse to come, plans were made to stage another Trial. This time the rendezvous was to be Elias Carpenter's house in Bermondsey, which stood on an islet called Jacob's island, formed by the River Neckinger and two canals specially constructed originally to feed the Bermondsey Abbey water mill.

Although only a mile from London, it seemed a delightfully peaceful spot, well away from the hurly burly of the city and a perfect setting for her Trial. Nobody told her it was known as the Devil's Neckinger. Thames pirates were once executed there and the rope that hung them became known as the Devil's neckcloth, or "neckinger" - hence the name of the river.

Blissfully unaware of these evil connections, she was full of high hopes, this time determined to be so well prepared that nothing would go wrong. So confident was she, that she even wrote to Joseph Pomeroy and invited him to attend. In a letter to Thomas Foley, he refused point blank, for no way did he want to get mixed up with her crazy schemes. On November 28, seven days before the first day of the Trial, Joanna received divine instructions to the contrary.

"Tell Pomeroy I have deferred the Trial to the last day. If he is not present, or sends none of his friends to appear on his behalf, he must trust to the judgement of myself and them that are present. As to his conduct, from first to last, it will all come into print with the witnesses' names. Let him know that. And the letter they send him must come into print."

She wrote to Pomeroy herself: "In your letter to Mr. Foley, you desire me to have the truth of my writings cleared up and tried by the test of the Scriptures, but to leave your name out of the questions. So what truth can be cleared up? Please direct your reply to Mr. Sharp, of 50 Titchfield Street." Pomeroy stood his ground. He would not be blackmailed into coming. He wanted nothing to do with the mad woman of Exeter. And that was that!

Mr. Jones, of Exeter, was sent to deliver yet another letter from Joanna.

He managed to slip it to a servant, but Pomeroy sent for him and returned the letter unopened. He complained angrily that Joanna's brother had written an impudent letter to him saying he ought to be horse-whipped. Despite this, Joanna remained optimistic, believing God would devise a way to make Pomeroy change his mind

> "He shall find I shall work for thee a way,
> To make his pride, like Jones' letter, lay
> Broken in pieces, he shall see the whole.
> His pride and wisdom shall together fall,
> Because, like Pilate, I did place the man
> And so, like Pilate, he thy judge became.
> For worse than Pilate, he must now appear.
> He cannot wash his hands and say he is clear
> From every injury he hath done to you.
> He sought by arts, thy honour to betray.
> But now by honour I will him condemn."

She was told she was not to know the reason for this new Trial. But it had something to do with Pomeroy and a lot depended upon his attendance. God told her: "It must come on between Pomeroy and thee and there is no time for delay. So, if Pomeroy will not be a just judge, let him be an unjust judge. Follow my instructions to Owen, Harwood and Hows, to write a friendly letter to Pomeroy to know the truth of letters being in his hands. Also that Joanna's Trial will never take place, unless he is present."

And so more letters were sent but still he stood his ground and, frustrated by her failure to move him, she sank into depression at the thought that this second Trial might prove as big a flop as the first one. She did not relish being made a fool of again. But God seemed to know exactly how she felt, for he quickly sent her more instructions to the effect that if the Bishops refused to come to the Trial then Joanna was at liberty to "go into the Highways and Hedges" and ask any others to come instead.

It was decided to approach the clergy direct. The Rev. Mr. Welsher went to three clergymen. The Rev. Hodgkin, of St. Thomas's, declined loftily with the remark, "I have no opinion of a Holy Ghost that could not write grammar." The Rev. M. Orme, of St. Gabriel, also refused and, to ensure the invitation was not repeated, offered his "absolute word" he would not serve any such undertaking under any circumstances whatsoever.

The third clergyman approached was the Rev. Mr. Draper, of St. Georges, who said he believed he spoke the sentiments of the clergy at large when he said Joanna's writings were blasphemous.

"I can see but one place where she is spoken of in the Scriptures and that is by the appellant of Jezebel, for Joanna is a Jezebel in the Church and as to prophets and prophetesses, in the present day I do not believe that there are any such creatures, though I must say this in her favour, that this is proof of the near approach of the Latter Day."

Even God was angry at this, for Joanna said he told her: "He who said you were a Jezebel out of his own mouth, I will condemn him for breaking the laws of God and man. How dare he say My Just Decree shall be prevented? How dare such a minister go into the pulpit, which puts all My Gospel in defiance?"

Foley approached the Rev. Robson, of Whitechapel. On being asked if he would attend Joanna's Trial as an opposer, he said he had destroyed the invitation.

"There is no occasion for such an examination as she already considers herself a second Eve," he remarked sarcastically. "I am sorry Mr. Foley is of the church, for he is not Christian and he should go home and get himself some water gruel."

Undiscouraged, Foley visited Mr. H. Foster, of Wilderness Row, who declared angrily, "As I consider Joanna Southcott a deluded impostor, I shall have nothing to do with her. I am very sorry, sir, that you are carried away with her nonsense."

Stanhope Bruce called on the Rev. Basil Woodd, of Bentinck Chapel, who went red, shook his head wildly and cried out in anger: "Stuff! Stuff! I shall having nothing to do with it." God apparently heard this and told Joanna: "I shall answer them from Mr. Woodd, that 'stuff' is his religion. Where is his love of God and Man?"

Upset by these rude rejections and what she considered to be disgraceful behaviour by the clergy, she noted huffily: "The letters were returned by the ministers with such infamous and blasphemous language, as though the Devil had either guided their hands or hearts. For such letters I should think could never be penned. For many of the expressions are so low, illiterate and indecent that it appears to me what we in Devonshire called Billingsgate language."

What was most infuriating was Pomeroy's stubborn refusal to attend the Trial or even send a representative. Since she came to London, Pomeroy had been left in comparative peace, although he still received tiresome letters, which he always threw in the fire. Now, he was horrified that she was trying to draw him into the forefront of her drama again. On January 18, 1805, Jane Townley noted that she had written to Pomeroy on several occasions "using every argument to induce him to come forward". But now she realised he wasn't worth bothering about and it was no longer necessary to try and get him to attend the Trial.

Joanna comforted herself by remembering that in 1796 she had forecast that the Methodists would act like the unbelieving Jews and the clergy would show contempt for her and be like "fruit that was fallen with the blunt end ruining them". She also prophesied that Pomeroy would turn his back on her and deny her, like Peter did to Christ, for fear of ridicule.

Yet a faint hope lingered that Pomeroy might yet turn up at the last minute. She fixed a date for her Trial - December 5, 1804. An Attorney was appointed to record the evidence of the witnesses and to give the affair an official feel. It was to take place over seven days and was advertised nation-wide. Believers arrived in the city in hundreds and congregated on the little piece of land surrounded by the water of two canals and the river Neckinger, known as Jacob's island, in Bermondsey. In the fields opposite, the sightseers gathered, spoiling for some fun at the expense of Joanna. Heavy rainclouds threatened to dampen the day's proceedings.

But not one opponent arrived to take part in Joanna's Trial - not a single Bishop or representative of His Majesty's Government, nor of his Majesty's personal staff, nor one single opposing clergyman.

Early that morning Joanna lay, weak with fear and trepidation, in her bedroom at Elias Carpenter's house, fortifying herself with glasses of watered-down Madeira wine. Her courage had failed her and she prayed frantically to God to give her strength to face her ordeal. But God was being curiously quiet. There were no voices in her head - just a vacuum of fear - and she felt horribly alone.

Chapter 12

Neckinger Trial

To those who had taken part in Joanna's first Trial, there was a familiar ring about the second one. It began promptly at 11am on Wednesday December 5, 1804 at Neckinger House, home of Elias Carpenter, on Jacob's Island, Bermondsey. The largest room was set up as a make-shift courtroom. Forty-eight people were there to carry out the proceedings. Hired Attorney, John Scott, wore formal black robes and a wig. His job was mainly to take down the evidence of the witnesses and to make sure everything was conducted in a professional fashion.

Many of her old friends had come from Exeter. Joanna, worried they might show her up by displaying ignorance of city ways, fussily wrote to Lucy Taylor: "I must beg you and Mr. Taylor to bring your gloves with you."

The comfortable chair, reserved for Joanna at the front of the assembly, remained empty on the first day. Joanna did not feel well! An early message arrived to say she was too weak to join them. She lay on her bed, elsewhere in the house, with the curtains drawn, tossing and turning and dreadfully sick. One or another of her women friends hovered close by. Frequently she sipped a glass of watered-down wine to replenish her strength.

Despite her absence, the Trial went ahead, starting with a roll call of all those participating. Every witness called was a sealed believer and, as was to be expected, each one loyally testified to Joanna's flawless character. Each speaker instinctively turned to address the empty chair. Joseph Pomeroy's name cropped up in evidence almost as many times as Joanna's and practically every witness went to some length to portray Pomeroy as a weak character and a traitor. Sometimes it was difficult to work out who was on trial, Joanna or Pomeroy.

John Trinity Symons, a printer, was the first to testify. He said he'd known Joanna for ten years and had taken dictation from her, often copying letters she had written to Pomeroy. He said she had a blameless character and was not deceitful. In 1801 Pomeroy told him he was certain no evil spirit was at work where Joanna was concerned. But in 1803 when he showed Pomeroy a pamphlet about Joanna he had printed, he laughed and exclaimed: "You had better have nothing more to do with that mad woman."

Symons told the meeting: "Mr. Pomeroy said we had troubles enough in my family, by believing in such nonsense. He was referring to the accidental death of my two sisters, in one week. He said Joanna Southcott's works were wrong and from the Devil. I asked him why, if they were from the Devil, he had previously told me to believe in her. He became angry and told me he wanted to get her to see sense and it would be better for me to believe only in the Church of England and burn all the Bills I had printed. I told him I should not."

Symons explained that ten months before this conversation, at his brother's funeral, Joanna told him that this was not the only calamity that would happen in his family. Her prediction came true. Within a year both his sisters were dead.

Next witness was Joseph Southcott, Joanna's youngest brother and the only member of her family prepared to testify for her. Joseph was still in awe of her. He was impressed by her wealthy and influential friends who seemed to regard her as important and clever. Sometimes he enjoyed basking in her reflected glory, but at other times was frightened at the way she seemed able to manipulate him.

Now he described how, as a child, Joanna had a placid, mild disposition and he had never known her to be false, uncharitable or inattentive to God. He didn't mention the time in Bristol when she almost ruined his life. Such incidents were best forgotten and, in any case, that was a family affair and he had no wish for his unfortunate term in prison to be brought to the attention of this illustrious gathering.

Joseph's testimony was followed by a flattering tribute from William Sharp, who arrived immaculately dressed and with a reassuring air of respectability. His evidence was not gushing, but calm and reasonable and merely outlined in a straightforward manner the work he had done in connection with Joanna's mission, such as copying, editing and publishing material by, about and to her. He added that Joanna was divinely inspired and her work beyond reproach. So the first day ended in an atmosphere of conviviality with everyone relaxed and smugly pleased with the day's events.

Next day they met at 10am. Joanna's chair was still empty but almost at once a message came to say she was in a state of "great agitation and excitement" and wanted to see the entire assembly in her room. This created some excitement. The thought was that something particularly significant must have happened, maybe even a direct message from God. Everyone obediently marched up to her room, where they found her sitting in a chair, flanked by her female attendants. She insisted upon shaking hands with everyone in turn, which took a while, after which she stood up and spoke for half-an-hour about nothing in particular.

Then the *Box of Sealed Writings* was brought in and she went on to explain how the writings came about. Most of the assembly already knew, of course. When she proceeded to follow this with a tedious account of her first trial at Paddington in 1803, those present began to find it embarrassing. But they waited politely until she had finished, after which there was an uneasy silence. Joanna gazed steadily round the room and fifty-five people stared back. What they wanted from her were profound words, inspired declarations, divine utterings. They were happy to listen to a tedious talk on mundane matters, as long as it was followed by a satisfactory climax.

If Joanna was playing for time, hoping for some unmistakable sign that she could say came from God, she was disappointed. Her mouth became dry and she felt that now-familiar sensation, like hot liquid flooding her brain. She put her hand out unsteadily towards the *Box*, as if to open it, and swayed. Ann Underwood caught her and she gratefully closed her eyes, blotting out the let-down looks on the faces of those present, and allowed herself to be helped from the room.

As Joanna recovered from her fainting spell, the trial continued without her, the proceedings mostly being taken up with glowing testimonials from her friends, Mrs. Taylor and her children Fanny and Charles; Mrs. Elizabeth Bruce; Jane Townley and Mrs. Mary Beaucraft.

But Joanna knew she had failed them all. They had expected something wonderful and meaningful from her. She had wanted her speech that day to be an inspiration. Tomorrow she would somehow have to deliver something relevant, or they might all lose faith and go home. Exhausted and genuinely sick, she spent most of that night praying to God for help. Her great hope was that he would send her into a trance in front of everyone and allow the Holy Spirit to speak through her. Such a performance would guarantee her credibility. She was even prepared to fake a trance. It could have been her intention that morning, but her courage had failed her. Most of the night she battled with the problem and finally fell asleep with it half solved.

The third day began with the dramatic announcement that Joanna couldn't join them because she was busy receiving an authentic communication from God. The message was that she wasn't sure how long this would take, but as soon as it was finished she would be down to deliver the holy words while they were still fresh in her mind. A ripple of hopeful excitement spread through the room. Outside, huge crowds had gathered and the news of the divine communication was passed on to them. It was what everyone had been waiting for - a message from God delivered to His very own divine prophetess. A sombre silence descended upon the little island near the Thames. Some knelt down to pray and sceptical onlookers on the other side of the river bank glanced at the darkened sky, fearing they might have misjudged Joanna Southcott.

At 11am Joanna, pale but confident, entered the room and sat down on the chair reserved for her. She had now got it all worked out. If she couldn't go into a trance in full view of everyone, then what she had to do was to pretend she had done so in private and had received a message from God. She delivered the message, therefore in the third person and spoke in a grave, detached manner, as if God was using her body as a vehicle for His Own Voice.

"Yesterday evening, Joanna was cheerful and meditated to herself how all shadows came before the substance of her writings. She was in hope that the shadow of her being taken ill yesterday would be the substance of throwing her into a Trance today. She told Ann Underwood, before retiring that night, that she was longing for the morrow more than she had ever longed for a day, but did not give a reason.

"She prayed all night that I would throw her into a Trance and I answered that she knew not for what she was praying. If she prayed for a Trance now, she prayed for her own death, for she would not live long after it. But if she died, she would return to tell her people what she had seen. Therefore, I told her that the men who prayed for this Trance might well say they were in mourning, for her Trance would bring about her death."

The message was silently absorbed. Of course everyone *had* been hoping she would go into some sort of trance. After all, they *had* come to the Trial expecting to witness a miracle. But here she was saying, in God's Name, that if she *did* go into the trance they all longed for, it would be the death of her.

Once she was certain she had successfully got this vital message across, Joanna relaxed. "If God was to throw me into a Trance now," she confided, "I shall never see the end of this year in this world. Then the stars will be sealed in sorrow and that will be the effect of your fatal curiosity."

From that moment on she had them in the palm of her hand. They protested that the last thing they wanted was to lose her and asked forgiveness for wanting visible proof of her divine gifts. She graciously forgave them all and made her exit, leaving them to continue the day's schedule without her. A short while later, alone in her room sipping wine, she contemplated her triumph and wondered why she still felt so depressed.

By Saturday, the fourth day, the crowds waiting outside hoping to catch a glimpse of Joanna, became restless and dissatisfied. Elias Carpenter had allowed them to shelter for the week in his paper mill, nearby, and over seven hundred men, women and children were there, having travelled from all over England to see Joanna. As their impatience grew, there were determined calls for her to show herself. It was feared that otherwise there would be a riot.

But Joanna was genuinely ill. She had been too nervous to eat and her only nourishment had been wine mixed with water. Consequently, her head hurt as well as her stomach and the prospect of facing a huge gathering appalled her. "I was overcome by considerable depression of spirits," she admitted. But, outside, she could hear them calling her name.

At last she was persuaded to get up. Ann Underwood helped her dress and she walked unsteadily over to the Mill. A few bales of hay had been hastily stacked together to serve as a platform and she was lifted up to face her followers. To her own amazement, she found herself possessed with unearthly confidence and, temporarily forgetting her sickness, spoke for an hour. Her words were of stirring quality and the crowd cheered her enthusiastically, reluctant to let her go.

She returned to her room, but that evening made a surprise appearance before her judges, telling them that the reason she had been able to speak with such strength that morning, even though she was so physically weak, was because "the Spirit of the Lord" had entered her body. The feeling of exuberance kept her going throughout the next day. Everyone was suitably impressed, and she was rigorously questioned for several hours.

That night Joanna did some serious thinking. The suggestion that she would die if she went into a trance, had had a sombre effect upon believers

- more than she had dared to hope for. She decided to return to the subject, emphasising how grave the risk was if their faith weakened. She felt confident now that she would be able to fake a trance and give them what they wanted. So on the Monday, the sixth day, she claimed that the Holy Ghost had said He would put her into a trance and, as warned, take her out of the world but then quickly return her. All this was to happen at a special ceremony that very evening.

With an air of cloying intimacy they all gathered together, at seven o'clock, when it was dark. Smiles and embraces were exchanged, wine and candles were brought in and distributed. Each person, holding a glass of wine and a candle, stood up to face Joanna and the *Box*. One of the judges read a command from God: "Thou hast forsaken the Law of the Gospel of the Lord to meet in the Church and receive the Sacrament from the hands of men. Yet thou has been a Law unto thyself and, drinking the wine in remembrance of Me with these words in thy heart and on thy tongue."

A large goblet, filled with wine, was handed round. Each drank from it and repeated the words: "May I drink deep into the Spirit of God, and may His Blood clear me of all sin." First Joanna drank followed by all the women present - symbolising the fact that Joanna had come to redeem the fall of women - then the men.

They were told that God's specific instructions were: "This is not a sacrament, yet let this be the desire of their hearts if they wish, for a double portion of My Spirit to be poured. After Joanna's death I shall strengthen the disciples that remain when she is gone. But while she is alive, all must come through her. And she stands trial for the whole world."

At nine o'clock the *Box* was sealed and returned to William Sharp for safekeeping. Joanna handed cakes to the women, which they broke up and shared as tokens of love and friendship. "All was a scene of joy and mirth," Joanna wrote later. Before the party finished, Joanna retired happily to her room. It had all been so merry and nobody mentioned that Joanna *hadn't* gone into the trance she had promised them earlier in the day.

The last day of the Trial was held outside, so that as many people as possible could watch and listen. The crowds were so huge, it was decided that Joanna would have to talk to them in an open field, elsewhere on the island, which was surrounded on three sides by the River Neckinger and two canals. On the other side of the river bank gathered angry mobs, yelling abuse at Joanna's followers. A few managed to wade through the shallower part of the river and break into the field. Some nasty incidents occurred. Joanna said she shuddered at the sight of people fighting.

The early part of the day was fine, which was regarded as a good omen. Joanna stood on a raised platform, gazing across the mass of faces, all turned towards her. But this time no inspiration came. Her mind went blank. All she could think of were a few quotes from the Bible vaguely referring to events of terrible significance which would occur if her prophecies were ignored. Luckily most of her words were lost in the wind, so it didn't really matter. People at the far end of the field, who couldn't hear, were content to watch and worship from a distance. It was more important, after all, to go home and say they had seen her in the flesh.

As she finished, ominous clouds gathered overhead and heavy rain spattered down, mercilessly drenching the crowds. She dismissed the assembly with a weak joke that, apart from all the other things she had warned them about, right now they must fear a storm and take cover. Aggressive mobsters struggled to cross the narrow stretch of water, which was now shallow because of the low Thames tide. An ugly mood had developed and Joanna's ample frame was hastily lifted down from the platform and, flanked by her male friends, Major Eyre took her arm and firmly escorted her through the crowd. Then the heavens opened and the rain poured down in straight sheets. Soaked bodies pressed oppressively close to her, many shouting abuse and scorn.

William Sharp said later: "The mob behind her were very invective with their tongues, but had not the power to injure her or her friends."

Some shouted they would like to trample her under their feet. Others threatened to throw her into the canal. A distraught woman carrying a child screamed she hoped the constables would get her. A man nearby yelled he didn't want the constables to have her, for he wanted to get hold of her himself. A woman cried with disgust: "If this be religion, it be time to put a stop to it."

To the modern reader, it might come as some relief to know that not everyone in London was taken in by her. Foley wrote that: "Many opinions were said respecting her as we came out of the field. However, she got through safely, without receiving any insult as they did not know her in person. When she came to the safety of the house, scores of her friends came to the door and, though fatigued, she went out to shake their hands, till the rain came a second time."

That evening a solemn report on the seven day trial was drawn up. Forty-eight people signed to say that they believed "individually and voluntarily" that Joanna's prophecies and spiritual communications came wholly from the Spirit of the Living God and not, as Joanna secretly feared, from the Devil.

A "book of the trial" was swiftly completed and rushed from the presses with a speed a modern-day publisher might well have been proud of. It was available in Elias Field's bookshop at 2, High Street, St. Giles, in less than a month. The one hundred and fifty five page book cost three shillings and there was such a tremendous demand for it in London and the provinces, it sold out within weeks.

Elias Field and Joanna's other bookseller, William Symons, regarded the Neckinger Trial as a total success, in financial terms at least. But less flattering details, such as her drinking, leaked out and she was again a target for hilarity and ridicule amongst city wits. Joanna found some consolation in the fact that the Trial had brought believers from all over England who, in meeting together and discussing Joanna's prophecies, had gone home with their faith not weakened but strengthened.

As if she didn't have enough to worry her, a woman named Dorothy Gott claimed that, while waiting for a coach, she heard a divine voice telling her to announce that the end of the world was nigh. Joanna would have recognised that Dorothy Gott had as much right to preach this message as anyone. But the problem was that she went on to publish a number of pamphlets similar in style and content to Joanna's, which enticed a tenth of her followers from her. Joanna was compelled to denounce Dorothy Gott as "extravagant and absurd" which brought further hoots of laughter from the more discerning public.

When depressed by such matters, Joanna often spent all day in bed, claiming exhaustion or a minor illness. The truth was she was just lazy. "I was prevented from rising, having a cold and my spirits low and too sleepy to get up. I was scared out of dreams for two nights and one day."

Even Satan thought her lazy. He told her on one occasion that she was an idle bitch. If she lay in bed till the Lord called her, he suggested scathingly, she would die in her bed. Her enemies suggested that if she drank less wine, she might not be so tired and constantly lacking energy. She often stayed in bed all day, unable to face the world, half drunk and indulging in splendid, prophetic dreams.

Another big headache was Elias Carpenter. He was rapidly losing faith in her. Joanna's performance at his house, during her second trial, had disappointed him. He had had the chance to see her in her true colours and he noticed how much wine she drank, which he felt was the cause of her unsteadiness and fainting.

Although he had previously written three pamphlets extolling her virtues, now he took to writing malicious and wounding letters criticising her authenticity. Elias was a man of "warm and rash temper", an enthusiastic, Bible-thumping man who required visible proof of divinity. He'd never seen Joanna in an actual state of possession by the Holy Ghost. He preferred prophets with more precise visions. Disillusioned by the Neckinger Trial, therefore, he gathered round him a bunch of weird psychopaths. One of these was Joseph Prescott, the young lad from the workhouse who had drawn frenzied pictures of his visions. Joanna, initially to please Elias, had even published a pamphlet about Prescott's fantasies, with her own interpretation of their meaning (*The First Book of Visions*). In it she reminded readers of Joel's words in the Bible: "The end will come by visions seen by young men and prophecies given by handmaidens."

Another of Elias's prodigies was an old man called Jerusha Dowland. He was a "humble, pious Christian, a man of timid nature, feeble in body and equally so in mind, but with the fear of God uniformly before his eyes". Elias had discovered Dowland, a 63 year old tramp, in September 1803 while Joanna was in Bristol being nursed back to sanity by Jane Townley. Dowland first tried to find warmth and shelter at one of the Southcottian meetings but he was considered too dirty and smelly to be allowed in. It was only when he threatened to kill himself, that he was accepted and sealed. Then he revealed that a divine spirit had given him a message to pass on to Joanna.

> "Come see, Joanna, see the saint arise.
> Burst earthly prison, soar above the skies
> To that bright world, where joys immortal grow,
> And life's unfathomed pleasures ever flow.
> There, robed in white, she'll join the heavenly train,
> The ransom'd throng for whom the lamb was slain.
> She'll share the glory of the sealed race,
> And bask, and triumph, in the God of Grace."

He had an unnerving ability to discharge streams of similar doggerel for hours on end and Elias Carpenter was impressed, particularly by the old man's amazing fluency when at other times he came over as a gibbering idiot. "Although there may be nothing in the style to attract the notice of such as pride themselves in their correct taste in composition yet, to those who know the man's simplicity, the whole was extraordinary."

Carpenter took the dirty old man into his own home. "I believe there exists not one who could give off-hand, as fast as a ready penman could possibly write, a number of lines on a subject with which he was unacquainted." He added that he felt Jerusha's output could not be matched even if "a month was given to a competitor for each hour he spent in writing". If an explanation was required, this feeble, illiterate old man with shaky hands and no learning "immediately replied in thirty, fifty or a hundred lines of verse". Dowland had won Elias over totally by declaring him a true Apostle. He even anointed him in oil and told him:

> "The power the Apostles had you now receive,
> My Spirit now, your soul shall never leave."

Joanna was more wary of this old man than any of her other rivals but, fortunately for her, he suddenly dropped dead without warning and so the immediate danger was averted. Elias, however, soon found a replacement, a man called Jared who called himself the "spiritual searcher". He was clever, with a degree of education and although Joanna accused him of being a fraud, Joseph Prescott, Elias's young prodigy, insisted God had told him Jared must be obeyed at all cost. For Elias Carpenter, this clinched the matter, for he had immense faith in Prescott's judgement.

Ever zealous, he opened up his luxurious home to interested friends and entertained them with more liberality than discretion. With his wife Catherine, he organised religious services, sometimes at his home or hired chapels. Although it was customary in those days to charge for admission to religious meetings, Carpenter allowed anyone in free. However, he did encourage his wealthier friends to contribute towards the expenses.

These favourites of Carpenter were only a few of many weird prophets emerging, it seemed, all over London and the provinces. A worrying aspect was that, because they were so numerous, there was a danger Joanna might be classed as just one of many religious cranks. Up to the time of the Neckinger Trial, Elias Carpenter was torn between loyalties. He had rented a Chapel near the Elephant and Castle, which he intended to be the new headquarters of Joanna's Mission. She had even advertised the opening by printing and distributing bills stating that: "The said place of worship is opened by express command of God, through me." Joanna had held only a couple of meetings there, when Prescott had a sudden, exasperating vision, in which God told him to "let Elias withdraw himself, nor meet the people more".

Elias immediately took notice and forbade Joanna to use the chapel, at which she furiously accused Prescott of being inspired by the Devil. Carpenter refused to return a letter she had once written to him on impulse, and which she felt would not be good for her reputation if he allowed the contents to be known. She was convinced he was going to use it against her. We don't know what was in the letter, but it must have been something extremely incriminating, for she was clearly worried.

She asked her divine spirit what she should do and was told soothingly that the letter was of no real consequence. It was all part of a divine plan, for God had actually ordered it to be put in Carpenter's hands for such a time as this, to illustrate the inconsistency of mankind.

According to Joanna's spirit guide, God was very angry with Carpenter. "Consider how long you concealed his frailties from the brethren," God pointed out to Joanna. "Now he is going from one evil to another." Having stooped to involve Himself in this petty dispute, God withdrew from the argument and left Joanna to sort it out herself.

Carpenter observed dryly: "In the year 1805 she had an unaccountable fit of being invested with some supreme authority, and directed certain proceedings against me for supposed acts of disobedience."

He was pretty angry himself at the way she was besmirching his character and called together mutual friends to discuss the matter, on the second floor of a Holborn lodging house. Twelve of Joanna's followers turned up and accused him of communicating with Satan through Prescott. Carpenter noted: "Those that were of her party believed everything through the youth was from an evil source."

One powerful figure who attended the meeting was one of Joanna's Devonshire disciples, the coarse and illiterate lay-preacher, William Tozer, famous for giving fiery sermons. Carpenter wrote of him: "He came from the country to publicly tell the inhabitants of the metropolis that nothing was to be received but through this woman, and that I was leading people by the Devil. That, had he not come to town, all were going headlong to the infernal regions.

"The simple people were alarmed, as though his satanic majesty had personally appeared. For he impiously said that he was spiritually taught by God, whilst I dared make no pretensions but to be an explainer of spiritual teaching. And, not withstanding his illiteracy, his gross language and repulsive manners, he prejudiced two-thirds of the people's minds against what, if understood, they would have firmly held as the pearl of great price, and made a breach which has never been healed."

Tozer defended Joanna to the hilt, although at first he had favoured Carpenter. Carpenter vehemently blamed him for the breach against Joanna. From then on Carpenter was not permitted to seal any more people on Joanna's account, but continued to do so on his own. Dr. Reece, one of

Joanna's medical advisers, accused him of selling his seals for financial gain, but when Carpenter threatened to sue him for slander, withdrew the remark.

It was all becoming sordid and petty. Carpenter felt Joanna was ungrateful. He had been very kind to her and helped her both financially and socially, introducing her to useful people, sacrificing "my friends, property, prospects, apparently for nothing". Joanna's believers turned against him too. Scarcely a week passed without hordes turning up outside his mill or his home in Bermondsey, to scream abuse at him. His windows were regularly smashed and rude messages scrawled on his walls.

By 1814 he was still feeling the effects of Joanna's wrath. "Nine years have passed," he wrote bitterly, "and still, wherever any knew me, even to the farthest part of Yorkshire, she has blackened me in the vilest and most infamous manner, and they who have heard and believed this envenomed slander have taken an equally active part in diffusing it to others, to display their fidelity."

The outcome was that Joanna lost both her new headquarters and Carpenter, who continued to hold services there for the next thirty years. Eventually he became obsessed with the spirit world and used the chapel for seances.

Spiritual experiences were becoming infectious amongst Joanna's followers. Peter Morrison came rushing up from Liverpool, to say he too had seen visions and had been told that nothing should be received but through Woman.

George Turner was also becoming an embarrassment, claiming to be in direct communication with God in much the same way as Joanna. In a letter to Robert Powell on December 22, 1806, he hints that Joanna's character was not as unblemished as she would have people believe.

Turner said that God told him "My handmaiden I will deliver from those that are too strong for her and my counsel shall stand. I have visited her in love and I have seen an horrible thing, the Adulterer with the Virgin of my Kingdom on earth."

Joanna was now without a headquarters. Peter Morrison found an abandoned chapel, in Duke Street, Southwark, which he rented and paid for it to be repaired and restored for Joanna to hold meetings in. William Tozer, as a reward for his stalwart defence of Joanna against Carpenter, was appointed lay-reader. He was an impassioned speaker with a voice of thunder that thrilled the congregation with a satisfying fear of the Almighty. There was even a choir formed and, with the added attraction of

Tozer's fiery preaching, the new chapel was crammed to overflowing each Sunday.

Joanna's friends had opened chapels in Leeds, Stockport, Bath, Bristol and Exeter. One of her admirers, Philip Pullen, compiled a special hymn book containing verses drawn from her writings and entitled "*A Hymn Book for the Sealed*". This handsome book was calf-bound and fastened with brass clasps and, though expensive, sold well to Joanna's wealthier followers. An enlarged edition was brought out in 1807 and a third in 1814 - this time entitled "*Hymns of the Millennium*".

But Joanna seemed unable to avoid scandal. Some of her disciples became involved with a confidence trickster called John King, a notorious Jewish money lender who had already served a sentence for blackmail. His usual terms for arranging deals was 5% per month with 1% commission.

He placed an advertisement in the newspaper: "A conveyancer whose fortune enables him to supply sums of any amount, has resolved to devote a portion of his wealth to the alleviation of misfortune and the cherishment of learning and industry."

William Sharp spotted it and, with Wilson and Eyre, contacted King with a view to interesting him in investing in Joanna's Mission. An unscrupulous scoundrel, King convinced them he was really a wealthy philanthropist intent on finding a good cause. He was so charming and courteous, the three men believed him when he said he wanted to build new chapels for Joanna's Mission. They gave King permission to borrow money on their behalf and foolishly signed Bills of Exchange promising to repay the money in a year's time.

However, once he had their signatures, King revealed he was not actually a moneylender, but a broker who sold the Bills for the best price he could get. To their distress they received sums for considerably less than the Bills of Exchange they had signed for.

Finally acknowledging King was a ruthless swindler, they were too embarrassed at first to admit they had been tricked and were reluctant to bring charges against him for fear of damaging Joanna's reputation. King was delighted when he realised he had three conscientious suckers in his grip and took advantage of them by continuing to swindle them in other things.

He had already cleverly prepared his case, should the matter come to court. His defence was to be that the three men were not as respectable as they professed, for they had been told by their prophetess that the world was going to come to an end well before their Bills of Exchange became due. King was planning to tell a jury that, because the prophecy miscarried, they were now trying to wriggle out of honouring a legitimate financial arrangement.

Joanna eventually found out about the swindle and insisted they sued. On January 1, 1807, she wrote a lengthy letter to King reproving him for his dishonourable conduct and quoting passages from the Scriptures in the hope his conscience might prick him.

He replied with a charming letter the same day, saying: "I admire your character and revere your doctrine and believe most devoutedly the divine authority you quoted." But nevertheless he refused to repent.

The case came before the court and King tried to sway the jury by referring to Sharp's religious views, accusing him of saying that the country would be in such a state of confusion in March, April and May that year, that it was as well to pay nobody and that the sealed would destroy those who were not sealed. Sharp was particularly upset when one counsellor remarked: "A new person has been presented to the court who, under the pretence of prophecy, has presumed to blaspheme the name of God." This was a reference to Joanna who had arrived to speak on Sharp's behalf. However, King argued brilliantly and won.

The whole matter reflected upon Joanna. She published a seething, seventy-two page pamphlet in which she urged the three men to fight on regardless and they followed her advice and appealed against the verdict, which went in their favour. But for months afterwards, Sharp was inconsolable because he felt the case had dealt a severe blow to his reputation and made him appear naive to his intellectual friends in the art world. Although their honour was restored and King shown up as a scoundrel, the money was never retrieved.

Chapter 13

Her Popularity Dives

A tiny scheming Yorkshire woman called Mary Bateman became the centre of another scandal which reflected upon Joanna. Although she seemed gentle, almost saintly, the truth was Mary had been making a good living for years as a professional confidence trickster and abortionist and was indirectly responsible for the deaths of a number of young girls. By the time she was forty, she'd built up an impressive reputation as a spellmaker and wise woman and ran a lucrative business from her cottage, next to a rowdy public house in the centre of Leeds.

One of her more sinister specialities was "screwing down" enemies for her customers. Mary asked for four brass screws and four gold guineas and the name and address of the enemy concerned. The guineas went straight into Mary's pocket, but what she needed the brass screws for was anybody's guess. No customer ever needed to ask, for within a short time the enemy's power to hurt mysteriously vanished - and sometimes the enemy did too!

When business was slow, she would drum up trade by popping into the pub next door to spread malicious rumours about "other women" to men's wives, or to invent tales about lustful young men intent on seducing innocent daughters. The alarmed parties would naturally appeal to her for help, which she gave most readily for an appropriate fee.

By putting on a facade of saintliness, she was able to continue her wicked practices for years and her ingenuity was often breathtaking. When Joanna visited Leeds in 1803 Mary Bateman, admiringly recognising a fellow trickster, naturally wanted to get in on the act. So she ingratiated herself by humbly confessing to Joanna a few of her own sins. Joanna succumbed to Mary's flattery in no time and personally sealed her.

Professing to now be a faithful follower, Mary took to preaching on Joanna's behalf. Her ingenuity surpassed itself when, in January 1806, she

Joanna Southcott
Wearing her best bonnet

An engraving of Joanna looking her best, with curls coyly escaping from beneath a fashionable and expensive-looking bonnet. Probably drawn during her affluent period, after coming to London. Portraits after her death were usually not so flattering. Artist unknown.

artfully produced an egg which had the words "CRIST IS COMING" inscribed on it, and claimed her hen had laid it fresh that very morning.

The word got round Leeds and soon there were dozens of visitors to Mary's house, demanding to see the miraculous egg. Joanna heard about it and it struck her as a perfectly reasonable and practical way for God to transmit a message and probably wished she had thought of the idea herself. On January 26, 1806, she wrote about the miracle to a friend, describing Mary as a woman who had previously been a person of bad character.

"The woman says she broke the inscribed egg to make a pudding with. The following day, the hen laid another with the same inscription on it. Some men from the public house, next door to where she lives, told her to hard boil it and then they broke it to see if it had boiled and it hadn't. They took the shell away with them. Some gentlemen of Leeds went to the woman and asked her to let them have the hen so they could watch it lay another egg. The woman agreed and the next day it laid another."

Joanna recalled a story about a maidservant who became pregnant by her master. The master wanted her to swear he was not the father but she refused. "When the child was born," wrote Joanna, "the name of the father was written on the child's face. If the Lord can mark the forehead of a child, why not an egg?" Of course, Joanna even wrote a verse about the incident.

> "So let them judge which way they will,
> The thing is deep, I tell you still.
> For Satan's hand was never there,
> To make the Egg that way appear.
> No, it was not done by man or me,
> The ending every soul will see."

The letter and the verse were published and Mary Bateman's esteem rose as a result of Joanna's approval. For two years, business in the brass screw racket boomed. Then, on October 8, 1808, Mary was arrested for the murder of one of her customers, a harmless little woman called Rebecca Perigo, from Bramley, Leeds. Becky believed unwaveringly in Mary's powers and for years had been paying to have evil curses put on those she had a grudge against. She was satisfied she got good value for her money. Apparently she paid out four guineas 17 times to Mary.

Becky's husband was not so gullible and was furious when he found out where his hard earned money was going. He went to Mary's house, accused her of fraud and threatened to tell the police. Mary was seriously concerned because the last thing she wanted was to appear in court, whether found guilty or not, for it would be bad for business. So she devised her own solution.

While the husband was at work, she visited Becky and took out of her pocket an envelope containing a white powder mixed with arsenic. She assured Becky the powder was harmless, but it had a magic component and, if mixed in with the Yorkshire pudding that Sunday, Mary would "guarantee to avert a great calamity". Becky offered her a fee, but Mary airily refused.

In Leeds, Yorkshire puddings were served at the beginning of a meal, thick like a pizza and covered in rich brown gravy - the aim being to blunt the appetite so that less meat would be eaten later. Becky mixed the pudding, adding the powder as instructed, and sat down with her husband to eat it. Both were overcome with stomach cramps and for several days were dangerously ill. The husband survived. Becky didn't but, before she died, she confessed her crime and the part Mary played in it.

Mary Bateman was brought before the Leeds Assizes and her life of crime and debauchery emerged. The prosecuting counsel painted a murky picture of her, saying she had a "knavish and vicious disposition" and, since the tender age of five, had been involved in theft, fraudulence, deceit and murder. She pleaded not guilty to all the accusations, particularly Becky's murder, and maintained it was an evil plot to disgrace her saintly reputation. A surprising number of people believed her and, when she was found guilty and sentenced to death, the rumour spread that a divine miracle would save her.

Mary clung to the hope that if she maintained her innocence to the very end, she stood a slim chance of a reprieve. On the day of her execution, dressed in a white gown, she made her way to the gallows with studied dignity and a crowd of 20,000 watched her play out her final act of deception. Many were convinced that an angel from heaven would appear and snatch her from the gallows. A Leeds newspaper reported: "She dressed in white for the hanging, and fully expected deliverance from the fatal tree."

There was no heavenly interference, but her story excited the ghoulish imaginations of Leedsfolk. The unsavoury undertaker lucky enough to be given charge of the corpse, charged threepence a peep as it lay on view in his parlour, and there was no shortage of customers.

It was reported that some were so moved by the saintly expression on Mary's face, that their faith in her was strengthened and, twenty years later, one old woman devotee was quoted in a newspaper as saying: "Ah, she will come again. She mun come again, afore all will be well."

Before she died, Mary Bateman claimed that she was one of Joanna's faithful followers, thinking this a point in her favour. Joanna, finding herself in compromising circumstances, had to come up with some sort of explanation no matter how unlikely. So she announced that Mary Bateman was under the influence of the Devil, but had been found out and punished. Therefore, those that said she, Joanna, was led by the Devil should take note that no punishment had been brought upon *herself.*

Conveniently disregarding the fact that Mary Bateman had been carrying on with her evil ways for forty years or more - much longer than Joanna had been doing much the same thing - she added: "Note the difference between us. How soon Mary Bateman's crimes were discovered and how short her power. How long the one stood. How soon the other fell."

Joanna didn't mention again the egg incident, which had so completely taken her in, but found she couldn't wriggle out of it that easily. Her critics brought it up at the slightest opportunity.

On March 15, 1808, Mr. Smith, a Calvinist Minister, preached a sermon entitled: "*The Lying Prophetess Detected*". He quoted I Kings, xiv, 6, which he altered to suit the moment: "Joanna, why feignest thou thyself to be another? For I am sent to thee with heavy tidings."

Joanna replied icily: "Who sent thee with heavy tidings to me?" and suggested it was Smith, not herself, who was feigning to be a prophet. Smith retaliated with a short verse, mimicking Joanna's own crude doggerel:

> "Thou mother of witchcraft and teacher of lies,
> Subverter of truth and deep in disguise.
> I dread not the curse, nor fear thee to tell,
> The whole of the system proceedeth from Hell."

All she could do now was ride the storm. But her reputation was tarnished. The general opinion was that she was a powerful witch. When an Exeter newspaper reported Joanna had prophesied the destruction of Bath on the following Good Friday, thousands decided that, although they didn't really believe such nonsense, it was best to play safe. That weekend the city was practically empty, although it was a holiday weekend. As a result, Bath was robbed of its Easter trade, which did not please the townsfolk who depended upon visitors for a living.

She was frequently accused of drunkenness, which she protested was "a crime I ever detest". But the slaggish tag stuck! In 1811 Hewson Clarke, a slick muck-raker and editor of a dubious journal called "*The Scourge*" wrote that Joanna had arrived, the worse for drink, at Elias Carpenter's chapel, dressed in diamonds and expensive furs. He also reported that she had had an affair with a candle-snuffer at the same chapel and had been seen in a passionate embrace after the service.

Jane Townley said Hewson admitted to her later that there was no foundation to these stories but, because she professed to be a prophetess, was therefore "fair game for anyone to shoot at".

It was bad enough when Joanna had to defend herself against reports which *had* some foundation. When faced with such barefaced lies, she was righteously indignant and wanted to sue but was advised that "judge and jury would view the case with prejudice as they would look on it as intended to decry fanaticism". Instead she noted wearily: "The natures of men have ever been the same with regard to revealed religion. True prophets have always been prosecuted and the false encouraged."

She was still gaining important converts, such as the Rev. Hoadley Ash, who had a reputation for being learned and pious. Ash was curate of Crewkerne and Misterton and, after joining Joanna's ranks, worked hard to establish a Southcottian community in his part of Somerset - concentrating on Crewkerne, Chard, Dowlish and Ilminster. What was referred to as "a cottage of worship" was established in virtually every village in the locality.

Ash's own parishioners were appalled and many decided he had gone mad. There was much resentment towards him but he must have thought it well worth risking his popularity for, on September 28, 1807, five days after meeting Joanna for the first time, he wrote her an enthusiastic letter, saying her communications were still vibrating in his ears. More in the tone of a lover than a disciple, he wrote: "A happier night I never enjoyed in this world - they have left a fragrance upon my mind and the remembrance of them is sweet."

After reading two of her books he said that: "Every step I took, the Word of God out of your mouth was a clear burning light unto my feet and a glorious lamp unto my path."

At last, he said, his search was ended. He marvelled that what his impressive learning had not revealed to him, was now made clear by an unlearned woman, and added earnestly: "For thirty-seven years I have diligently searched the Scriptures in seven different languages and consulted all the commentators, with the hope of finding the truth."

Although it was normal to charge an entrance fee at most chapels, Joanna criticised Mr. Huntingdon, a popular Calvinist Minister, for selling tickets in excess of seats available in his chapel. Joanna was annoyed when she attended one of his meetings and, after paying for her seat, found that the place was full. But, recognising it as a useful way of acquiring income, she introduced a ticket system in her own chapels - on the pretext that she wanted to discourage unauthorised worshippers and hecklers from attending.

She explained to William Tozer: "It will prevent great confusion amongst the people if they all took their seats and everyone had a ticket. Then the people who may come out of curiosity or to make a disturbance, will be prevented from filling the place with disorderly people, as they cannot go into any place of worship to take away the seats from those who have paid for them. This keeps all churches and places of worship in order."

Peter Morrison, one of the original disciples, was in her bad books because he had been prophesying on his own account which "mortified and grieved" Joanna. "I cannot stand joined with any that will not follow the directions that are given to ME." Morrison was the brother-in-law and close friend of Joanna's bookseller, Elias Field, and lived in the wealthy suburb of Mansfield, Nottingham. On December 21, 1806, Field (who had also tried his hand at prophesying) wrote to Morrison about his predictions. "I received your curious letter and I sent it to our Mother (Joanna). I shall leave her to determine as she may think proper. What you say has astonished the Friends, so it seems you and I are two astonishing fellows."

They were both too useful to Joanna for her to get stern with. Field was clearly doing good business out of Joanna. He asked Morrison to send him his list of sealed converts, to pass on to Joanna, before the last day of the year 1806, and wrote: "I am obliged to you for your intention of sending the money with the lists - that will do very well. I will send you what books you want, with the new books, as they will soon be ready."

He added with satisfaction that the demand was so great for Joanna's latest production "*Sound the Alarm*" that they had been obliged to print 4,000 copies. "I have pleasure in informing you that I have lately sent 1,000 seals on demand to Leeds, and 1,050 "*Sound the Alarms*" to Samuel Hirst only and am so very busy I have no time to write you any more news." A year later, business was waning and on September 26, 1807, Field wrote gloomily to his brother-in-law: "It is uncertain when we may have a new book, but one is at present going into print."

Field had also been somewhat depressed by family matters. His wife Anne's sister-in-law, a youngish woman, had suddenly dropped dead. Joanna had predicted her death six weeks earlier, by suggesting "she would not spend next Christmas" with them. Ann Field, shocked by the accuracy of Joanna's forecast, miscarried the baby she was expecting.

A sinister aspect to all this was the fact that the dead woman owned a seal which her brother, a Mr. Spring, had bought for sixpence from John Middleton, one of Joanna's disciples. Joanna publicly expelled him from her Mission with the firm statement that: "If Middleton received any money for delivering the seals, then he is entirely cut off from anything to do with my work, because he sinned knowingly, since I had said no money at all should be taken for the seals." Furthermore, she told Spring that, since he paid for the seals for himself and his sister, then the seals would be a curse and not a blessing and they would both suffer.

As a result of the scandal, the old charge was revived that she was making money selling seals for sums ranging from 2s 6d to twenty-one shillings. She again insisted that this was not true. "There are thousands desirous of having them. If these were purchased for a shilling each, the gain would be great. But I have never received anything for a seal in my life and neither would I."

So again sealing was halted for a while. Then Field wrote that Joanna had given permission to begin sealing people again. Since Morrison, in Nottingham, had thousands clamouring to be sealed, Field said he would send him a thousand copies of the seal by coach "as I thought you would rather pay the coachage than keep the people in suspense". Which makes it all sound very commercial and difficult to believe that a racket in seals was not going on.

It had become fashionable to be signed twice as a sign of renewed faith. Field told Morrison that he and his wife had done so. "But it is no use signing their hands unless their hearts go with it," he warned.

The Leeds Mercury reported that devout possessors of the seals had been promised by the prophetess that "they would live at least a thousand years". When one of the sealed, a Mr. Joachim, was murdered in London, many felt betrayed because they thought the seals were a guarantee of safety from all mortal danger.

So Joanna issued a stern warning: "Let this be a caution to believers, not to run themselves into danger, but let them remember how often I have warned them, to avoid danger in every way. If they simply suppose the seals were made as a wall about them, that no dangers could come near them, then my warnings and caution would be in vain. Let them discern how dangers are laying in wait for the just and the unjust, for believers and non-believers."

Joanna, what with the sale of her books and perhaps of the seals as well, was rumoured to have a tidy fortune tucked away. She must have been quite comfortably off, for when she made her Will about this time, she was able to leave a life income of £10 to one of her sisters and her brother, and £10 in lump sums to a sister-in-law and niece. Tokens of "love" to old friends totalled over a thousand pounds. The bulk of her estate she left to Jane Townley and Ann Underwood, because she said they had a joint interest in her published books and "all debts and credits appertaining thereto".

Joanna was a natural business woman. It was Joanna who, when her father let the farm in Gittisham go to rack and ruin after his wife died, went through the books and put everything to rights. She once said that, if she hadn't become a prophet, she would have certainly been a successful businesswoman.

To these suggestions that she raked in a good living from her books, she replied: "I stand one hundred pounds worse than I should have done had I never took pen to hand."

She said she did it all for God, and reminded everyone that she was an upholstress by trade and could, if necessary, support herself. "I should have placed myself in business years ago, had I not been ordered by God to leave all, to follow Him. So I have done as Peter did, and launched into the grand deep."

Even so, she took a keen and earthly interest in book sales and wrote anxiously to one agent: "Sales have gone off very irregular. I shall be glad to know what there is left of every thousand in your hands, that I may know how to reprint the First again, and any of the thousands that may be nearly out."

She ordered all her booksellers to report to her monthly, so that she could assess sales. Elias Field did so well that Joanna put him on a regular salary of one and a half guineas a week - more than £100 a year - instead of commission. Joanna was delighted when he ordered "fifty whole sets of the Divine Works".

Sales rocketed when Joanna introduced a lucrative new law. No-one, she said, was allowed to be sealed unless they owned at least *one* of her books. It was not enough to have read a borrowed one. She later compromised by allowing a husband and wife to own a book between them. In Teddington, Middlesex, records show that Edward Baker commanded a congregation of Southcottians consisting of 69 women and

54 men. Of this number 44 were single and there were 35 families. The families possessed between them over fifty of Joanna's books, and only two couples didn't own any but relied on borrowing. Of the unmarried ones, four of the men and one of the women had a complete collection. In all, the Teddington congregation had a total of 1,460 copies between them.

If this was typical of other Southcottian groups in the country, it is an impressive indication of how well she was doing as a best-selling authoress. Her sister Susanna wrote to her that she'd heard reports in Ottery St. Mary that Joanna had made between £10,000 and £15,000 from sales. Joanna indignantly denied it yet once wrote to Foley promising she would send more books if he could persuade believers to subscribe for them and, as an incentive, offered to pay the postage out of her own profits. But the shrewd business woman and the saintly prophetess were only two sides of her complicated character. Like a frightened little child, she suffered awful nightmares which she blamed on evil spirits. However, she believed she had worked out a practical way of telling the difference between a good spirit and a bad one.

She explained how in a letter to Townley in October 1807. A good spirit could be identified "by the heavenly joy within, which takes all fear and terror from us. This I always experience - my fears vanish and my comfort increases. But when evil spirits come to consult me I always feel fear, terror and dread and though the Devil may come as an angel of light, yet he brings horror with him".

In 1811 a comet appeared in the sky. Joanna was fascinated by comets. She believed they were sent by God and that the Star of Bethlehem was one. A comet was seen in the sky on the night she was born and the most famous comet of all - Halley's Comet - made a spectacular appearance when she was seven years old. The comet of 1811, discovered by German astrologer, Johann Franz Encke, was named after him and was visible for about eighteen months. Described as of great magnitude, its progress was eagerly reported by the newspapers. Sensationalists blamed it for almost all notable disasters - floods, storms, fires and warfare. But its very sighting filled Joanna with gloomy foreboding. She believed all the stories she read about it and was convinced it heralded the beginning of the *Final Millennium*. And she wasn't ready!

A sense of urgency overwhelmed her and she was torn between fear and impatience. She felt that she couldn't afford to waste time. The end of the world was near and she needed to hurry up and put her plan - although she wasn't quite sure what it was - into action before the Day of Judgement finally dawned.

Chapter 14

Curse on George III

The man Joanna probably hated most in all the land was poor old mad King George III. It was a very personal hatred. She had written to him - letters she said God had ordered her to write. She had sent him invitations to her Trials. She had asked him to acknowledge her as a divine prophet. His Majesty had deigned not to reply - not even to a request for the return of all her unanswered letters.

She considered this disrespectful, not only to her but to God Himself. It was a sin to disobey her because, she always stressed, it was just like disobeying God. All her disciples had signed statements swearing they would do exactly as she told them in all things. And the King was, after all, head of the Church of England and therefore should have known better.

Despite his mental condition, she had decided early on that even kings must be punished and convinced herself that his madness was the result of a curse she had placed on him. True or not, the King's bouts of madness increased over the years and he became violent and a danger even to those who loved him. He was often put in a strait-jacket and pinned down by brutal surgeons. Hearing stories of his sufferings left Joanna with a smug sense of satisfaction that justice was being done and God was punishing him on her behalf.

She was particularly jealous of the affection shown him by his subjects - affection she considered rightfully hers. He was basically a good and conscientious King who genuinely tried to identify with his people. Since assuming the throne in 1760, he had lived a private life of homely domesticity with his rather plain wife, Queen Charlotte, and had always made clear to his people that his family were of the greatest importance to him - a new concept in court circles but one which won him popularity and affection. His son and heir, George, on the other hand, was constantly shocking the nation with one scandal after another.

King George had the power to order the Bishops to examine Joanna's writings, to insist she be shown proper respect. Yet all he did was treat her with contempt and encourage others to do so too. It is small wonder that she hated and reviled him and showed no compassion for his madness. For how can one mad person sympathise with another's plight?

Her deep seated resentment towards the King made her depressed and uncontrollable. Jane Townley decided she needed rest and seclusion and John Smith's suggestion that she went to stay at Rock Cottage, in Blockley, was welcomed. Their relationship had strengthened and Joanna felt secure enough to send Jane Townley and Ann Underwood to lodge elsewhere in the village, leaving her alone a great deal with Smith.

It was a tranquil phase of her life. Much of her time was spent cutting up bits of material and sewing them into a patchwork quilt. The quilt, apart from being soothing therapy, was symbolic of a "complete covering for the Perfect Man" which could, she said, only be achieved after all nations had been cut asunder.

It was also a productive period, for she received numerous communications which she dictated to Ann Underwood, describing her divine guide as the "still, small voice" inside her. These notes were sent back to London to be published, and the new book which emerged was a sell out. It was not only believers who clamoured for it, but also the amused, the credulous and the curious. Joanna was an enigma, a legend in her own lifetime! Everyone wanted to know more about her.

Towards the end of 1809 plans were announced for the nation to celebrate King George III's Jubilee the following year. He was being treated by a wiser and more sensitive doctor, Dr. Willis, who tried a new soothing treatment and the King seemed to recover completely. Plans to install his son as Regent were dropped.

But news of the King's recovery and the Jubilee plans enraged Joanna. She considered it an insult to God that a king who, by rejecting her had virtually rejected God, should be considered worth rejoicing for. She made up her mind to increase his suffering by foul means or fair.

The first indication that God held the same views as herself came on October 1, 1809. "I am God, source of happiness, and by Me Kings reign and Princes decree justice," God told her. "I have gone again and again to the rulers of this land, England, and made known what all evil, through disobedience, will bring upon the nation. But I am not regarded and shall My word fail, disobedience will be punished. I will make them bow unto

Me, for I will be honoured in My invitations. I am not a man, to lie, or the son of man, to repent. No other way will they escape the evil and distress that will surround them on all sides. For I *will* be obeyed. They have greatly rejected My Word. Therefore shall they smart. Those that deprive and regret My invitation, shall greatly feel My wrathful displeasure, for My curse shall come in their store. I will drain their wealth and turn it into dross, that they may know that I am the Lord.

"Let no-one marvel in their hearts that I should prolong the life of the King to have a jubilee kept for him. The shadows of all things may appear before the substance to the Grand Jubilee that I shall bring to man. They saw no more room to rejoice at your birth, than they saw room to rejoice at the King's reign, because the great enemy was not destroyed and therefore I tell thee it is but shadows in both. But the fifty years of the King's reign will not be up until October. And when he is let loose again, My fiery indignation shall destroy him and then shall he be judged and rewarded according to his deeds, being cursed above all beings."

It was an angry, jealous and wrathful God who spoke through Joanna, coincidentally echoing her exact feelings of bitterness and resentment. The dreadful curse, directed at the King of England, was treacherous and indeed a hanging matter. Joanna's defence - that it wasn't she who placed the curse, but God Himself - wouldn't have carried any weight had the news got out.

On October 28, 1809, came another allegedly divine outburst. "Let no-one marvel in their hearts at times such as this, when your nation is surrounded with every burden and oppression, that some should be inclined to propose a Jubilee being kept as a Jubilee to Man, as a day of thanksgiving and rejoicing, which to many appeared as madness. Shadows will come round in the ten years I placed to thee, but here thy own pondering thoughts go deep that, soon after the time is up, come in the change of the four figures."

Within the cosy seclusion of Rock Cottage, she worked on her patchwork quilt, painstakingly cutting up squares of material and with her nimble upholsteress's fingers, sewing them deftly into place. She had started the quilt on first arriving in London, because she said she couldn't bear to be idle.

She explained the connection between the quilt and the curse she and God together had put upon the King: "The meaning of the four figures is this. It was said to me, when I began to mark the patchwork quilt, that the name was to be put in the middle." She said that God told her to sew into the middle of the quilt the date **1811**. For thread, she used her own light brown hair. That was the date, she believed, when the King would receive his just punishment. Joanna's patchwork quilt can be seen today at the Royal Albert Museum, Exeter.

The statement of the curse was first read by Joanna's closest friends, who were alarmed at how easily it could be interpreted as an act of treachery. They feared that if anyone in authority saw it, it was quite likely she would be arrested and charged with plotting against the throne, and flung into jail and very likely hung. Richard Brothers had been imprisoned for saying much less. The ultimate punishment for treachery was death. So no copies of the statement were made, and it was circulated within a very tight circle of trusted disciples. "It must not go out of London," Joanna warned.

After a few days the enormity of what she had done, and the risks she had exposed herself to, dawned on her. She worried it might be seen by a member of Parliament and so she ordered Ann Underwood to write another note of caution to close believers. "Dear Friends, I beg you will observe Mrs. Southcott's instructions and not let the communications concerning the Jubilee be copied off, as she will not let it go out in London and therefore wish it not to be sent."

Whether or not Joanna seriously expected the curse to work, is debatable. She certainly hoped it would. But there seemed chilling proof of her powers when the following year, before the King's Jubilee could take place, his favourite daughter, Amelia, was struck down with a fatal illness. The King couldn't come to terms with her death and in no time he was seriously deranged again and incapable of governing the country. The Prince of Wales, at that time in Joanna's good books, became Prince Regent in 1810.

The Regency Bill was passed in 1811 and the King was privately confined, having gone blind as well as mad. He lived his final years in misery until he finally died on January 19, 1820. Ten years previously Joanna had embroidered the date of the King's downfall (**1811**) with her own hair, in the centre of her patchwork quilt. Her divine guide commented approvingly: "Mark my mind, what hath befallen the Head of your nation."

Joanna was friendly with George Troup, who came from Blockley and was John Smith's cousin and also a fervent Southcottian. For forty years he had been page to the Prince of Wales. When George Troup mentioned to him that Joanna Southcott was staying at a cottage in Blockley, the Prince asked if he could meet her, perhaps feeling it necessary to appease Joanna in some way. In 1807, while staying at Ragley Hall, not far from

Blockley, the Prince paid her a secret visit "to assure himself of the truth of her claims". It was said he had "made some generous gifts to help the Cause" or, more likely, to insure Joanna didn't put any curses on *him.*

It was a brilliant display of diplomacy by the new Prince Regent and temporarily absolved him of all sin in Joanna's eyes. Despite his wayward life, she felt he was infinitely preferable as a ruler than his father. Unfortunately, he didn't maintain his friendly attitude and it was not long before he too became a target for her curses.

In 1812, one of her followers, James Cosins, died leaving all his money and worldly possessions to Joanna, Jane Townley and Ann Underwood. During the summer of that year Cosins had, apparently, promised Joanna he would leave everything to her, apart from a few small legacies.

On November 15 he was suddenly taken ill and Joanna rushed round to see him with unseemly haste, to make sure he kept his promise. As she feared, no Will had been drawn up! God apparently promised her Cosins would regain sufficient strength to sign a Will. So Joanna remained at his bedside praying and, sure enough, next day he was well enough to be propped up with pillows. Meanwhile, Joanna had had a Will compiled, leaving everything to herself and her two companions. Cosins weakly signed it, in front of witnesses. The following morning, November 17, before taking his last breath, Joanna bent her head close to his and said he whispered to her: "I shall die happy in this faith, but should not in any other."

She received from another disciple a legacy of £250 a year, which left her fairly well off and no longer dependent on the charity of friends. No matter how the Mission fared, she would now be financially secure for the rest of her life. She made a Will of her own, including with it a glowing account of herself - describing herself as "abstemious". There were many who did not hold the same high opinion of her.

Dr. P.Matthias, an eminent surgeon called to attend to her professionally, remarked with disdain: "I never could learn that she either fasted or prayed. On the contrary, she passed much of her time in bed in downy indolence, ate and drank much and often and prayed - never." Joanna heard of his opinion of her and was not pleased. Maybe he regretted his words for, directly after Joanna's own death, he committed suicide.

The Press became curious about Joanna and her whereabouts and set out to hunt her down, but without much success. Journalist Johnson Grant reported that because of her mental state, Joanna had to be locked in a secret chamber and was seen by only a few friends - which was at least partly true. Richard Hann wrote a pamphlet entitled "*The Remarkable Life, Entertaining History and Surprising Adventures of Joanna Southcott*". He began by saying she was born in Getsham and Joanna replied icily that, as he began without accurate knowledge, so he continued in *everything* concerning her.

She kept herself occupied, sometimes issuing very shrewd advice. For instance, some of her followers had been fined for speaking or preaching without licences. So she defined exactly what was required to keep in line with the law. Those wishing to preach, she said, should be licensed as a Protestant Dissenter and the meeting place should be licensed too. However, it wasn't worth the money to licence a meeting room if there wasn't a licensed preacher, especially if the numbers were small. "But if you meet together to read the writings and compare them with the Scriptures and neither use Prayer or Hymns, they cannot hurt you for that."

She still wrote regularly to Lucy Taylor, who adored her and sent her presents such as a "beautiful quarter of Lamb". Lucy's daughter, Fanny, was married to a Mr. Luscombe, who disliked Joanna and objected to his wife's association with her. Consequently, relations between Joanna and Fanny became temporarily strained. But Joanna wrote to Lucy: "I would be glad of a few lines after your long silence. We will excuse the past, if you promise not to forget us for the future."

She was often consulted on purely practical matters. Lucy Taylor never made an important decision without consulting Joanna. When Lucy's husband, Robert, was involved in a legal dispute with a man called Mills, who claimed he was overcharged for upholstering materials bought from Taylor's shop, Joanna showed a canny wisdom. She advised him to ask another upholsterer to arbitrate, rather than risk going to court. Her reasoning was that if the law upheld Mills' claim, then "every man that wishes to cheat a tradesman out of his money may make a pretence he hath bought his goods too dear". She pointed out that Mills had been told the price of the goods before buying and only after delivery did he accuse Taylor of overcharging. If the law considered this permissible "then all business would be at an end".

Joanna had disliked the courts ever since her harrassment case against her employer in Exeter, William Wills, even though she won. She once told Thomas Foley to stay away from the law over a financial matter, warning him that it was too easy to lose hundreds of pounds in legal fees "when once you get into their claws. I myself have seen so much of it". This sort of down-to-earth advice was something Joanna excelled at.

She spent three years altogether at Blockley, with John Smith as her companion and their daughter, Sarah, who was passed off as his niece. They reason they didn't marry was probably because Joanna still believed she was destined to marry Joseph Pomeroy.

Eventually the novelty of cosy domesticity wore off and she became bored, impatient and vaguely disappointed with herself. She had not achieved what she had set out for - to be accepted by the Church as a genuine divinely-inspired prophet. She could not rid herself of resentment towards the Church, and she was still smarting from the disdainful attitude of the Bishops. Then, out of the blue, she received a huge shock which made her temporarily forget everything. A country newspaper reported the sudden death of the Rev. J. Pomeroy, as he was about to preach from a church in Bodmin.

Joanna was shattered. She had been assured by her divine spirit that Pomeroy was the man chosen by God to persuade the Church and the King to listen to her. It was incomprehensible, therefore, that God would allow him to die before he had carried out his task. Despite all the rebuffs she had ever received from him, she had always believed that he would eventually succumb to God's wishes and persuade the Church to examine her writings and accept her as a wife. She noted it in verse:

> "In vain may Pomeroy try to flee,
> He ne'er shall shun his call."

It had not occurred to her he might evade his duty by simply dropping dead. She had regarded him as invincible. Yet here it was, in black and white, the cold statement that the **Rev. Mr. J. Pomeroy**, of **Bodmin**, was dead. Joanna was inclined to believe implicitly everything she read in the newspapers and accepted it had to be true. She went into shock, suffering violent convulsions. Her divine spirit kept telling her Pomeroy was alive. The newspaper said he was dead. She was not sure what to think and was unable to handle it.

The newspaper reported that Pomeroy arrived at church one morning to take the service and Mr. Kendall, the chaplain, noticed his manner was strange. Kendall offered to take the service, thinking that perhaps Pomeroy was drunk. Pomeroy accepted his offer and started to take off his surplice to hand to him, when he staggered and Kendall caught him in his arms. He was carried to his house nearby and a doctor certified him dead. "I was startled, in that I thought he would live to see the awful trial," noted Joanna.

When the report appeared in the London newspapers as well Joanna decided it must be true. So, in her *First Book of Wonders* which was almost finished, she added at the beginning: "All these things worked together a strong feeling in my mind and heart, to pity the man and to love him. In my heart, I felt deep love for him." She appealed to God:

> "Now suppose that he is dead,
> As in the paper it was said?
> The way his death did then appear,
> Wilt thou then see the mystery clear?"

Her book was published. Copies had already been speedily despatched all over England when the stunning news came that Pomeroy wasn't, after all, dead. One copy of Joanna's book had already reached Joseph Pomeroy, at his home in St. Kew, Bodmin. What astonished him more than the report of his own death, was the passionate lament from the woman he loathed and who had ruined his life.

It transpired there were two clergymen living in the Bodmin area by the name of Pomeroy, which was a common name in those parts. It was the **Rev. John Pomeroy** who had died so suddenly, not **Joseph Pomeroy**. Joanna looked silly, felt silly and was excruciatingly embarrassed. She had been made to look a fool before, but this was deeply personal and made her seem like a love-sick old woman.

Unable to face up to her dilemma, she relapsed into more fits interceded with periods of calm. Visitations came fast and furious and Jane Townley and Ann Underwood had their hands full, one minute trying to cope with her violent outbursts and the next taking divine dictation as fast as they could. Every day fresh "wonders" were revealed to her by God and she said she was constantly surrounded by angels. Her two friends were incredibly patient and tolerant, clinging to the blind conviction that no matter how crazy she seemed, she was always divinely guided.

Joanna described a bizarre dream she had on April 3, 1806, which she considered deeply significant, as dreams often do in the middle of the night. She dreamt that she was told to boil her Bible, so she tied a piece of string round it and dropped it into the boiling pot of water. She said she saw the Bible float to the top of the pot. She fished it out with the string, laid it on the table and opened it at the Psalms. The soaked Bible started to disintegrate and she was reluctant to risk opening it more. But she said her divine voice whispered to her that she was to have another trial but this time there would not be so many as attended the Neckinger event.

People were curious about how she conversed with God. Asked what God's voice sounded like, and how she replied to Him, she told Richard Hann that her divine voice spoke as distinctly as any human voice, although only she could hear. She wrote an ecstatic account of *how* she received her communications at the cottage in Blockley.

"I am awakened in the morning, between three and four o'clock. I sit up in my bed and have communications given to me. When the day breaks, I rise and go down into the dining room by myself. The moment I enter the room, I feel as though I am surrounded by angels, feeling a heavenly joy which takes me from my appetite. For three weeks past, I could not take any breakfast or dinner. Neither could I drink my tea in the afternoon."

One morning, at about five o'clock, she said she was sitting up in bed when there was a flash of light. "I thought it was the candle that blazed before going out," she said. But it was only God, to say she had to buy new clothing for all her female friends and twelve new gowns for herself.

Then she was told: "The time of your departure draweth near. For thy sands are nearly run!" She said this pleased her, because she was weary of the world, as the world was of her. "I cannot enter into particulars of what else was revealed to me, as it was ordered to be sealed up in the presence of seven friends and put into the *Box*."

She was right about the world being weary of her. Her Cause was going through another bad patch. Even the newspapers regarded her as old hat and no longer carried stories about her. The novelty of Joanna Southcott had worn off! The number of believers was dropping rapidly and, worse still, book sales were low. "We may see what a falling away there has been among the sealed, when we consider that 14,000 were sealed before," she wrote as she racked her brains to think of ways to revive her movement.

Joanna's "still, small, voice" within her hit upon a grand notion that she hardly dare specify. It was so outrageous she wasn't sure she had the courage to utter it aloud. She still clung to her hope that the Church would take her seriously and the Bishops would judge her at a proper trial. On the other hand, she had already had two trials and both times she had ended up a figure of ridicule. This idea forming in her mind was so much better than a trial. If she managed to pull if off, the Church would *have* to take notice of her.

Cautiously, she first of all told her friends about the divine instructions for them all to have new clothes and professed not to know why. Next morning she revealed that the new clothes were to be for her own wedding. Understandably, everyone was startled, for she was now bloated, old and dithery. The idea of her getting married should have struck her followers as hilarious. But no! In their eyes she was infallible and they listened to what else she had to say with appropriate awe. "I must enter into a marriage union with a man. I have been kept for the man whom God had designed for me. When I was told, all my nerves shook and my head was like the rivers of water."

Usually when her brain seemed to liquefy in this way, everything she said sounded like gibberish. On this occasion she remained articulate. "Whether in my senses or out of my senses, I cannot tell. For my spirits are so confused I can hardly speak to my friends when they come. I dread the thought of marriage at this time of day. Considering my age and the happy life I now live single, I am agitated with sorrow. I look upon matrimony as worse than death."

This was not exactly true! She would have jumped at the chance of marrying Pomeroy. Because she had it fixed in her mind that he was the man God had chosen to be her husband, she had refused to marry anyone else, not even John Smith.

As her mind fluctuated from rational to irrational, she claimed to be a virgin still and when this was disputed, protested that "malicious inventions have been raised against my character". Her reputation had been scandalously abused, she said. She could deal with accusations that she was a witch, that she was mad and influenced by the Devil. But when her chastity was questioned, she chose to react like an indignant young girl. Reports circulated that she was the common-law wife of John Smith and they had a "base-born" child.

Joanna lived at Rock Cottage, Blockley under the name of Mrs. Goddard and not many knew her true identity. Jane Townley and Ann Underwood, lodging elsewhere in the village, helped her keep her secret. "Here, my dear Miss Townley, you see what a strict charge is given to you, not to reveal my abode; neither must you let my friends in London know what place you have taken me, or where my abode is."

Another time she complained: "I am compelled to flee, not only from my enemies but from my friends, to conceal myself in a place of safety where I am not known by any person and my name I am obliged to conceal."

Rock Cottage was her home, on and off, from 1804 to the time of her death. John Smith would commute to London, where his business was, but returned regularly to join Joanna at Blockley. He also worked very hard for Joanna's movement and was totally committed to her, yet his name was never mentioned in any of the letters or communications, until a few months before her death, when she decided she would marry him officially, since there then seemed little hope of a marriage with Pomeroy. She needed an earthly father for the holy child she claimed to be carrying, and John Smith was suddenly presented as a casual acquaintance instead of her intimate companion of ten years.

Suggestions that she was a whore, a loose woman, upset her more than most things. "These malicious slanders and reports came strong into my mind," she wrote hotly, "and burned like fury on the one hand, and love to my friends burned strong on the other." God soothed her with an assurance that "my innocence and injured honour could be cleared by a marriage union. I thought I could freely go to the flames and die a martyr, sooner than my enemies triumph over me."

Sometimes in her mind she confused Pomeroy with her first love, thinking her bridegroom would be Noah Bishop, with the same strong, handsome body he had had as a youth. And God told her that she, Joanna, would be miraculously transformed into the lovely eighteen year old he had courted all those years ago. This cheered her up no end. Especially when God went on to say that all the mistakes she had made over the years were not her fault. It was all pre-ordained. She would have been powerless to organise her life any other way. She wouldn't have been able to marry Noah under any circumstances, because God had decided she must not.

God proceeded to explain that He ordered her to write a history of her life, so that men might realise how He had kept her in His power. "They will see from the history that thou couldst not act in a spirit of thine own. I permitted Satan to deceive thee, to see if thou wouldst be led by a wrong spirit. And I found thou wouldst not, but saw that thou was wounded and cut to the heart fearing what step to take."

A trial, she decided, was no longer necessary. She accepted that the Devil had indeed influenced her entire life, but only because God had told him to. All those times she had feared the Devil was within her, she had been right! But it was part of God's mysterious plan!

Although Joanna was not eating, she was drinking watered-down, refined wine throughout the day and, consequently, she was having strange illusions. Her excuse was that, since she wasn't eating, she needed something to give her strength. There were suggestions that she also indulged in straight rum.

On August 6, 1805, she had a curious dream - the sort one might have after a heavy bout of drinking - and considered it awesome enough to not only write it down, but to illustrate it too. "I dreamt I kicked a coal of fire. It ascended upward and I woke. Perfectly, before my eyes, there appeared a round, ball-like fire, nearly as high as the tester of my bed. It seemed to come down in streams of fire, round the ball in the manner I have drawn it. Sparked abroad as I have drawn it. Like a rocket at the bottom, as I have drawn it. Some sparks appeared at the top and it fell down upon the floor and seemed to cover a large place. It looked like a fire was exhausted at the top hole.

"This would have alarmed me if I had not known it was a vision. It was explained to me that the vision alluded to Carpenter and others. For none would the fire stream down, or love or anger, and if Elias Carpenter was not now convinced that Joseph (Pomeroy) was wrong and I was right, to have it burn in streams of love, he would burn in streams of anger, for that vision would be fulfilled one day. But now, it is said to me the time will come when the truth of the vision will appear in the hearts of friends and foes, some for me and some against me. For now the Coal of Fire is kicked that will burn like fire in man. This Vision I was ordered to draw."

Other visions had erotic overtones. She dreamt she was in a large room with ranks of men before her. The front rank was her enemies and the back rank her friends. A man at the back put his hand in his bosom and said, "I will show you what is in my heart" and he pulled out from his shirt a handful of pink coral stones. Joanna colourfully described them as like "small hearts hanging on stems, almost a teacupful".

Tactfully overlooking her odd behaviour, her friends prepared for the mysterious wedding they had been told was to take place. The wedding dress was bought and gowns for the women who were to attend her - all paid for by the wealthy Jane Townley. Joanna was consoled, pampered and worshipped as ever, as she waited hopefully for God's promise, to transform her into a lovely young thing, to come true.

But she remained old and fat and no young Noah appeared. In her confused state, she began to doubt herself, and consulted her Bible for guidance, turning to the *Book of Revelation*. For years she had suspected she was the woman in chapter twelve - the woman "clothed with the Sun" who would bring a man-child into the world. This child, the Bible said, would be "caught up by God" immediately after its birth. She had always presumed that the child was meant to be symbolic.

In March, 1814, God told her formally that she would give birth to the child prophesied. "This year, in the sixty-fifth year of thy age, thou wilt have a Son by the power of the Most High and thy public trial will not appear, for thee to be called forward in a solemn assembly to testify the truth of the Child, before thou canst go with the Child in thine arms, while milk is in thy breast, that men may know thou hast not deceived. They will know that thou art the Woman mentioned in *Revelation*, to bring the man child into the world. I had the power to take Man's nature upon Me, in the Virgin's womb, to be born as a child, for the Son of Man. I have the power in the end to create that likeness again to fulfil the Gospel."

She at last found courage - and the nerve - to tell her friends. They were prepared to believe anything from her, but this news that she was to be dramatically elevated by God to the same sacred position as the Virgin Mary, took a while to adjust to. It was difficult to accept immediately that, like the Mother of God, Joanna was to produce for the world a second Messiah, the Prince of Peace who would redeem the world and set the Jews free. However, as the message sunk in, they warmed to the idea. They very much wanted it to be true, for they all yearned for salvation and an eternity of peace in heaven. So they accepted the news as Gospel Truth, and from then on she was addressed as Mother Joanna. As an extra precaution, however, they called in doctors to confirm the pregnancy.

It was unanimously agreed that the new Prince of Peace would not be born in poverty as on the first occasion, but in comfort, showered with love and accorded every possible luxury. Joanna would be confined at 17, Weston Place, St. Pancras, London home of Jane Townley and looked after tenderly until the end of her pregnancy.

Joanna was thoroughly enjoying all the attention she was getting and congratulated herself on her brilliance. She had already worked out roughly how she would handle the situation when the child's birth became imminent, but not the finer details. She calculated that there was plenty of time and was even confident enough to issue a public statement that, if she didn't have a Holy Son within the year, then the Gospel was a lie and therefore the story of Jesus Christ and the Virgin Mary was a lie too. Thousands blissfully accepted the story, but Joanna was generally considered by the Church and others to be a blasphemous witch. Even Mary Bateman, who duped Leedsfolk with her miracle eggs, would have hesitated at such an ambitious scheme. But then, she wasn't insane - just wicked. Joanna, it appeared, was both.

It was easy for Joanna to convince others that a miracle that occurred two thousand years ago could repeat itself in modern times. After all, it was clearly promised by God in the Scriptures. And, as for her age, that was no barrier for it was recorded in the Bible that Sarah and Elizabeth both conceived in their old age. What God had done once, He could do again. And if he didn't Joanna had already made plans to ensure that it all came true. So Joanna became big news again, and her popularity as well as notoriety, soared. Newspapers took to carrying even the most trivial story about her.

What everyone wanted to know, of course, was when the immaculate conception actually took place. There were various pet theories. Some people in Devon came up with the story that she was impregnated many years ago, when she was a young girl, and had been carrying the seed within her all her life. What made this vaguely credible was a superstition in Honiton, a market town a few miles from Gittisham. The town had a borough seal on which a pregnant woman was seated under an outstretched hand, perpetuating a tradition that a night spent in St. Mary's Chapel, Honiton, would make any woman a mother, no matter what her age.

It was surmised that, in her youth, Joanna might well have spent a night there. She was so pious in those days, that she would sit for hours in church and lose track of time. She had relatives in Honiton, who she often visited, and she once worked there. An immaculate conception might just feasibly have taken place many years ago, when Joanna was too young and innocent to understand.

While a few fondly toyed with this idea, Joanna was prepared to supply much more specific details of her immaculate conception, which succeeded in making many of her woman friends blush.

Joanna's Patchwork Quilt

It took Joanna Southcott ten years to sew this magnificent 62-inch square quilt. Composed of a variety of coloured chintzes, into each patch she vented her hatred of the Royal Family, particularly George III who refused to answer her letters. She put a curse on him, embroidering the date of his downfall, **1811,** in the centre of the quilt with strands of her own hair. Now at the Royal Albert Museum, Exeter.

Chapter 15

Immaculate Conception

Up to now, in God's Name, Joanna had managed to get away with a lot - but her latest scheme was positively outrageous. Even to her *own* astonishment, people actually believed her and from there it didn't take much to convince *herself* it was true, particularly in her moments of madness. Once she even half believed, it was not difficult for her to elaborate in her own audacious manner. And she was certainly not shy about going into detail about the affair she said she was having with God. "I am going to lay before you one of the most important and delicate cases that ever a woman had to lay before Mankind," she wrote boldly to George Turner on February 25, 1814.

She went on to describe, with startling frankness, how on October 11, 1813 she experienced a "powerful visitation working upon my body" and was alarmed because she thought that the pleasant sensation was wrong and that Satan himself was making love to her. Her divine guide assured her that it couldn't possibly be Satan, for he was unable to invade the human body without causing acute physical pain and what she was feeling was acute physical pleasure. And anyway, it was candidly pointed out to her, she was no longer attractive enough to draw an evil spirit as a lover.

"Then I thought to myself that it might be an invisible spirit of a man," she continued, referring to the time Satan told her that in her youth the spirit of a man called Follard had invaded her body. But her divine guide assured her that if the spirits of men departed had the power to come again, no woman would ever be at rest "after a man that had loved was deceased."

What Joanna probably experienced was an involuntary orgasm while asleep and, being ignorant of such matters, could be forgiven for thinking either God or the Devil had visited her in bed and had his way with her. So, with the amorous incident still delightfully fresh in her mind, she told

Turner firmly: "No! My visitation *was* from the Lord, not in anger but in love to show me his power, which I had taken in question."

At Rock Cottage, Blockley, on October 14, 1813, she said she was told by her divine guide to spend the night in a room alone. First her "still, small voice" spoke soothingly to her.

"What I was told that night, I shall keep in everlasting memory and not forget the Giver of Blessings I enjoyed. Many extraordinary things were revealed to me. I sat up until about midnight, and then looked at the candle. There was something like a large bowl behind it, with a point towards the candle, which was flaming and bright. A ring as red as scarlet circled round the middle of the flame. Immediately there appeared a hand as white as snow that came between the candle and the bowl, and pointed at me.

"I trembled, but was answered - Fear not! It is I! I was then ordered to put on my glasses, and the hand appeared a second time, more brilliant than before. But the flame seemed parted in two and looked different than the first, which burned very bright. The hand was pointing towards me a second time, as white as snow and a red cuff was on the wrist." As the vision faded, Joanna said she was left "weak with joy".

She considered it so important that she immediately drew an illustration of it. Modern Southcottians still hold special services to commemorate *"The Night of the Everlasting Remembrance"*. It was the second visit she had had, with sensuous overtones, from her spiritual suitor. An outright proposal of marriage soon followed:

> "All to refuse, no man thou'lt chuse,
> I know, to wed, but me.
> So I'll appear thy husband here,
> That every soul shall see.
> As Lords have stooped so low to wed,
> I'll stoop to wed with thee."

Another visit came a few weeks later. Joanna was sharing a bed with Jane Townley, as she often did when distraught. Jane wrote an account of the first part of the visit.

"After a hard contest with the Devil, Joanna fell asleep at last and, whether awake or asleep, she does not know but she remembers she was quite awake when she felt the Hand of the Lord upon her in a heavenly and glorious manner and she felt joy unspeakable and was full of glory. She felt herself laying, as it were, in Heaven in the hands of the Lord and was afraid to move, fearing she would remove His heavenly hand, which she felt as perfect as any woman felt the hand of her husband."

Joanna continued the account: "In this happy manner, I fell asleep and in my sleep I was surprised at seeing a most beautiful and heavenly figure arise from the bed between Townley and me. He arose and turned Himself backwards towards the feet of the bed, and His head almost reached the tester of the bed. His face was turned towards me, and it appeared with beauty and majesty, but pale as death. His hair was flaxen colour and in disorder round His face, which was covered with strong perspiration and His locks were wet, like the dew of night as though they had been taken from the river.

"The collar of His shirt was unbuttoned and the skin of His bosom appeared white as the driven snow. Such was the beauty of the heavenly figure. The robe He had on was like a surplice, down to His knees. He put out one of His legs on mine, that was perfectly like mine, no larger with purple spots at the top, as mine are with beating myself, which Townley and Underwood are witnesses of. Methought, in my dream, He got Himself into that perspiration from being pressed to sleep between Townley and me.

"I asked Him if He was my dear, dying Saviour, come to destroy all the works of the Devil. He answered yes. I called Underwood and waked Townley to look at Him, which they did with wonder and amaze. I thought I would get out of my bed and fall down on my knees before Him, to return Him thus for His mercy and goodness.

"But as soon as the thought entered my head, He disappeared and a woman appeared in his stead. It gave me pain to see Him gone, but the woman told me many wonderful things that were coming into the world and what was coming to the Devil. Yet I grieved at the loss of my Dear Redeemer, for I saw no beauty in the woman and though the woman reasoned strong with me, her reasons I did not like. In this confusion, I awoke and heard the bell tolling for the dead, outside."

Passion mounted, as her spiritual lover recalled their amorous meetings:

> "The vision, see, was shown to thee,
> Wet with the dew I'll come.
> Thou knowest My hair did so appear,
> And I no coat had on.
> So every way I now do say,
> The likeness doth appear.

Thou saw'st the sweat upon My face,
With wet, disordered hair.
With tears within, thou dost begin,
My perfect love to see,
And I thy love would stronger win,
But weakness I do see.
When I impart to thee My heart,
How it in love is come.
To waken all, to hear thy call,
That unto Me will turn.
Under thy head, My hand was laid,
My left hand did appear.
My right hand see embraced thee,
When breathing strong was here."

From here, Jane Townley took up the story and said Joanna then fell asleep, with "the strong breathings that were over her head, which she found impossible to describe and which took her senses away. And whether awake or asleep, she does not know, but she remembers that she was awake when she felt the hand of the Lord upon her".

Joanna wrote to George Turner. "A further visitation came to me at Christmas, which I kept to myself and which astonished me more, by far, than the shaking of my whole frame. I was meditating on what people had said concerning the birth of Our Saviour and that it was impossible for the Virgin Mary to have a child without the knowledge of man."

Her divine spirit promised: "Thou shalt feel how it was possible for life to be created in the womb *without* a man's seed but by the power of the Lord."

"After this," wrote Joanna, "to my astonishment I not only felt a power to shake my whole body, but felt a sensation that is impossible for me to describe, upon my womb. This alarmed me greatly, yet I kept it to myself. From the answer that was given, that I should not be alarmed, and had nothing to fear for IT WAS THE POWER OF THE LORD WORKING UPON ME. That I should remember I was the spiritual bride of God as well as the temporal."

Joanna added coyly: "I thought it could never be that the Lord would condescend in such a manner, to work upon a woman's feelings. And therefore feared that it might be some spirit or other unknown to me."

But she said her divine spirit insisted it was impossible for her to know in what way the Lord could work upon the human frame and create feelings "according to his good pleasure".

"I was told that if my visitation *was* from any but the Power of the Lord, I should be so alarmed with fears, that I should be afraid to sleep in a room by myself."

Joanna was, in fact, going through a period of untroubled sleep, in a room by herself. She was no longer having nightmares, and claimed that this was an indication of how clear her conscience was.

Such erotic spiritual encounters were mere preliminaries to the actual immaculate conception which Joanna maintained took place in March 1814. A divine spirit was in bed with her, when she felt an orgasm which she described as a "quickening". Some of her friends felt her specific description was indelicate.

"All of a sudden, the Spirit entered in me with such power and fury, that my senses seemed lost. I felt as though I had the power to shake the house down and yet I felt as though I could walk on air at the time the Spirit remained in me. But I did not remember many words I said, as they were delivered with such fury as took my senses. But, as soon as the Spirit left my body, I felt weak as before."

Love affairs never had gone smoothly for Joanna and this heavenly involvement was no exception. Minor flirtations occurred. Once Joanna said she amorously embraced a handsome angel and even exchanged kisses. On another occasion she dreamt she was in bed with someone, who lay close to her and put his arms round her. She turned round slowly, to see who it was and, as she did so, a "good looking youth sprang off the bed". Her divine lover was jealous of these lovers, and referred to Noah Bishop as "my rival foe".

> "As Noah here, I'll now appear,
> And thy first love now see.
> Because thy heart he did ensnare,
> And gained the love of thee.
> But it was I, that dwelt on high,
> That kept thee from that man.
> For, in the end, 'twas my intend,
> I, in that name, should stand."

God warned her that all the doubts she had herself experienced would be bound to be felt by many "when the knowledge of My Visitation is made known, which cannot be long concealed." Anticipating that the news would incite anger as well as joy, she felt she had better prepare the general public for what was to come. In January, 1814, she cautiously hinted that something would happen of tremendous importance that year "something that was never seen in England".

It occurred to her that men might accept that she was pregnant, despite her age, but lay the blame on some seedy alliance with an earthly lover. She couldn't bear the thought of being considered a common whore. God told her he too was anxious to protect her good character. "And so now you see the justice of My threatening to the Bishops if they refuse to come forward at a time like this? For the strict examinations thou must go through I will not suffer to be done by vulgar and ignorant men. And therefore, I have fixed them that they will act with prudence. For it is through shame I shall take *your* shame away."

Anticipating the inevitable accusations that she had had sex with an earthly lover, she forbade any men to come near her, except for the Bishops, who declined to anyway, and Joseph Pomeroy. The ban on men was to be dropped once the pregnancy was confirmed. Joanna still wanted Pomeroy for a husband and for this reason included his name amongst those men allowed to visit her. If aspersions had been cast that *he* was the real father, she would have been delighted.

"I will work upon Pomeroy's heart and convince him to make him thy judge, otherwise thou couldst not go through the strict examinations that thou must go through, to explain every particular to a stranger," promised the Lord.

On February 25, 1814, a letter was sent to Pomeroy explaining the matter, but he found the contents distasteful and ignored it. A note, with a copy of the letter sent to Pomeroy, was taken by John Hows to the Archbishop of Canterbury. His Grace coldly sent word there was no answer. Similar approaches were made to the Archbishop of York and Bishop Hurd of Thomas Foley's Diocese.

Whatever the opinion of others, the story of the holy romance thrilled Joanna's women friends. Ann Underwood remarked happily: "All the friends say they never felt such joy in their hearts as they did from what was laid before them."

But Joanna bided her time before telling the world in general. If we are to believe one of her doctors, she was working very hard to make her body show all the appearances of pregnancy. One trick was to suck her own nipples so hard and vigorously, day after day, that eventually something resembling milk appeared and the breasts became swollen and the nipples red and raw. She also practised retention of urine in her bladder for long periods so that her stomach became distended. With practice, she was soon able to control her bladder to such an extent, she was able to make the contents appear to resemble the movements of an embryo in the womb.

She was gaining weight rapidly in any case, due to her eating so well and spending most of her days in bed. Occasionally she went for an airing, but in Jane Townley's carriage, so she got very little exercise.

But she was prepared to see visitors. "If any serious enquirer or warm opposer, that will bring forth arguments founded on the Scriptures to show their reason why they judge my prophecies from the Devil, they are at liberty to come and bring forth their argument and I will bring forth mine." Anyone whose arguments proved too clever and convincing, she dealt with smartly by condemning them as liars and proclaiming indignantly that "a liar shall not tarry in my sight, if I know it".

Some "ladies and gentlemen" she said offered her money to tell their fortunes. "To such I answer - they and their money shall perish together. My soul shall never come into their secrets. Their gold and principles I abhor and despise."

She found no difficulty, however, in abandoning these principles when money and gifts were offered to her by admirers. An "elegant suit of clothes" was sent to her "from one who professed it was done in love to the Lord, to strengthen my hand to carry on this work". She accepted the suit, but said she returned it, after having worn it several times, when the giver lost faith.

She convinced herself that the imagined pregnancy could become a reality, if not by a miracle at least by fraud. So she considered what name to give the child. In *Genesis, Ch. 49, verse x*, she read Jacob's statement that "the sceptre shall not depart from Judah, nor a lawgiver from between his feet, until Shiloh come; and unto him shall the gathering of the people be". She had never come across anyone called Shiloh, ancient or modern, and the name "Shiloh" lingered tantalising in her mind. It had, she thought, a prophetic ring about it. So she announced that God had ordered her to call her child Shiloh. Unfortunately, Joanna in her ignorance misinterpreted the Scripture, for Shiloh is not the name of a person, but in fact a place.

Having found a name, she began to think of him as, not a fantasy, but a real person. She was showing convincing signs of apparent pregnancy, lying in bed all day lethargically dictating to her attendants her *Third Book of Wonders*, in which she officially announced the imminent birth of the Prince of Peace and glorious Redeemer, Shiloh.

"When the fullness of time was come, God sent his son, made of woman, made under the law. A mystery no man can explain. If it began with a woman first, it must end with her at last and now I am ordered to put in print, the woman in *Revelation* xii is myself. Therefore, it was written by Isaiah - **REJOICE, THOU BARREN, THAT DOES NOT BEAR**. Christ is compared to a second Adam. Therefore must come a second Eve to bring the Godhead to Manhood, to perfect likeness. For his Bone was taken from Man and made Woman in Man's likeness. Then Christ is the second Adam and must have a Bone taken from Him also, to fulfil the law of God and the Gospel of Truth."

Engraved on her personal seal, the one she found in Mrs. Taylor's shop in Exeter and kept, were two stars. She decided that these were symbolic of the Morning Star (Christ) and the Evening Star (Joanna), and clearly proved she was the equal of Jesus.

"They'll find the Spirit and the Bride are come.
They'll find the Root of David too.
And then the Morning Star you made so clear,
Is when the Evening Star arose to shine."

She said God told her: "I must come in the body as a perfect man first and in the spirit of My Second Coming I must come made of woman, made under the law, to redeem those that were under the law." The awful doggerel gushed out:

"Then tell Me whence the Heir did come?
Is it from Woman or from Man?
And now like Man I do appear,
To prove that Woman brings the Heirs
That must possess My every crown."

Everyone was now calling her Mother Joanna and she liked it. The Holy Ghost also seemed to think it appropriate, and well suited to her elevated status.

"So you may call her what you will,
A prophet, Mother - but stand still.
I said a woman did appear,
That I bring in my every Heir.
And by her name you all shall see

That Mother doth with her agree.
But now, again, the second time,
I happen to appear.
And blessed is the Barren Womb,
That never yet can suck.
Because the time is happening on,
They will find her with milk.
For milk will be, they all shall see,
Although the breast seem dry,
For as I made the water wine,
I will bring it so this way."

This was the way Joanna chose to announce to the world the coming of the Second Messiah. It lacked the simple beauty of the announcement in the New Testament of the coming of the First Messiah. Some people were unkind enough to suggest it was confused nonsense and, if God *had* felt inclined to convey such an important message to the world He would have done so less crudely. Undeterred, Joanna went on to boast that God had promised that her child would be treated like a prince and not a lowly beggar, as Jesus had been.

"No more you see the despised Galilean
But in His father, King, His son.
No more the infant will be had in scorn,
But joyfully received where He is born.
No more in swaddling doth the Infant lie,
But now He come in glory and bright array."

Joanna's ruthless stimulation of her own breasts produced results. Her women friends were delighted to find what appeared to be genuine milk, which came out in yellow spurts when they squeezed her nipples. Her stomach had grown large and hard, as in pregnancy. Ann Underwood wrote to George Turner in Leeds to say that she and the other women were all "well satisfied that we can feel the Child as strong to move as we have ever felt one of our own outwardly".

George Turner took time off from his business to come to London to see for himself whether the astonishing report he had received was true. He wrote back to Yorkshire: "I can only say she increases much in size and I think will be a beautiful sight by the time she is eight months."

She still needed a professional diagnosis from a reliable source, so she called in Dr. Mathias, who had once accused her of "downy indolence". If he, one of her worst critics, could be persuaded to confirm her pregnancy then she really would be able to congratulate herself.

Before showing him up to Joanna's room, Jane Townley tried to prompt him by asking: "Would you believe that Joanna could have a child by a divine agency, if you saw a child at her breast?"

Dr. Mathias merely replied that "seeing is believing". After giving Joanna a rudimentary examination, his verdict was forthright, scornful and contemptuous. No! She was definitely not pregnant! At which point, Joanna abruptly dispensed with his services.

Her women friends told her that he didn't know what he was talking about. Mrs. Lock, a respected midwife, and Mrs. Foster, a doctor's wife, gave her intimate examinations themselves - much more extensive than she would allow any male doctor to give - and they coyly confirmed she was "in the family way". As the ladies sat chatting together by the fire, Joanna said she could feel "the life working inside me". Mrs. Foster confirmed she could see the baby moving in Joanna's stomach, from where she sat, and excitedly put her hand over the spot, saying she felt the life of the baby as strong as she had ever felt any of her own.

Heartened by this, Joanna called in two other doctors and both cautiously agreed, at her instigation, that "if such symptoms occurred in a young woman, she would be pregnant". This gave her confidence to write to the Prince Regent, two Archbishops, and the Dukes of Gloucester and Kent, enclosing copies of her *First Book of Wonders* and engraved portraits of herself. She invited them to send their own physicians to "pass judgement whether they think it likely for such an event to take place".

When these distinguished people ignored her invitation, she called for more doctors. Among them was Dr. Richard Reece, M.D., M.R.C.S., of Bolton Row, Piccadilly, whom she had known for some years. He was one of London's leading surgeons whose highly regarded Medical Guide had reached a seventeenth edition and become standard work. He was a professor of chemistry and had a "magnificent shop" at Bullock's Museum. Joanna coveted his good opinion, for his reputation was second to none. If his examination proved positive, then surely none would dare doubt her.

On August 7, Dr. Reece was invited to Weston Place for the first time in connection with her pregnancy. He said the house was full of busy people. "In the front apartment, several of her proselytes were engaged in folding up her pamphlets." He exchanged polite words with Jane Townley before being shown into a small front room. Joanna rose demurely from her seat and "politely received me with an air of unaffected simplicity". He said he was impressed by her at this first interview and, although outwardly sceptical, was determined to remain open-minded.

Joanna told him what her symptoms were and added that she had not had her "regular monthly appearance" for at least 15 years. When he asked to examine her, she modestly declined and instead asked the same question Jane Townley had put to Dr. Mathias - if she had been a woman of 25 with such symptoms, would he consider her pregnant? Recognising this was a trap to make him appear to confirm her pregnancy, he agreed that if there was milk in her breast it was a sure sign, but he was not prepared to commit himself without an examination.

Frustrated, at this point Joanna lost her temper. "That will not satisfy the public," she screamed at him. Convinced she had taken leave of her senses, he hurriedly left the house.

Dr. John Sims was the next to visit her. She allowed him to examine her a little bit more closely than the others, explaining that her child would be born "before the harvest was over". She showed him her bare breasts and told him that until a few months ago they had been flabby and shrivelled with the nipples inverted. He reported: "They are now plump, the veins large and visible, the nipples red and protruded. They do not, however, have the elasticity natural to the breast of a pregnant woman and the areola is pale, part covered with a little whitish scurf. It put me in mind of the breasts of an old woman grown corpulent."

He was allowed to feel her stomach, but from outside her clothes. She did let him insert his hand under the night-gown and place one finger on her bare navel. He said it was sunken in, not protruded as it would have been had she really been pregnant. He said he couldn't feel any movement, although she insisted there was a strong kicking. She told him about the nausea, violent stomach pains and an extraordinary craving for asparagus in spite of a loss of appetite generally.

But she was unable to sway him. His verdict was firm: "I did not hesitate to declare that Joanna Southcott was *not* pregnant."

She complained petulantly that he was the first medical man that had seen her, who had said she wasn't. Patiently, he went on to explain he believed her uterine organs were diseased and that the breasts, sympathising with those parts, had been stimulated by an increased quantity of blood.

She must have charmed him somewhat, for he added generously: "I am convinced this poor woman is no impostor, but labours under a strong, mental delusion." He conceded that if by some remote chance he was wrong "such an event would not be hid in a corner".

Dr. Reece was called back on August 18, 1814. Joanna wanted him to eat his words. He was such an established figure that she badly needed his confirmation of her pregnancy. Out of curiosity he came back, and again told her that if he was to satisfy himself that there was a child, he had to examine her internally. This was unthinkable, she told him. However, she finally let him examine her through her thick, flannelette nightie. He insisted she exposed herself even more and Ann Underwood helped her uncover her breasts.

Dr. Reece said he was astonished by their appearance. "They exhibited the picture of a woman in the seventh month of pregnancy, being equally full and plump and expanded. This fullness, on closer examination, consisted of a real enlargement of the mammary glands, that part peculiarly destined for the secretion of milk. There was no appearance of disease or tendency to irregular enlargement, morbid hardness or scirrhosity. The nipples also were elongated but with the scaly surface which is apt to cover it at an advanced period of life."

He examined her stomach and said its expansion equalled that which normally takes place in the seventh month of pregnancy. "I felt a hard tumour not less than the size of a man's head and bearing the shape of the womb. It was peculiarly hard to the feel and, she complained, acutely painful to the slightest pressure." She allowed him to keep his right hand over her stomach for ten minutes in order to feel the child moving, but there was no movement.

She then said Shiloh was always quiet in the presence of a stranger, but particularly troublesome when she ate. Ann Underwood obligingly placed a piece of peach into her mouth, which Joanna chewed. Dr. Reece felt something move under his hand in an undulating motion, appearing and disappearing in the same manner as a foetus.

On this evidence, Dr. Reece said he was prepared to agree she was pregnant though "it would have been more satisfactory for me to have formed my opinion from an internal examination".

Later he confirmed that "there is no doubt she is with child" and even wrote to the *Sunday Monitor*. "The appearance of her mammary glands I considered to be a leading point in her favour. I saw no reason for supposing the smallest deception."

Unlike Dr. Mathias, he was impressed by Joanna and said he found her to be a woman of mild temperament and simplicity of manners, with a "motherly kindness that distinguished her behaviour". He said her living quarters were "paltry and mean" and added that she did not appear to be loaded with the delicacies of life.

He called in nine medical practitioners to back up his verdict. Six of them pronounced without hesitation that she was definitely pregnant. The other three declined to give an opinion on account of her age. After his examination of her, Dr. Joseph Adams, of Hatton Gardens and editor of the *Medical Journal*, signed a certificate saying positively: "I am decidedly of the opinion that she is pregnant." News of the examinations got around and aroused tremendous curiosity in medical circles. Doctors queued up for the privilege of examining her. Altogether, twenty-five doctors agreed she was pregnant.

Thomas Foley, who had lurking apprehensions, decided to come to London to see the evidence for himself. On arrival, he went to see Joanna at once and said all doubt vanished when he set eyes on her. He and his wife, Elizabeth, had children of their own. He knew what a pregnant woman should look like, with or without clothes. He noted: "Joanna, thank God, was large and far gone in pregnancy."

He sought the opinion of others and recorded in his diary, on Friday, August 18, 1814: "Had an interview with Dr. Adams. He said he would not hesitate in pronouncing her pregnant, were she a woman of twenty-five. But, at the same time, he had seen many cases where strong appearances of pregnancy in women showed themselves and suddenly disappeared. On Saturday, Col. Harwood and myself waited on Mr. Foster (a surgeon of 24 Mount Street, Lambeth and a close friend of Joanna's). He said, from his personal examination, he had no doubt she was pregnant. We then went to Dr. Reece who had no hesitation in saying she was with child. He at once gave his reasons - the state of her breasts, the enlargement of her womb and the fact that he distinctly felt a living child in her."

Mr. Mealin, a surgeon of 2 Devonshire Street, Portland Square, said he believed she *was* with child but, as to the miracle, he knew nothing about that but this he *was* sure of - that the united efforts of all the men in London could not have gotten her with child. Described by Foley as an infidel, he added that if she *did* have a child at the age of 65 "then I must believe in a divine power". Foley added in his diary: "Met Mr. Wetherall, the surgeon. He gave his firm opinion she was with child. Mr. Phillips, the surgeon, confirmed this."

Dr. Wetherall, who lived in Highgate, was a disciple of Richard Brothers as well as Joanna. He had once said, of the faithful: "They will reign with Christ in his earthly Kingdom during the *Millennium* and have a sure passport to Heaven". It is probably this comment that gave rise to the idea that Joanna's seals were "Certificates for the *Millennium* and Passports to Heaven". After examining Joanna, he confirmed her pregnancy and said he based his diagnosis on the fact that her breasts and nipples were like a young woman's, that her womb was much enlarged and rose two inches and, most conclusively, he had distinctly felt a living child.

Particularly sceptical was Dr. John Hopgay, of 130 Ratcliffe Highway. Foley first met him at Weston Place and was unnerved when the doctor "fixed his eyes very strong on me for several minutes". After examining Joanna he said emphatically that she was certainly not pregnant but, recognising that Joanna, Foley and all her believers were determined that she should be, wryly acknowledged that his opinion was "not worth tuppence".

At the final count, over thirty doctors confirmed she was pregnant. Such positive confirmation from so many eminent men, removed lingering doubts from the minds of cynics. Joanna relaxed. With support from those who were not even part of her Mission, she felt more secure. Towards the end of August she tempted providence by calling in the doubting Dr. Mathias again, to see if she could get him to change his mind.

After examining her, he told her curtly she was suffering from "biliary obstructions" and that her excess weight was due to lack of simple exercise. He was so firm in his opinion, that she came near to tears. "If I am not pregnant, then could something be wrong that might kill me?" she asked with sudden fear. Dr. Mathias agreed that this was possible, and gave her some medicine for the biliousness - a strong preparation of mercury and bitters. Afterwards Joanna remarked wryly that if she took it "it would be bound to bring on mischief".

Dr. John Hopgay, the surgeon who had given Foley a "strong, penetrating stare" perhaps in the hope he would bring him to his senses, wrote to the *Times* saying he had examined Joanna and she "most decidedly was not in the situation she wished to impress upon the minds of those who follow her".

On August 30, a letter from J.W. of St. Pancras, was published in the *Times*, pointing out that the newspaper was wrong to give Joanna so much publicity. "The more this imposture is brought forward, particularly in respectable newspapers like yours, the greater attention does it excite till at length many weak persons whose hearts are better than their understanding, begin to wonder and become credulous.

"I wish the parish officers or the magistrates would put a stop to the mischief at once, by taking this deceiver as a common cheat and placing her in a situation where all the silly fools who now come from all parts of the Kingdom to pay her homage, may be prevented from having any access to her without authority. For it is a fact that, in consequence of what the newspapers have for some time been relating about this woman, shoals of enthusiasts with more money in their pockets than brains in their skulls, are now pouring into London and its vicinity to behold this chosen vessel."

Despite unabashed sensationalising by the press, the medical profession was not unduly influenced. To most doctors, the miracle was that a woman of her age could become a mother at all, they were not the least bit interested in whether Joanna was a virgin or not, or who the father of the supposed child was. On the other hand, it was essential to Joanna and her followers that her purity was undisputed in order for the immaculate conception to ring true. So she let it be known that she had not been in the presence of any man for twelve months, until the time she was visited professionally by her doctors. Therefore, she maintained, her conception could only have been from the Holy Ghost.

"I can take my solemn oath that I never had any knowledge of man in my life, so that if the words of the Spirit are fulfilled in me this year to have a son, it is by the power of the Lord and not of man. And this sign is said to have proved the truth of the Gospel, or the Gospel is not true. For this I am answered. If the Visitation of the Lord to me does not produce a son this year, then Jesus Christ is not the son of God, born in the manner spoken of by the Virgin Mary. But if I have a son this year, then in like manner our Saviour was born." In other words, if she was a liar, then so was Mary and Christ.

God told her: "Let them look on thy age and the manner I have confined thee from any man coming in thy presence and to prevent many saying that a man came in women's clothing, I have forbidden all thy female friends to come into thy presence likewise."

There were attacks from all quarters. Coloured prints, ridiculing Joanna as the pregnant prophetess, were printed and circulated. At Horbury, near Wakefield, Yorkshire, an effigy of her was carried through the village, shot at and burnt, head downwards, signifying she was on her way to hell.

Meanwhile Joanna, confined to bed at Weston Place, was often in great pain. Whatever she was doing to herself to invoke symptoms of pregnancy, was not good for her. To make things worse, she was having disquieting dreams.

On May 10 she dreamt again of Joseph Pomeroy. "I was going to some place to be examined and thought Mr. Pomeroy must be there. Mrs. Pomeroy came to me and said, we will go together, and she put her arm around my neck. Mr. Pomeroy looked at us but did not speak. There were a vast number of men standing, with Mr. Pomeroy in the middle. One man looked very steadfastly at me and asked how many Gods there were. I replied only one, the creator of the Universe. He answered that he had contrived to rock the Cradle. I thought to myself, doth he mean this in mockery? Everyone was silent and did not speak a word afterwards. This dream I thought so simple, that when I told Underwood of it, she laughed, but in the morning I was ordered to have it penned."

God explained that the dead Mrs. Pomeroy appeared in her dream in such a friendly manner because "the dead know all". And, being dead, she would naturally appreciate that it was necessary for Pomeroy to marry Joanna in order to fulfil God's wishes. Therefore she would have shown no jealousy, only approval and understanding.

> "In this creation, now see clear,
> The way that he contrived the whole.
> To bring the Cradle now to all,
> That soon shall rock the hearts of men,
> When once the child therein is seen.
> Then all these jestings will be o'er,
> And my creation must appear.
> To see how I've contrived the whole,
> To shake the hardened, stubborn soul.
> To shake my foes that now do mock,
> Because at first I've rocked thee,
> Which from thy youth they all may see,
> How I have rocked thee to sleep,
> And all thy lovers I made weep.
> Because I drew thee from mankind,
>
> Thus from the cradle all shall find,
> How from thy youth I drew thee on,
> Till to old age thou art come,
> And so I've rocked thee at the last.
> In me put thy every trust.
> But now, I'll tell thee of his wife,
> Whose arms around thy neck was placed.

Thou knowest thou didst not her resist,
But kindly did together go,
I'll tell thee why thou dreamt it so,

Because the dead who know the whole,
Would now rejoice to see
If he received his every call.
I have contrived to bring a life,
When I prove every call,
How it is done by my own hand,
My outstretched arm appear,
To prove the cradle now shall stand,
When my FIRST BORN is here.
But yet thy pains they must remain,
Before the end is come.
For if awhile I stop them here,
They will turn back again,
So, simple as thy dream appears,
I tell thee it was deep."

Ann Underwood confirmed that this communication came at about eight o'clock in the evening, while Joanna was in agonising pain. Then, for the next two days, she felt much better but, as warned by God, the pains returned with a vengeance.

She wrote reflectively, in her *Fifth Book of Wonders*: "I have felt life increasing more and more from the 16th of May to this day. But never having had a child in my life, I leave it to the judgement of mothers of children, who attend me, who give their decided opinion that this is perfectly like a woman that is pregnant. Then now, I say, it remains to be proved whether my feelings and the judges be right or wrong, whether there is a child or not. Which a few months must decide, or the grave must decide for me. For I could not live to the end of the year, with the increasing growth I have felt within so short a space, without deliverance."

Newspapers reported that, when the end of her term of pregnancy arrived, she had arranged for a new born child to be smuggled into the house, which Joanna would say had been delivered from her own womb.

Other reports stated that there were several pregnant young women hidden in the house and, whichever had a boy child first would hand it over to be passed as Joanna's. The workhouse was another place where a new born child could easily be procured and it was said that Townley and

Underwood had already made arrangements to pay the first woman to produce a male child at the right time. "People invent such lies," protested Joanna, worried that these rumours were too near the truth for comfort.

Nevertheless, as the time drew near, an electric excitement took over London. Thousands, hearing about the Immaculate Conception, clamoured to become one of Joanna's Sealed before the holy baby arrived. New followers flocked to the city to witness the big event. Samuel Jowett colourfully recalled the euphoria of those months:

"Our eyes were so dazzled with the glorious prospect set before us, of those things taking place immediately, we became like the man taken out of a dark room and placed in the radiant beams of the sparkling sun, the light so overpowering him that he could not see.

"So it was with us! The idea of having one of the Godhead reign over us was overwhelming after being so long tyrannised by man, under evil influence, that we could not calmly and deliberately consider what was delivered unto us, because of the bright shining picture of the illustrious era which was present to our view."

Impostors also flocked to London to cash in on the event. Some claimed to be the prophetess herself and extorted money from the gullible, so Joanna ordered that her portrait, copper-etched by William Sharp, should be distributed throughout London, so that people would know exactly what she looked like. "There are women of bad character going about London calling themselves Joanna Southcott, by which means I have been represented as a strange looking woman."

There was another urgent and very practical problem to overcome. Joanna was supposed to be pregnant, but was unmarried. No handsome Noah had appeared, as God had promised, and Pomeroy still adamantly refused to marry her. Joanna didn't want to appear to have given birth to a bastard, out of wedlock. Illegitimate children were still described on baptismal registers as "base born" and their mothers labelled whores. If God or providence didn't sent her a husband soon, then she would have to tackle the situation herself. She needed a flesh and blood man to marry her and give her respectability. It wouldn't do for a child she claimed her own, to have only a heavenly father to refer to for a name and protection.

Chapter 16

Health Deteriorates

The *Sunday Monitor* was quick to realise Joanna was big news. Consequently, readership figures boomed as they proceeded to publish the slightest newsworthy titbit about her. *The Times* pompously accused them of dishonourable conduct, but the *Monitor* congratulated itself on its tolerance and said it was sour grapes because they had not cashed in on the story earlier.

"The mood of public applause and the unparalleled increase of circulation which has attended our impartiality, are the most encouraging tributes which can be paid to our rectitude and independence," stated an editorial in the paper.   It pointed out that Joanna Southcott was hot news and the sole interest in the minds of many throughout the country, even with the American war being waged and the fate of Europe undecided.

"If the dome of St. Paul's had collapsed or a fourth of the city been destroyed by an earthquake, the excitement could not have been more intense," continued the editorial. The editor invited readers to submit their views and letters poured into the newspaper's offices. The paper became the one everyone read to obtain up to the minute information about Joanna.

Her pamphlets were selling like hotcakes and shops were stocked with cheap souvenirs, such as "Joanna Southcott cradles" draped in pink calico with a trim of silver lace and a tiny doll inside to represent Shiloh. Street entertainers sang ballads, some laudatory but most rude and mocking, about Joanna and Shiloh. Many were angry at Joanna's blasphemous claims. On August 22 a mob arrived outside Weston Place, where Joanna was living, and tried to break down the door. Others were attracted to the scene as a result and for the rest of the day dozens came to stand outside in the street, staring at the windows hoping for a glimpse of the miracle woman.

From then on it became a daily event and anyone entering or leaving the house was mobbed. Ann Underwood wrote that: "We are beset with men, women and children and everyone looking up at the house calling out for Joanna, and abusing her with shocking expressions."

Foley recorded in his diary: "There was a great riot and they threw violently many stones and brickbats against the house and doors and those within were much alarmed. Joanna was told by the Spirit that it was not safe for her to continue there, as her life was in danger."

Hecklers continued to shout abuse and throw stones and suggestions were made that one of her male disciples was the father of her child. Joanna and her two companions were terrified and stayed up all night, fearing they might be murdered in their beds. Next day they slipped out by the back door and took refuge in a house in Leicester Square, but the secret leaked out and the mob came and hurled more bricks.

George Turner said: "Now let the mockers be silent for, if she is a deceiver herself or is deceived, she has now completely committed herself. Let them wait the issue of the event!"

To quell the mass anger a low profile was sought. All Southcottian chapels were closed and notices pinned up outside with the message: "No more meetings until after the birth of Shiloh." At the final service, at the end of August, a huge crowd gathered outside the chapel in Duke Street to hear William Tozer speak. Those that couldn't get in waited outside. Dr. Richard Reece said Tozer was: "good looking, rather tall and lusty, little cultivated but possessing good natural abilities and, on the subject of Joanna, his conversation bordered on insanity."

Told that the crowds were getting restless, Tozer spoke from one of the chapel windows, where he could be seen by everyone. His style was fiery and intense. In his thunderous voice with a heavy Devonshire accent, he told how great events were to take place and that someone was coming who would prepare the way for the *Final Millennium*, when all mankind would live in unity.

But the crowd wasn't there to hear a sermon. What they wanted was news of Joanna. Tozer obliged by saying he understood the child would be delivered in the middle of October and was rewarded with an appreciative round of applause, which he loved. He bowed continuously to the crowd, giving them his thanks and calling down God's blessing on them all.

Followers were advised to "wear nothing by which they could be distinguished". The sealing of the faithful was halted and Joanna's influential friends were asked to be more cautious about what they printed, to avoid controversy. Few people doubted she was pregnant, but there was general alarm that she was claiming that God was the father. An exchange of letters between doctors was published in the *Morning Advertiser* and other London newspapers, debating the subject at length, which fostered even more interest.

Meanwhile, unperturbed by the medical arguments, Joanna's thousands of followers prepared for the Birth. Women knitted caps, shawls and bootees. Collections were made to buy presents. There was a magnificent Bible in red Moroccan leather - "the most beautiful bound book ever produced". A Birmingham engraver sent a tray, inscribed "Hail, Messiah, Prince of Salem". Souvenir christening mugs were manufactured.

One newspaper reported: "Joanna Southcott has literally been overwhelmed with presents. Lace caps, embroidered bibs, worked robes, a mohair mantle which cost £150, a splendid silver pap spoon and candle cups (one shaped like a dove) have been pressed on her." Readers were told that a lady of rank was said to have given Joanna a solid gold font along with other objects of similar costliness. Those who could ill afford it made sacrifices. A poor tradesman was reported to have bankrupted himself by sending £20. A blind woman gave sixpence and a little girl two roses. Other gifts included a comb, a piece of flannel, a night cap, a pair of socks, a dozen napkins, a pin cushion, a shilling, a robe, a shirt, a pair of shoes and a small foreign coin.

Cradles and cribs were made for the holy infant but the most splendid of all was the one from Mr. Seddon, a carpenter of Aldersgate Street, London. A journalist described it in detail. The pillars on each of its sides were tapered with ribbons of gold entwining them. The head cloth was of blue satin with a celestial crown of gold embroidered upon it, underneath which appeared in gold the word Shiloh in Hebrew.

And this was only the manger! The actual crib hung on a swivel. It was made of satinwood fitted with cane work, through which passed a cord of gold to a pedal, so that the cradle could be rocked from a distance, thus avoiding the necessity of anyone leaning over the manger - which might not be properly respectful for a holy child. The crib and the manger cost upwards of £200. Today it is looked after by the *Panacea Society* in Bedford, although they don't actually own it. It belongs to the Salford Museum, donated in 1860 by John Hows. In 1924 the *Panacea Society* "borrowed" the crib on a semi-permanent loan and have never returned it.

That the child might have to perform natural functions and risk making a mess of all this finery had been overlooked. It certainly made a sharp contrast to the humble crib, lined with straw, hastily constructed for the Baby Jesus in a stable eighteen hundred years previously.

Three pregnant, destitute women were allegedly kept hidden in Mrs. Townley's cellar and the plan was that the first male baby to be born in good health was to be sneaked upstairs to Joanna's room. One newspaper claimed to have a confession from Ann Underwood, explaining how a baby would be smuggled into Joanna's bedroom hidden in a warming pan.

The *Morning Chronicle*, on December 6, 1814, reported: "Last week two of the followers of this antiquated virgin were discovered to have been negotiating with a poor woman for one of her twin children, which they intended would be passed off as the true offspring of the prophetess. The fraud being prevented by the discovery, the negotiators and the prophetess were paraded about in effigy through the streets."

Despite these criticisms, Joanna was feeling secure and satisfied. Her plan, if it was a plan, was working admirably. Her popularity had soared and her books were selling better than they ever had. "I acknowledge," she wrote, "that I am very comfortably situated and I have a number of respectable and worthy friends."

But to have a child and not be married was a shameful thing. Even her divine spirit thought so. "The union must have a reputed father, to adopt him as a son when he is born. A base-born child is a reproach to a woman. They would say that thou had a base born child in thine old age and therefore thou must have a husband to do away with this reproach. For without marriage taking place before the child is born thou wouldst be looked upon as an adulteress."

But there were more practical reasons that her child should have an earthly father, which Nathaniel Halhed and William Sharp recognised. The Law did not give bastard children any entitlement and therefore it was essential the child's birth should be legal so that he could inherit all that was due to him.

She claimed her immaculate conception had taken place at the beginning of the year. By the end of August she was still unwed. Joanna, now huge and not well, became fretful. She still wanted Joseph Pomeroy. He had, after all, the same name as the first Messiah's earthly father. So, swallowing pride, she sent John Hows to Bodmin to propose to Joseph Pomeroy on her behalf. She convinced herself that, with the Lord's help, he would recognise what a privilege it was to be asked. But Pomeroy, disgusted at the very thought, stiffly declined.

On September 15, 1814 Joanna was "seized with a violent sickness, so that I was obliged to go to bed and spent a very restless night". On the Friday morning, when she felt she could bear it no longer, her divine spirit apparently told her: "Thy deliverance will take place before the end of September." But this turned out to be a vain promise.

Joanna fondly envisaged the high respect she would receive once the baby was born. "Many respectable gentlemen and ladies will be truly convinced by the birth and will become faithful friends and true believers, and you will have nothing to fear of being established in a comfortable situation," she was told by her divine spirit. This reassured her, for she had a deep fear of poverty and was still haunted by the dismal circumstances of her own father's death.

"You must let them know from your feelings that Death or Life must end the Strife and that thou canst not live a long time in the situation thou art in without a deliverance. So if thou art deceived they will find out thy deception in death."

Journalists, as irrepressible then as they are today, soon discovered her whereabouts. They gathered in the street and waylaid visitors for information about the Shiloh. So Joanna was smuggled out and taken to another secret address, 38 Manchester Street, Marylebone. Jane Townley wrote on October 13: "Mrs. Southcott removed to the house that was taken last Saturday and bore her journey very well and is as well as we can expect considering the time draws near. But we hope soon the birth will take place. A marriage has not yet taken place. All we know is that it will take place before the birth and all things will suddenly come on, but this is the hour of silence and we must wait patiently. We know the Lord will fulfil all things in his appointed time."

The lack of a husband still irked her. She was now past yearning for Noah Bishop or Pomeroy. What she wanted was good old-fashioned respectability. To find her a husband was now a priority. Possible candidates were interviewed, eager to fill the exalted position.

Turner came rushing up from Leeds, saying excitedly that he had been told by a "voice" that "thou art the man". Joanna didn't like Turner. He was a rough-voiced Yorkshireman with fiery eyes, so she icily told him that his information was from the Devil. She turned down all the other offers. The worry made her ill and on November 14 Ann Underwood wrote to Thomas Foley to tell him that Joanna was "confined to bed and cannot take any food and constant sickness and pain - neither medicine or anything else kept within her stomach but a little Malmsey Madeira and water is, and has been, her chief support."

By the beginning of November, a husband had still not been chosen. Then Ann Underwood noted that a "worthy and humble-minded man, a respectable friend of ours about her own age, an independent man" came to her and said he had been thinking about Joanna's situation and he was willing to be the adopted father of the holy child.

This "respectable man" was none other than the same John Smith, ten years Joanna's junior, who had been living with her, on and off, since 1804 at his cottage in Blockley. Joanna said her Spirit told her not to refuse him. The next day, Saturday morning, he came to discuss it.

"He was eager to have it all settled immediately," wrote Ann Underwood. "He wished everything to be done that day that could be done. A paper was drawn up of a contract of marriage. And he read the service over himself and she repeated her part of the ceremony in presence of me and others."

By now she was very weak. Fearing that it they waited any longer she might be too ill to participate, the ceremony took place in her bedroom before hurriedly assembled witnesses and was described by Ann Underwood as a "private marriage". No Registrar was present and no official documents signed. It was hastily organised by Member of Parliament, Nathaniel Halhed, who believed it necessary to legitimatise the Holy Child for practical reasons. Approval of the Bishops was sought, to no avail. They had no wish to be involved.

Joanna's pains got worse and there were hopes that labour had commenced. Ann Underwood, in her letter to Foley telling him about the marriage, ended: "I have given you as much as I can in this letter, though in a blundering manner as our Dear Friend is in great pain again and I am up every five minutes. I pray to God you may hear of her safe delivery before the week is out."

It was decided to keep the marriage secret until after the birth. John Smith was kept out of the way. An impression was deliberately created that John Smith and Joanna only knew each other slightly. Joanna could not risk harming her reputation at this crucial point of her career. She didn't want the truth of her intimate relationship with him over the years to leak out.

She felt driven to defend herself and earlier, from her hiding place, had written bitterly: "I am compelled to flee not only from my enemies, but from my friends likewise, to conceal myself in a place of safety where I am not known in person and my name I am obliged to conceal to protect myself from the malicious and inveterate enemies who threaten to set the house on fire where I live, and to take my life if they get any means in their power.

"The public newspapers have been for some time past filled with the most vindictive abuse and invented lies of various kinds, which none but the Devil himself can put into the heads or hearts of man. The wrath of men is against me, calling me a mercenary impostor, that I sold seals for a guinea and 12 shillings each. But I never received anything for a seal in my life. Likewise, that I announced that a miracle was to be performed, by raising a corpse to life. This, with my ascension to heaven, was to take place in Bath, are their own inventions. I have never stayed in Bath! The workings of these miracles I have never pretended to.

"Another report says I have had presents to the amount of £30,000 for the Child that is to be born to establish the Jews in their land. And that I was going to leave the country taking these presents with me to France. But I have ordered that if there was a possibility of me being deceived all should have their presents returned to them."

Joanna said people would recognise she was the woman mentioned in *Revelation, chapter 12*:

"And there appeared a great wonder in Heaven; a woman clothed with the sun and the moon under her feet, and upon her head a crown of twelve stars. And she, being with child, cried travailing in birth and pained to be delivered. And there appeared another wonder in heaven; and behold, a great red dragon having seven heads and ten horns and seven crowns upon his heads.

"And his tail drew the third part of the stars of heaven and did cast them to the earth; and the dragon stood before the woman which was ready to be delivered, for to devour her child as soon as it was born. And she brought forth a man child who was to rule all nations with a rod of iron; and her child was caught up unto God and to His throne."

Joanna read these words over and over. The bit that terrified her was about the Devil devouring her child as soon as it was born. But God assured her He would protect it by catching it up to heaven, as it said in the Bible. Nonetheless the agonising death of Jesus Christ haunted her. She dreamt she saw Him nailed to the cross, His face wracked with pain. She didn't want to endure such pain.

Her divine spirit assured her: "Thou wilt *never* be put to death as I was, neither will thy believers be put to death, as *MY* disciples were."

In her crazed moments she believed wholeheartedly in her own divinity. It was only when her mind cleared and she became rational did she face the truth - that she had irrevocably become entangled in a web of lies. Eating little and sipping wine continuously, her mind was rarely clear and consequently she became more and more confused, finding it difficult to differentiate between fact and fiction. Weird visions plagued her and her friends were alarmed as her health took a turn for the worse.

Meanwhile, her disciples were looking for a suitably luxurious place for the delivery of Shiloh. Joanna's divine spirit ordered that an advertisement should be placed in the *Morning Chronicle* for a "large, furnished house" where Shiloh could be born in a princely manner. The paper announced next day that a "great personage" had offered the "Temple of Peace in the Green Park". *The Bristol Mirror* reported that believers had purchased land near Regents Park in order to erect a palace for King Shiloh.

Ann Underwood said two illustrious visitors arrived unexpectedly. One was Count Lieven, who she said was the Russian ambassador to London, and the other was Count Orloff, who she said was an aide-de-camp to the Emperor Alexander. "They behaved in the most feeling and polite manner, bowing to her," she wrote. "There was something of the appearance of serious awe as they went up to the bed. The ambassador, when he took his leave, stood at the foot of the bed and wished her a happy deliverance."

One journalist who said he interviewed her, described her as "portly but not uncomely". "Joanna's cause has been, in London, for some time in a flourishing state. She has a chapel, in Duke Street, St. George's-in-the-fields, where they have been preaching every Sunday. They administer in their chapel the Sacrament of the Lord's Supper, the first Sunday in every month, and profess themselves to be members of the Church of England."

She was asked to explain to the journalist how her divine spirit spoke to her. At first she said it was as man speaks to man, then said that when the spirit was about to impart a command she felt an agitation within.

"Then the prophetess, the secretary and the witness range themselves in one group," went the report. "After this, the Spirit begins to speak, addressing Himself not to the witness, nor the secretary but to Joanna within. So the Prophetess has simply to sit down and talk to herself. The secretary takes down what she says and then the witness signs it. Joanna sometimes dictates a line only, sometimes a sentence, speaking till it is perfectly committed to writing. While, however, she is receiving the instructions of the Spirit, her thoughts are given to wandering, which induces her to play a game of cards to confine them."

The writer points out she used the initials "IC" on her seals. "I can only understand them to mean Infernal Communion, believing that Joanna acts under the immediate direction of Satan. She dreams much about the Devil, whom she declares she once saw as a pig, with his mouth tied. Another time she wrote that she skinned his face with her nails after a fierce battle and that she had bitten off his fingers and his blood tasted sweet."

The Church up to now had felt the best policy was to ignore Joanna. But some parish priests could keep quiet no longer. The Rev. William Wates Horne, Vicar of St. Luke's Chapel, South London, dedicated his sermon for Sunday, August 21, 1814 "in repudiation of the presumptuous pretensions of Joanna Southcott".

A stern man whose sermons were tedious and long, he considered Joanna Southcott so distasteful that he recoiled from even mentioning her name but finally decided that no matter what his personal feelings, he had to speak out. He accused her of blasphemy, witchcraft and ignorance of the Scriptures.

"It seems that our salvation depends upon the birth of her imagined child. I know not of which to be most astounded - her ignorance or her blasphemy. Pronouncements to substitute her son, if a son she should have, for Christ, suggests she denies His resurrection of Christ."

He summed it up by describing her claims as: "the most consummate proof of ignorant incoherence and misrepresentation that ever proceeded from the lips or the pen of the most inveterate enemy in Christianity. It is either the daring audacity of the subtle deceiver or the pitiable madness of the self-deluded prophetess. Her blasphemy assumes familiarity with the Lord Himself, making him speak with all the freedom which one creature would to another upon the most trivial and unimportant business. She claims to have frequent conversations with Christ. Compare this with the sacred awe, deep humility and affectionate fervour of soul displayed by the holy men of old in their approaches to the Eternal Throne. How shocking are the pretensions of this woman."

Unabashed, Joanna's followers continued to refer to Shiloh as "The Promised Seed" and before she closed her own chapels, *Southcottians* were singing enthusiastically:

"Shiloh, to our faith is given,
On this bright auspicious morn.
Shiloh, choicest gift of heaven,
For a faithless world is born.
Hail, Joanna, favoured mortal,
Chosen maid of Heaven's love.
Thou canst open the blessed portal,
Of the joyful seats above."

And, to the tune of *Rule Britannia:*

> "Come, loud hosannas let us sing,
> By all the earth let praise be given.
> Praise God for giving us a King
> To make this world resemble Heaven.
> Rule, King Shiloh. King Shiloh, rule alone.
> With glory crowned on David's throne."

Shiloh's Cradle

Made in 1814 by Mr. Seddon, of Aldersgate Street, London for Joanna's professed holy son, Shiloh. Owned by Salford Museum but in prolonged temporary custody of the Panacea Society, Bedford.

Chapter 17

Facing Death

Straw had been strewn on the cobbles outside 38, Manchester Street, Marylebone, to deaden the sound of passing carriages and horses' hooves so that Joanna was not disturbed. A curious crowd gathered outside. Some were believers. Most weren't sure what they were waiting for. Some were there to mock. Most were just drawn to the spot determined to be around should a miracle occur.

But each day the crowd grew bigger, and there wasn't much room for traffic. Joanna wasn't aware of them. She was too ill. She couldn't keep food down and a glass of fortified wine no longer comforted her. Her believers were not discouraged by her illness because they had been told that God had warned her: "Thy sufferings will paint Mine to Life, when the Child is struggling in the womb to get life. As I suffered for the transgression of Man, in childbearing thou wilt suffer for the transgression of Woman."

Dr. Richard Reece came to check on her and while he was still there, Monsieur Assalini, according to Ann Underwood a distinguished professor of midwifery in Paris and accoucheur to the Empress of France - Napoleon's cherished Josephine - paid an unexpected visit. He had heard about the pregnancy and had come to see for himself.

Joanna was impressed by his visit and made an effort to compose herself, even allowing him to examine her. After confirming the pregnancy, he asked if he could check her internally. When she refused he remarked that he was astonished a person in her condition should "oppose a man such as himself". When she explained that she was taking on all this suffering for the benefit of the human race he suggested curtly she should save her strength for the delivery of her child.

But Joanna no longer felt very pregnant - just lonely and disappointed and a bit of a fraud. Despite her weakness, her mind was clear and rational.

Joseph Pomeroy had been telling her for years, first out of kindness and then in anger, that she was deluded and her "voice" came from the Devil. Feeling she was losing her grip on life as well as her strength, she considered again whether he might have been right. Perhaps she *had been* deluded! Maybe she was, after all, influenced by the Devil and not God!

She agonised over what would happen should she die. Unless she confessed, she would more than likely go to Hell and be eternally damned. Yet if she *was* to die soon, this might be her last chance to make amends. It was difficult for her to admit to anything, for these were only doubts and she still *wanted* to believe everything she had ever preached. How could she reject it all now? How the world would ridicule her!

For several weeks she was in a pitiful state as she struggled with her conscience. On Monday morning, November 7, 1814, her divine guide had spoken encouragingly to her: "Before the end is over," she had been told, "everyone's faith will fail them, for thy sufferings will be so great, thou wilt appear as dead. But the faithful must not despair. Caution is given to keep them from sinking for He that hath began the Word will carry it through. No violent means must be used, however great the dangers appear, to preserve the life of the child, by taking thine."

These words came back to her, now death seemed uncomfortably near, and brought her some consolation. She didn't want to die! She didn't feel noble enough to sacrifice her own life for the child's, who now seemed so real to her. But her still small voice had assured her that this would not be necessary. Both lives would be saved. "Let no-one be alarmed if thou appear as dead, for after a while I shall raise thee again." In other words, if she *did* die, she would be resurrected after a few days, as Jesus had been. What was more, at the moment of her apparent death the child, Shiloh, would be snatched back into Heaven by God's angels, as prophesied in the *Book of Revelation.*

On November 19 she had a fit of vomiting. Fear of death gripped again and she clung to the thought that her Spirit had promised her resurrection. Then it struck her that, unless someone was told that God had scheduled for her to be resurrected, she might be buried and wake up in her coffin, six feet below ground. In sick panic, she called Dr. Reece to her bed-side to let him know what he must do in the event of her death. He noted she was "weak and dejected" and unable to speak clearly, but instructed him feverishly not to allow her body to be buried immediately after death. It had to be kept warm, at body temperature, with hot water bottles and warming pans. She explained to the astonished doctor that she was to be brought back to life by God, after four days in a trance, and therefore it was necessary for her body to remain in good condition.

She added that if, after four days, there was definitely no sign of life after every conceivable test had been carried out, then he could perform a post-mortem on her body to determine whether there was evidence of pregnancy. "You *will* find something alive in me which will prove to my friends that I am *not* the impostor I am reputed to be," she insisted defiantly.

Finally, Joanna called her closest friends to her. As they gathered round, she tried to sit up but was too weak, so Ann Underwood gently propped her up with pillows and carefully placed a large white handkerchief in front of her. Nervously fidgeting with it, Joanna displayed unaccustomed humility as she confessed that she had been having serious doubts about herself.

"Some of you have known me nearly 25 years and all of you not less than 20," she said. "When you have heard me speak my prophecies you have sometimes heard me say I doubted my inspiration. But, at the same time, you would *never* let me despair." Then she added wistfully: "Yet, when I have been alone, it has often appeared delusion."

Jane Townley and Ann Underwood, the most caring of her friends, suggested that she was showing signs of her old mental illness. But she shook her head tearfully and said: "No, when the communications were made to me, I did not doubt." She added despairingly: "Feeling as I do now, that my dissolution is drawing near and a day or two may terminate my life, it all appears a delusion."

She wept into the handkerchief they had given her and remarked wryly: "It is extraordinary that, after spending all my life investigating the Bible, it should please the Lord to inflict this heavy burden on me." Her distress affected her friends and some of them cried.

Mr. Howe, from Exeter, told her tenderly: "Mother, your feelings are human. We know that you are a favoured woman of God and that you *will* produce the Child. And, whatever you say to the contrary, it will not diminish our faith." He promised that her instructions to Dr. Reece would be written down there and then and, in the unlikely event of her death, would be carried out with utmost dignity.

This display of loyalty distressed Joanna even more. Dr. Reece said that several times during the strange scene, she seemed strongly tempted to make a complete confession of her sins and, if he had been alone in the room with her, he felt she would have done so. Faced, however, with the unquenchable faith of her friends, her courage failed her. A document was finally drawn up and signed by Dr. Reece and four witnesses, agreeing to honour her final instructions.

The *Sunday Monitor* issued an "official" bulletin as a response to the "many most pressing enquiries relative to Mrs. Southcott". The Bulletin sent out at 8pm on Saturday, December 4, 1814, read: "On Thursday night, Mrs. Southcott rested better than she had done for some weeks past, being entirely free from pain and restlessness and she continued so on Friday. Last night, however, she became restless and uneasy. She took one of the opium pills, which composed her till near two o'clock in the morning, when she awaked in very great pain and continued so for an hour. It then went off and she slept for a short time, then waking in great pain. In this manner she has continued the whole day. The pain is not of a long duration, as she very soon goes to sleep again. Though her sickness has not returned, her appetite does not improve. She is free from fever, but is faint and low."

On December 6, Dr. Reece visited her again and noted that in his opinion she wouldn't live much longer, despite the fact that she said she felt the child stronger than ever and hoped the labour would come soon, for she was now well into the tenth month of her alleged pregnancy. He felt her stomach for movement and for the first time was uneasy about his original diagnosis. "There was a sudden action of the diaphragm or midriff and abdominal muscles - apparently produced by an act of the mind or a voluntary impulse for the sake of deception. I decided that perhaps the laudanum prescribed to quell the vomiting had affected the head. Her stomach was now reduced to that state of weakness as to retain nothing but a little Madeira wine. Everything else is rejected."

"I *have* felt the child move," she told him plaintively, as if trying to convince herself. Dr. Reece asked if she did die, would she want him to try and save the child, to which she burst into tears. "If it is the work of the Lord, He will deliver me. And, if it is not, it is fit it should die with me." She turned her face to the wall, and he prescribed laudanum and kali for her retching and sickness.

Dr. Reece was beginning to worry about his own reputation. He pressed her again to allow him to give her an internal examination which would establish beyond doubt she was pregnant. After all, he had supported her and risked his good name and reputation to do so, so it was her duty to grant this simple request. Joanna told him sharply that in her present state of health a very short time must determine her situation one way or another, and an internal examination at this stage was unnecessary.

Ann Underwood wrote anxiously on December 10, 1814: "Her weakness seems rapidly to increase."

Joanna was frightened that she was close to death, but Colonel Harwood, who had been at her bedside continuously for weeks, assured her she was not and would soon give birth. "All that happens is far out of the common practice of medical men and they know nothing about it," he told her, refusing to acknowledge obvious signs of deterioration. He assured the others that "all true believers will see her, as promised, with the child in her arms and milk in her breasts."

On December 16, Dr. Reece paid an impromptu visit and expressed astonishment that all signs of pregnancy had vanished and she was sallow, cadaverous and dying. "Damn me," he exclaimed. "If the child is not gone. There is nothing there but the working of the muscles."

Up to this point, he had always told Joanna and her friends that there was no doubt about her pregnancy. His letters to newspapers stressed that he had examined her extensively and was positive of his diagnosis. Now, confused and embarrassed, he tried to backtrack. He announced to the Press: "I found her with every mark of approaching dissolution."

According to Colonel Harwood, Joanna was upset by Reece's lack of confidence but was able to muster a show of bravado by commenting: "Well, it is of no consequence. I shall shortly produce the child and all I ask of him is to act like a man. If he were a believer, he would not be a proper witness and the most improbable the event, the firmer will be his conviction that it is the work of the Lord."

Reece was ultimately denounced by the Press as a rogue who took fees from the *Southcottians* in return for substantiating Joanna's claims. In his own defence, he published a pamphlet setting out the events precisely. But his reputation was already tainted. He tried to wriggle further out of his predicament by accusing her of calculated deception and laid the blame on her. "To the last," he said, "this unfortunate woman made no confession of her error."

Joanna was now certain she was really dying. There was no way she could deceive herself. Constantly giddy and drenched in perspiration, she said she felt a dreadful sensation in every nerve of her body. She struggled to remain conscious fearing she might die in her sleep, and protested weakly to her friends: "What does the Lord mean by this? I am *certainly* dying."

Blind loyalty still prevailed. "No, no," she was told by the ever confident Colonel Harwood. "You will not die. Or, if you do, you will return again." But now Joanna was not easily convinced.

On December 17 Dr. Reece found her rambling and restless. He said she placed her hand "emphatically" to her forehead - "an effort I have never before observed in a person in that convulsive condition" he remarked. Later, when he attributed her illness to "mischief of the brain" he seemed to think her gesture significant. He left, saying he doubted she would survive more than two days.

On Christmas Day, which fell on a Sunday, she turned to Ann Underwood, squeezed her hand and whispered defiantly: "I am not afraid to appear before my God, as I have done nothing but what I believed to be in true obedience to my Lord." Later that day she awoke in pain and murmured deliriously: "The child is coming and the head is in the world. He is making his way out through my side."

Her nurse felt the spot she indicated and reported later that she had felt a tumour as large as a man's head which suddenly gave a distinct kick. On Boxing Day, December 26, she appeared to rally a little and hopes were raised. Ann Underwood and Jane Townley stayed by her and prayed. But that evening, she had a relapse.

Harwood, exhausted by his long vigil, withdrew for a short rest and asked the nurse to tell him if she became worse. Her breath was now coming in painful gasps - "the death rattle" her mother Hannah had called it. He was called back to her room at 3 o'clock in the morning and watched her struggling for breath for another hour. He told his wife: "I saw her last breath go from her mouth, exactly as the clock struck four."

Ann Underwood recorded: "To all appearance, she died this morning as the clock struck four." She assumed, as did others, that Joanna was merely in a suspended state between life and death and God would miraculously restore her to them within a short while. Harwood wrote in his diary: "I shall always think of what I have done and what I am doing, as a duty to the Almighty." He firmly believed God possessed the power to "raise his instrument from the dead".

The Press reported Joanna's death with relish. Since publicly announcing her Immaculate Conception, she had been hounded by a ruthless media who delighted in ridiculing her. All sorts of bizarre stories had appeared in the newspapers about her. Her last words were reported to be: "Oh England! Oh, England! How I have deceived thee."

Southcottians faithfully complied with her wishes to keep her body warm for four days, on the assumption that on the fourth day she would return to life, as prophesied. Ann Underwood sent a strange note from 38 Manchester Street, to Dr. Reece. "You desire to be present at Mrs. Southcott's accouchement. It has taken place as expected" - indicating that she considered that the child had been born and snatched back to Heaven by God.

She went on: "The friends consider it is their duty to inform you and all medical gentlemen who have an interest, that to all appearance she died this morning exactly as the clock struck four. Care has been taken to preserve the warmth in the body, as she instructed, and it is the wish of her friends that you will see her in her present state."

Joanna's followers reasoned it was essential for her body be examined without delay by professional doctors, to establish she was clinically dead. They didn't want a situation where, when she *was* resurrected on the fourth day - as they were confident she would be - she might be accused of faking death. Already there were rumours she was pretending to be dead to escape the humiliation of her mysteriously vanished pregnancy and that, when the hue and cry had died down, she planned to escape to France with all the money and valuables she had been given for her child.

Dr. Reece called to see the body and said Joanna was lying in the same position as when she had died, wrapped up in flannel blankets and surrounded with hot water bottles. But there were no faces of woe to greet him. All twelve people present wore radiant smiles and were buoyant with happy optimism. Jane Townley, beaming joyfully, insisted Joanna *would* return to life.

William Sharp grabbed hold of him, took him into a corner of the room and told him he realised he had an arduous task to perform but the result would enhance his reputation and honour, for the soul of Joanna would return having only gone to Heaven to legitimatise the child which *would still be born.* The general feeling was of excitement that the fulfilment of Joanna's prophecies was imminent. Reece was asked teasingly by Sharp, if Joanna *was* resuscitated and she did produce a boy, would he *then* believe in Joanna.

"In my present frame of mind," replied the bewildered doctor who must have felt he had entered a room full of lunatics, "it would to me appear as reasonable as to expect the building of St. Paul's to ascend into the air."

"Ah!" said Sharp patronisingly, "You only take a professional view of it, but *I* take a spiritual one."

Jane Townley was asked what attitude she would adopt if there was no child. "If it should turn out to be so," said Townley fervently, "I would burn my Bible and declare the whole fabric nonsense."

By the third day, Reece said the body had become highly offensive and the lips and fingers had assumed a black appearance, but even this did not shake the faith of the followers. He pointed out to them that the situation was now unhygienic because the intense heat of the room had accelerated the process of putrefaction. But it was like talking to a brick wall. Common sense could not penetrate their aggravatingly stubborn faith. Sharp said comfortingly, "Don't be uneasy. You will not suffer by it for, depend on it, she *will* return to the body."

"If you think so," said Reece with studied sarcasm, "then you should endeavour to keep it sweet for her reception for, should the ceremony of her marriage in Heaven continue two days longer, the tenement will not be habitable for her return."

"Well then," said Sharp with unabashed delight, "greater will be the miracle. The God that raised Lazarus can raise her up also."

The body lay on view at Miss Townley's rented house in Manchester Street, watched over by her friends and 15 doctors and invited members of the Press. By the fourth day, the heat from the hot water bottles and the fire in the room, caused the flesh to putrefy disgustingly. The smell was so bad, visitors had to wear masks and the watchers smoked heavily to disguise the sickening stench. Finally, after four days, it was reluctantly conceded there was a genuine danger of disease, and hope was abandoned.

But not quite! Believers agreed to allow Dr. Reece, in the presence of those eminent doctors prepared to brave unpleasant conditions in the interests of science, to perform a post-mortem to establish the cause of death and to find out whether there *had* been a child in her womb - immaculate or otherwise. They still nursed a vain hope that God had some devious plan, and the operation would reveal the final miracle.

Dr. Reece arrived at 1.45pm but was not allowed to start even a second before the appointed hour of two in the afternoon, to give Joanna's spirit every last chance to return to her body before it was mutilated by the surgeon's knife. Colonel Harwood insisted he should adopt a Caesarean method of operation in order that the body would not be spoilt, just in case she returned *after* the autopsy. William Tozer begged him tearfully to take care not to harm the child. No attempt had been made to prepare the body for burial. Dr Reece said Joanna was still wearing the same flannelette nightie she had died in and the rings on her fingers and other jewellery, had not been removed. The body was so putrefied that it had to be transferred to the hastily set up operating table on a sheet, for fear of disintegration.

Witnesses eagerly grouped themselves round the table, some smoking tobacco to combat the odour of the body. As the dissecting knife was inserted, the stink from the putrefying flesh became so unbearable that one or two observers ran retching from the room. Dr. Reece, his face hidden behind a mask, held his breath and valiantly carried on.

"The believers were all on tiptoe to see Shiloh appear," he wrote later. "And those who could not have a view themselves were most anxiously making enquiries of others. No promised child, however, appeared, which so confused the rest that they gradually left the room abashed and dismayed."

Dr. Reece, sensitive to the anxious curiosity of the faithful, first examined the womb. "It was the size of a small pear," he wrote with a trace of scorn, "and considered by the medical gentlemen as remarkably small." There was no mark of disease and no sure evidence Joanna had been pregnant. He did discover that the gallbladder was filled with stones, which he felt could have accounted for her stomach problems. Because of the state of the body, the doctors felt that they had done their duty in opening up the abdomen, and could not stomach the ordeal of dissecting the brain, where Dr. Reece later said he felt all the mischief probably lay.

An account of her death appeared in a London newspaper, written by a reporter from a medical journal who had been allowed to observe from the sidelines. "On Thursday, December 29, nine medicals viewed the corpse and examined the countenance and felt the arm for the pulse and, without hesitation, bore evidence of her death. Her believers in her mission erroneously supposed her to have gone into a trance. Dr Reece, this day, pronounced that putrefaction was rapidly taking place. The body was opened on Saturday, December 31, in the presence of 15 medical gentlemen, - including **Dr. Joseph Adams, Dr. Sims, Messrs. Want, Taunton, Dr. William Roundell Wetherall, Cook, Phillips and Catton**. No disease appeared in the womb. The substance on the side had also disappeared. Only a small enlargement of the abdomen was evident. The body is now in a complete state of putrefaction. It was removed at 9 o'clock from Manchester Street, to an undertakers for private interment."

The fifteen doctors at the post-mortem signed a paper stating that: "No unnatural appearances were visible and no part exhibited a natural appearance of disease sufficient to have occasioned her death."

Joanna's close friends were stunned, not just by the shock of her death - for they were suddenly without a leader - but with the realisation that the whole affair had turned into an appalling farce. For months they had diligently prepared for Shiloh's birth and had believed in him as implicitly as they believed in Christ. Now they were being made to look foolish and some found it difficult to bear. Yet they were reluctant to condemn Joanna herself, believing that if they remained loyal to her memory she would still show them the way. Most reserved judgement and waited for a sign, either from God or the departed Mother Joanna. Amongst those who finally couldn't take it was Colonel Harwood, who had been with Joanna throughout her months of sickness. He managed to restrain his distaste sufficiently to arrange the funeral and follow Joanna's coffin to her grave. Finally he went off, bitterly disappointed and appalled at his own gullibility, to cut himself off forever from the sect.

The two who mourned her most were Ann Underwood and Jane Townley, for they felt a deep personal grief and, for a time, were inconsolable. Both tried hard to understand the situation and to read some good into it. But it was difficult. Ann Underwood wrote: "The friends, I am glad to see, appear to derive comfort thinking all is right, but I cannot see anything to warrant it." It took some time, if ever, for her to come to terms with the situation.

Richard Law, still in love with Jane Townley, described Joanna as "the most ungrateful woman that ever was befriended by man". In a letter to Jane, he said: "Many a rich present she got through the instrumentation of such men as myself, but she forgot us in her Will, nor even left us a single trinket." With bitter satisfaction, he added: "Mother is gone to Hell and her gentlemen and ladies will soon follow her."

Dr. Reece, ridiculed by the Press and members of his profession, finally boiled over. "Both Dr. Sims and I were made dupes of imposture and artifice, systematically laid and carried on by this apparently artless woman who, one would suppose, must have been tutored in medical instruction. From this imputation, I entirely exclude her followers, who were no less deceived than ourselves. Indeed, her apparently artless behaviour I consider now as the chief engine of her deception and whoever accurately examines her portrait, as delineated by Mr. Sharp, will perceive a certain archness of look about the eyes which tends to confirm the opinion."

Dr. Reece was acknowledged by his peers to be a brilliant doctor. So it is a mystery just how this simple, uneducated woman could ever have hoodwinked him. Richard Reece himself was baffled. Smarting with the humiliation of it all, he went over the situation again and again and finally arrived at what he considered a rational explanation. He decided that the tumour he had noticed in her stomach was none other than urine deliberately retained in the bladder for hours on end. He recalled how she had stubbornly refused to have any doctor examine her internally.

"Was it not ridiculous," he asked, "to suppose that delicacy could operate in the mind of a woman who freely exposed every other part without a blush and refused compliance with a request less indelicate and which alone would have discovered the imposition?"

He believed that the supposed movement of the child in the womb, observed by so many, was deliberately contrived by quick and instantaneous muscle movements. He suggested she managed to enlarge her breasts by constantly and fiercely sucking her own nipples - which would account for their unusual length. This stimulation encouraged rushes of blood to the mammary glands which not only served to increase the breast size but also resulted in the secretion of what appeared to be milk. He said the fact that, previous to announcing the pregnancy she admitted spending weeks locked up alone in her room, substantiated this.

Joanna's devious plan had been to smuggle a child into her room from the poorhouse and, he said, this was why she often changed her dates, in order to fit in with some destitute expectant mother paid to give up her child at the moment of birth. Reece believed she made arrangements with several women all due to come to the end of their term of pregnancy at the same time. However, Joanna could not be sure that one of them would deliver up a boy, or that a healthy live child would result. "She was probably foiled in her projected design on several occasions," he suggested.

In a final burst of disgust at the whole affair, which he regretted ever getting mixed up in, he said: "To introduce a human being as the Son of God is a blasphemy which beggars description - the bare idea chills the blood." He reckoned the reason why she deluded so many intelligent people was because she managed to conduct herself with more decorum than the average fanatic. "Joanna was apparently quiet, correct and decorous," he pointed out. "Her warning Spirit was mild and gentle and spoke to her in a whisper and communicated with the soft still voice of inspiration. But she is now gone to the Tribunal which forms the true judgement of all human conduct."

The Press meanwhile were having a field day raking up damaging stories about her and her followers. Anyone who had ever believed in her was inclined to keep silent. Those still loyal to her withdrew into their homes, shrinking from the scorn.

Joanna's corpse was placed in a plain pine coffin, the lid screwed down and sealed with black pitch. Her grieving friends waited until after midnight before smuggling the coffin out and carrying it unceremoniously to an undertakers in Rathbone Place, where it remained until the funeral. But news soon got round it was there and huge crowds formed outside, either non-believers out for some fun, or ghoulish sight-seers. Some were genuinely indignant Christians angry still at the blasphemies they felt Joanna had preached.

The funeral took place on New Year's Day, 1815. It was a gloomy, furtive affair. A black hearse pulled by two horses drew up outside the undertakers. As the body was carried out of the undertaker's parlour, hooligans hurled abuse and obscene vilifications after the coffin, accompanied by hails of stones and rotten vegetables. Despite this excited mob, it ended up a lonely and sad burial. Her friends were afraid the event would be turned into a circus by graveside aggressors and Joanna's name disgraced even more. They wanted her interment to be dignified in order to preserve her immaculate image, at least to themselves.

The grave was booked in the assumed name she had used at Blockley - Mrs. Goddard - which in Old English means "God's Dear One". Even the venue was kept secret, though the mob determinedly followed the hearse until the horses broke into an unseemly gallop and left them behind.

On that cold New Year's Day, only three people officially saw her off, muffled up in great coats buttoned at the chin, with collars raised and scarves pulled over their faces, partly to avoid being recognised and partly because of the bitter cold. Led by a grim-faced Colonel Harwood, they followed her coffin to the graveside at the bleak St. John's Wood cemetery, site of an old plague burial ground.

It was situated in what was then the country, several miles from the select, wealthy new suburb of Marylebone where Joanna had died. The brief ceremony was held at the recently built chapel attached to the ground, which had only been adopted as a cemetery for the new parish of Marylebone six years earlier. The chapel, designed by Thomas Hardwick, was not consecrated when Joanna's funeral service was held there. Consecration took place later in the year.

Scattered around the cemetery grounds, believers watched from a discreet distance as the coffin was lowered into the damp earth. After a few hurried prayers, the soil was thrown swiftly upon it and, with an air of shame and furtive concealment, the three official mourners skulked away almost before the first shovelful of soil hit the coffin lid.

Joanna Southcott
after death

This portrait was sketched by a witness immediately after Joanna died in 1814. Her disciples believed she had merely gone to heaven for her marriage to Jesus and she would be restored to life after four days. Her body was kept warm in a heated room and Dr. Richard Reece remarked scathingly that if the marriage ceremony lasted two days longer the tenement would not be habitable for her return. To which William Sharp replied gleefully: "Well then, greater will be the miracle."

Joanna Southcott died here.

Number 38, Manchester St., Marylebone, London, where Joanna lay in bed in a first floor room overlooking the street, waiting to give birth to Shiloh, the child she said was to be the Second Messiah. Straw was laid down outside to soften the noise of passing traffic. She died there at 4am on December 27, 1814. Her disciples said the child **was** born the previous day, but in spiritual form.

The Laughing Gargoyle.

Satan once explained to Joanna that he was a "lively, cheerful spirit, full of mirth and gaiety, which God could not tolerate". This laughing gargoyle above the door of 38, Manchester Street, fits the description remarkably well.

Chapter 18

The Big Disappointment

Angels in heaven may have rejoiced on the night Joanna was born, but only the Devil's own imps could have been there at her death. "Mother has gone to hell," gloated Richard Law, and he was not the only one who thought so! Most of London was enjoying the macabre joke of Joanna's phantom pregnancy.

A detailed account of her bleak burial appeared in the *Morning Post*, describing her as a notorious woman who, in conjunction with others, had long practised on the ignorance and credulity of the lower classes. "Gross and impious absurdities have originated from this woman and her followers, and we lament that very many persons of respectable condition in life, from whom better things might have been hoped, have suffered themselves to be deluded by her most irrational and abominable pretensions."

Neither the Minister who conducted the funeral or any of the people connected with the church, knew the identity of the corpse until the funeral reached the chapel. The grave itself was in common ground, where there was a rule that no monument could be erected. "In a short space of time," reported the newspaper with satisfaction, "from the vast number of persons interred there, it will be difficult, if not impossible, to mark the exact spot where the body of this deluded woman has been deposited."

From his pulpit in St. Mary's Church, in Ottery St. Mary, the Rev. Joseph Turnbull delivered a scathing sermon, grimly referring to the death of Joanna Southcott, christened in that very church 65 years previously. He asked scornfully, "What Christian would wish to see his adored Saviour rocked, even in a silver cradle, by silly women instead of beholding Him in his triumphant chariot, shining resplendent?"

A fortnight after the funeral found the Rev. Thomas Foley back at Old Swinford, licking his wounds. His pride had been severely bruised - the sniggers from his parishioners he found particularly hard to bear - and he hid himself away until Sunday, January 15 when, mustering courage, he took his place in the pulpit to preach for the first time in months. Needless to say, Old Swinford Parish Church was packed for the occasion, despite it being cold and wintry. Thomas Foley had become a curiosity and everyone wanted a glimpse of him.

His wife, Elizabeth, sat stiff and upright in her pew watching nervously as he quoted fervently from *Corinthians*. "We are troubled on every side, yet not distressed. We are perplexed, but not in despair." His parishioners had been hoping he would by now have come to his senses and abandoned his cranky beliefs. But no! After the service, he wrote, "many of the congregation were much disappointed, but that is of little consequence to me."

His stubborn attitude prevailed and, despite the advice and pleadings of those close to him, he stuck to his guns. But Elizabeth was stunned and shamed by the ridicule and scorn. She rued the day they had ever set eyes on Joanna and tried, in a wifely way, to talk to him about it, but to no avail. An icy atmosphere developed in the Foley household. The day after his sermon, he wrote: "I am truly grieved to say that my wife and self are now quite opposite in our opinions respecting Joanna's works and most uncomfortable is our present state - for one of us must be going deeply into sin."

The quarrel persisted all that week and on the Wednesday Foley wrote miserably: "I had a violent breeze with my wife after dinner, about Joanna's work, and she asserted a most gross lie for which, and other exasperating language, I was obliged to put her out of the room." Next day he noted "most miserable and wretched we are at the moment".

Happily, by June of that year a compromise had clearly been reached and matrimonial harmony restored, for Foley mentions that he and Elizabeth made a trip together to London to do some shopping and enjoy a few days' pleasant relaxation.

Other disciples kept a low profile. Some of them, like Colonel Harwood, had renounced the Southcottian mission, but others who really loved her - Foley, Jane Townley and Ann Underwood - searched their souls for some rational explanation which might serve as a salve for their emotional wounds. Slowly, very slowly, the hurt subsided and, as they recovered, they came up with various explanations. Astonishingly, few were prepared to blame Joanna in the slightest degree for the non-appearance of the child. It was unthinkable to them that she might have deliberately deceived them, so certain they were of her unblemished character. "I have gone through many severe trials within the last four months," confessed Foley, "but blessed be God for it. He has most mercifully carried me safely through them."

He described how, at the end of June, 1814 he went with his wife, Elizabeth, to St. John's Burial Ground to see the plain memorial plaque set in the ground marking the spot where Joanna was buried.

"You may imagine how my feelings were hurt when I saw it's a little removed and most carelessly placed upon the ground. I then, at once, made up my mind to have it for the future properly secured, and I endeavoured through a few friends to have it railed round. But the Churchyard is divided into two parts by iron railings - one part for the rich and the other for the poor - and our dear Joanna was buried in the poor's ground, where raised monuments are forbidden.

"The Trust have allowed a tablet to be fixed in the wall, about 22 feet from the grave. The expense will be between £30 to £40 and it would be instantly raised among a few. My dear friend Malkin has been very zealous indeed in accomplishing this praiseworthy business."

In a letter to Foley, John Malkin wrote from his home at Rock Place, Kingsland "nr London": "I have made all the necessary arrangements, by paying the fees for the Stone and also I have orders to the Mason to prepare a handsome black marble tablet. The letters, after they are engraved, are to be handsomely gilt with gold, with a star at each corner on the top of the tablet. The size of the tablet to be five feet long and two feet six inches wide and three inches thick."

Foley was keen that the words on the stone should be startling enough to catch the attention of passers-by and make them stop and think. "The people that read it would see that we still have strong grounds for retaining our faith in this glorious cause we are engaged in. Even after the Great Disappointment which befell us in December 1814, when our dear Spiritual Mother, Joanna Southcott, died! We have selected three verses from the Scriptures - and they are very strong in our favour."

The words he chose were from *Esdras, Chapter 7, verses xvi, xvii.*

"Behold the Time shall Come, that these Tokens which I have told Thee, shall come to pass: and the Bride shall appear - and she coming forth shall be seen, that now is withdrawn from the Earth. And whosoever is delivered from the aforesaid evils, shall see my wonders."

And from Habakkuk, Chapter 2, verse iii.

"For the Vision is yet for an appointed time. But, at the end, it shall speak and not lie. Though it tarry, wait for it. Because it will surely come."

Foley was satisfied with his choice. "The verses are clear, full and appropriate to the times we live in and must make a deep impression on many that will read them."

However, the memorial stone was not erected for another fourteen years, because they had difficulty raising the money. In 1828, a small group of *Southcottians* who met every Sunday in the porch of the church, finally arranged for it to be put up twenty-six feet from the spot where she was actually buried, by the railings on the Western side of the cemetery. Newspapers suggested that this was to guard against body-snatchers and ghoulish trophy hunters. The verse on the tablet read:

> "While through all thy wondrous days
> Heaven & earth enraptured gazed,
> While vain sages think they know,
> Secrets **THOU ALONE** can shew,
> Time alone will tell what hour,
> Thoul't appear in **GREATER** power."

On October 2, 1874 a barge called the Tilbury, carrying five tons of gunpowder, exploded with devastating results just under Macclesfield Bridge on the newly built Regent's Canal. All that was left of the bridge was a pile of bricks ten feet high out of the water, and nothing was ever found of the crew of three. Today it is still known as *"The Blow Up Bridge"*. The explosion was so horrific, it damaged buildings for miles around.

As far as *Southcottians* were concerned, the most significant result of the incident was that the tablet erected in memory of "Mother Joanna" cracked almost in two. They read it as a sign of God's wrath at the world's rejection of her and hopes were revived that Joanna would soon return to finish her work. The stone deteriorated over the years so that eventually the words could hardly be read and in 1964 a replacement was erected on the same spot. It can be found on the western path of the Old St. John's Wood cemetery, behind what is now St. John's Wood Parish church, with the back of the stone blankly facing the busy Wellington Road, opposite Lord's Cricket Ground. Today it is looked after by the late Alice Seymour's

Southcottian Group, who took it upon themselves to tend her grave in 1927, when £3.10 was raised for its restoration.

Witty poets composed odes to her. One (author unknown) entitled "*The Broken Bubble*", was printed in London by James Baker.

> "Johanna, the Virgin, Oh! Where has she fled?
> Escaping, alas, is her nose so red.
> And eternity's truth has gone in its stead.
> The Holy of Holies when she was young,
> The worst of her members confessed was her tongue.
> For their fraud and folly continuously hung.
> At length works to madness, her craft knew no stay,
> She became a soothsayer and flourished away,
> With visions all night and the bottle all day.
> When arrived at the climax of all her deceit,
> She swore a sweet spirit had given her a treat,
> Of a nice china bowl full of rum, good and neat.
> Now Towzer began to stare with surprise,
> And eagerly swallowed her fanatic lies,
> For he cried, "Sure the woman has got bigger in size."
> But some who with Towzer were not quite in tune,
> Thought she was the mountebank, he the buffoon,
> And laughed at young Shiloh, his cot and his shoon.
> The sealed and the doubtless grew wondrous hot,
> Some said the old woman the dropsy had got,
> Some said she was pregnant, some said she was not.
> Pain and sickness came on, she was carried to bed.
> Ere she yielded to nature, softly she said.
> Till I stink like a pole cat, don't think I am dead.
> And now, ye sage doctors! How altered each strain.
> Since ye gave your opinions so light and so vain.
> To prove what?   Why, your noddle's deficient of brain."

More accomplished poets were also inspired to scorn. In *Canto 3* of his poem, *Don Juan*, Lord Byron refers to Joanna in a criticism of Wordsworth's poem, "*The Excursion.*"

> "But Wordsworth's poem, and his followers, like
> Joanna Southcote's Shiloh and her sect,
> Are things which in this century don't strike

> The public mind, - so few are the elect;
> And the new births of both their stale Virginities
> Have proved but Dropsies, taken for Divinities."

John Keats, in a letter to George and Georgina Keats in 1819, called Joanna and those like her "nuisances" sired by the Devil. By way of an answer to these scoffing poets, a new hymn was composed by the Southcottians.

> "Oh yes, although no Shiloh has appear'd
> And fancied triumphs glad your laughing minds,
> Soon shall your jest and mirth no more be heard.
> Despair, you scribbling liars of the Times.
> What if Joanna's wrath on scoffers hurl'd,
> Implores the Powers above to change her doom?
> Serenely quits a persecuting world,
> And sinks content to a lamented tomb.
> Shall these things for a single moment make
> A *true believer* venture to complain?
> No, tho' mysterious, like her prophecies,
> All shall at last be clear to vulgar eyes;
> All doubt, in time, be gloriously solved."

Also buried in the St. John's Wood Cemetery, not far from where Joanna lies, are the remains of her rival, Richard Brothers. William Sharp once believed Brothers was the New Messiah who would one day lead an army of believers into a splendid new Jerusalem. He died nine years after Joanna, on January 25, 1824, and was buried on the wealthy side of the new St. John's Wood Chapel - so was therefore allowed railings round his stone to protect it from vandals.

Modern members of the church fondly refer to these two as the "Marylebone Fanatics" and are very pleased, in the interests of history, to direct curious parties to their graves.

Joanna's Memorial Stone

In 1828 Thomas Foley arranged for a memorial to be erected, at a cost of £40, near the spot where Joanna was buried in the new cemetery at St. John's Wood, Marylebone. In 1874 a barge blew up under Macclesfield Bridge, on the newly-built Regents Canal, and the force of the explosion cracked Joanna's memorial in two. It became more dilapidated over the years until, in 1965, modern Southcottians put up this pristine new replacement. Joanna's actual remains are buried under a crumbling stone slab, 26 feet from the memorial, concealed by bushes.

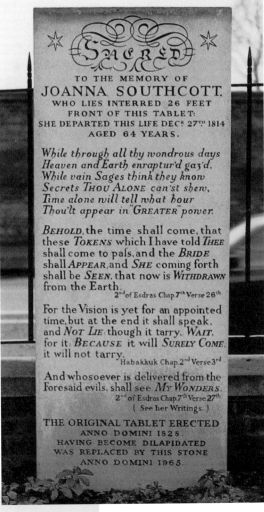

SACRED

TO THE MEMORY OF

JOANNA SOUTHCOTT.

WHO LIES INTERRED 26 FEET
FRONT OF THIS TABLET:
SHE DEPARTED THIS LIFE DEC.ᵣ 27ᵗʰ 1814
AGED 64 YEARS.

While through all thy wondrous days
Heaven and Earth enraptur'd gaz'd.
While vain Sages think they know
Secrets THOU ALONE can'st shew,
Time alone will tell what hour
Thou'lt appear in "GREATER" power.

BEHOLD, the time shall come, that
these TOKENS which I have told THEE
shall come to pafs, and the BRIDE
shall APPEAR, and SHE coming forth
shall be SEEN, that now is WITHDRAWN
from the Earth.
        2ⁿᵈ of Esdras Chap.7ᵗʰ Verse 26ᵗʰ

For the Vision is yet for an appointed
time, but at the end it shall speak,
and NOT LIE though it tarry. WAIT,
for it: BECAUSE it will SURELY COME,
it will not tarry.
        Habakkuk Chap. 2ⁿᵈ Verse 3ʳᵈ

And whosoever is delivered from the
Foresaid evils, shall see MY WONDERS.
        2ⁿᵈ of Esdras Chap.7ᵗʰ Verse 27ᵗʰ
        (See her Writings.)

THE ORIGINAL TABLET ERECTED
ANNO DOMINI 1828.
HAVING BECOME DILAPIDATED
WAS REPLACED BY THIS STONE
ANNO DOMINI 1965.

St. Marylebone Parish Church, built 1814 and designed by Thomas Hardwick. Joanna's funeral took place there a few months *before* the chapel was consecrated.

Joanna Southcott
as a Figure of Fun

A MEDICAL INSPECTION.
or MIRACLES WILL NEVER CEASE

Crude cartoon of Joanna vulgarly displaying her pregnant belly, by Thomas Rowlandson (1756-1827), one of the most brilliantly perceptive caricaturists of the time. It sums up the ruthless scorn and ridicule that followed Joanna's extraordinary death, embarrassing her stunned believers to the point of despair.

Chapter 19

Fighting Disillusion

The dizzy euphoria which had been buoyant during Joanna's "confinement" was followed by a period of chilling apathy. Shocked numb, those who had been close to Joanna were at first at a loss to know what to do. Then, gradually, each found their own way of coping.

George Turner convinced himself he was Shiloh. William Tozer, who loved to preach and was loth to give it up, spread the word that Shiloh had arrived on earth but was biding his time before making an appearance. Ann Underwood grieved for the friend she had lost. William Sharp became disillusioned. Colonel Harwood went off in a huff. Foley, whose bubbling enthusiasm couldn't be dampened for long, withdrew to Old Swinford but within months was as eager as ever to renew the campaign against the Devil.

Jane Townley shut herself away at 17 Weston Place, with Ann Underwood. With Joanna, they had been dubbed The Three Women, united spiritually to carry out the fight against the Devil. But Ann and Jane had been accustomed to taking orders from Joanna, even over trivial matters. Without her to lead them, they were like lost children.

"But if I had not been thus mercifully blinded," Jane later said defensively, "I could not have supported myself during those anxious days between her death and dissection. Through the blight that followed, the confusion and distress of my mind were greater than I can express. But in mercy to me and my friends, I was enabled to meet them the following morning and it was made clear to my mind that it was a spiritual, not a temporal birth, we were to look for." In other words, Shiloh *had* been born, but his spirit had entered into the body of a living being and *not* into a body of his own. This was why, Jane concluded, there was no sign of anything physical when Joanna's womb was dissected.

It dawned on her that there was only one person in England qualified to be "The Man Child" or Shiloh. The Prince Regent himself! Not only had he the power to ensure Joanna's prophecies were properly examined, he was the only member of the Royal Family to have shown the slightest interest in her. It was *his* body, she decided, into which Shiloh had manifested. She wrote his name down, sealed and dated it and asked friends to witness it. Then she confined herself to her house "so as to be at all times ready, in case any inquiries concerning the mission should be made."

William Sharp, now 67, was thoroughly disillusioned with Joanna. He decided his faith was not strong enough for him to remain custodian of *Joanna's Box* and, in 1816, asked Jane Townley to take charge of it. She was delighted, believing it was God's way of showing that He wanted Ann Underwood and herself to continue where Joanna left off. For six years she studied Joanna's writings, reading into the garbled verses and prose deep significances of world-wide importance. Deprived of fresh air and sunshine, she became nervous and mentally ill and fellow *Southcottian*, Dr. William Pughe, was called in to attend to her.

Jane brooded about one of Joanna's prophecies, which stated that when the Prince Regent assumed the Crown, he would be the last King to sit on the Throne of England. This seemed unlikely, since next in line was the warm-hearted, popular Princess Charlotte, the Prince's only legal child. She was happy, healthy and in love with Prince Leopold of Saxe-Coburg. In May 1817 the young lovers were married and almost immediately Charlotte became pregnant - apparently ensuring the continuation of the royal line.

But, as Joanna predicted, tragedy soon hit the Royal Family. The lovely Princess, apple of the Prince's eye and second in line to the Throne, died on November 5, 1817, giving birth to a stillborn boy. Then, on January 29, 1820, King George III died after spending his last years in miserable isolation never having recovered his senses. The Prince Regent became King George IV, assuming real power and control over the land and, if Joanna's awful curse was to be fulfilled, the last King to reign over England.

The new King had domestic problems. He hated his consort, Queen Caroline, but she liked being Queen and refused to divorce him. Although not invited to take part in the Coronation, she nevertheless arrived on the porch of Westminster, only to be refused admission by embarrassed Heads of State and Church. The squabbles ended with her death on August 7,

1821. Jane Townley, thinking that now the King would be able to concentrate on serious matters, waited patiently to hear from him.

She confessed to a startled Ann Underwood that she had been having little chats with Joanna's own divine guide, who had told her that on an unspecified date she would go into a holy trance, which would be a sign to the Bishops to examine Joanna's prophecies. Ann Underwood, who had become somewhat sceptical about Joanna, nevertheless humoured her.

Jane believed she had taken over from Joanna, as God's representative on earth. When she told Foley this, he accepted it without question. His faith was as unswerving as ever. Right up to his death, in 1835, he expected the Day of Judgement was imminent. But others were jealous and suspicious of Jane. William Tozer, the rough, powerfully-voiced peasant preacher from Devon, bluntly told Jane that he saw the Devil in her and had long seen it. This hurt her, and she was advised by her Divine Guide to have nothing more to do with him.

Jane let it be known that George IV would be the last King to reign over England. When news of the prophecy reached His Royal Highness he was alarmed, because of the bad luck that had hounded his family since Joanna's death. A message came that he was very upset. William Pughe, who was acting as Jane's paid secretary as well as her doctor, hastily explained that the prophecy had been made by Joanna, not Jane, and was part of a secret communication which had been sent to a selected few. What Joanna actually meant was that George IV would be the last King to reign *under the Satanic Power.*

"Mrs. Townley is surprised that the believers did not see the manifestation of the Lord's power at the Coronation," said Pughe. "Joanna was instructed to seal up the King and half the nations that was loyal to him, when the mist was over the earth, and these words alluded to his present Majesty and not the late dead King George III. Therefore no believer is justified in condemning the King."

Pughe decide it would be a good opportunity to clear up a few other misunderstandings. When Joanna wrote about the branch that would be cut off, this referred to the Princess Charlotte. "By the event came disappointment to the nation, like the disappointment to Joanna's believers concerning her child." He added that the words "I'll surely cut your land" in one of Joanna's books was originally meant to read "I'll surely cut off your King". Because the Bishops did not "awaken" or take notice of Joanna's writings, "the sceptre was shaken" over the late King. In her Sealed Prophecies, Joanna wrote: "If Priests and Bishops do not awaken, then the King's heart I'll make tender." The sceptre (the King) was shaken by his illness and he died without being restored to his senses.

On August 24 Jane had a "mysterious and distinguished visitor" - the new King himself - who came to tell her that he had heard of her visitation and repented his sins. Jane told him God was pleased by his humility and forgave him.

"He was so overjoyed that he wept aloud," said Jane. "I then, in confidence, gave him the Key to the Writings." After he left, she wrote again that she was sure he represented the Paul (the name she now used for Shiloh).

Preparations for her proposed Trance and a new examination of Joanna's writings were well in hand. Joseph Pomeroy had been sent for, for it was assumed that when the time came for the writings to be examined, Pomeroy would be required to finally acknowledge the truth of them.

Jane Townley and Paul (the King) were to go into trances simultaneously, during which Joanna would miraculously return and lay on the bed with them, appearing "much like a ghost". She was to remain in that state until the spirit of the Lord entered her, giving her power to dispute with and pronounce decrees against Satan - to establish that Joanna was merely an instrument of God and not divine in herself.

"Who is the Man Child for the present, is concealed," she said. "But that person who is taken in a trance, at the same time as me, is the Man Child, or the Spiritual child of Joanna, who will reign and rule temporarily as the Representative of Christ and by His Spirit."

Her divine guide gave her a firm date for the trances. January 12 was the day the King would send for her - the 20th anniversary of Joanna's High House trial. She began to brood about the accusations made by some and worried that an evil spirit might be controlling her. "In my distress, before I was up this morning, I formed a plan that, if I was being deceived, I would retire to a distant part and live the rest of my days amongst strangers." As a precaution, she even arranged with a captain in the navy to command the ship "that is to take me abroad afterwards". For the next few months she worked herself into a panic and, as time passed and there was still no word from the King, consoled herself with the thought that the place and time of Joanna's Neckinger Trial in 1804 was kept secret until the day previous - in order to counteract Satan's evil.

"It was put to me - how could the Bishops become alarmed fearing they had done wrong, unless there had been circumstances or time not given nor understood by them?" On Sunday morning, January 5, she became nervously ill. Tension spread to the rest of the household and, by January

12, a general feeling of anxiety reigned. At two o'clock, after dinner had been served, Jane rose, smiled brightly and said she felt her spirits rising - then burst into tears, insisting they were "tears of joy and not of sorrow".

All evening the little group waited for the King to arrive and the *Sealed Writings*, having been taken out of the *Box*, lay on a table. The minutes ticked by and soon the night passed and it became clear he was not coming. The writings were returned to their "plain, wooden box" and sealed up again. An endorsement was added: "Enclosed are the papers which Mrs. Townley was commanded to deliver to His Majesty King George the Fourth, if he announced himself the Paul, before twelve o'clock at night of January 12, 1823."

Next day, displaying a calmness she did not feel, she dictated a letter to Dr. Pughe to be sent out to believers. "The 12th January is past, without us hearing anything. Therefore Mrs. Townley has nothing more to say. She sends her love and hopes you will not take the ways of the Lord in question. She is resigned to His Will."

She finally broke down and for days lay weakly on her bed, longing for oblivion. "Greatly oppressed in spirit by the events mentioned," she wrote miserably. "I began to think of putting into execution my plan for living in seclusion." Most disheartening was the fact that, although up to now she had been in daily communication with her divine spirit, it seemed she had been abandoned to face the humiliation alone for, after January 12, she received no direct communications.

Although fey and neurotic, Jane was basically honest and genuinely detested deceit. She needed to explain herself to the world, especially now she felt her work on earth was finished. She wrote a confession to her once close friend, the Bishop of London. Since her letters to him were always returned unopened, she offered it to the *Courier,* the *Times* and the *Morning Herald* for publication. They all rejected it. Whether or not the Bishop of London ever got to read her sad words is uncertain, but it was a genuine cry for help. She desperately wanted guidance from the Church and bewailed the fact that, when she wrote to him in 1814 about Joanna's visitation she begged him, if he thought she was wrong, to tell her in what way. "This, from our former friendship, I had a right to expect," she insisted. "But your Lordship did not even answer my letter. Therefore I concluded your silence was acknowledging me to be right."

She reminded him that, in 1814, she had promised that if ever she lost faith, she would announce it to the world. Now she found it necessary to do so. Since Joanna's death, she said, she had been guided by the same spirit and up to now everything had been perfectly fulfilled. She went on to describe how the same spirit had advised her that Joanna's writings would be demanded by a "Paul", who she believed to be the King, who would "mind no loss, nor fear no cost, but to the purpose come."

"I was told that His Majesty would summon the Bishops to take the cause in hand. But as the month of January is past, without fulfilment, I have nothing more to say." She added, with struggling pride: "I have acted upon the strictest principles, for the honour and glory of God and for the good of mankind, and I have neither disgraced myself nor my family."

She finally decided against running away and even began to think that God had been merely testing her, since many said that as a result of the disappointment, their faith, far from being weakened, had been strengthened by a new light. To her relief, on May 10, 1823, the divine voice made contact again and confirmed this.

In 1823 a meeting of the Church Council discussed Joanna Southcott's writings. Their verdict was that she was an impostor, an enthusiast and a madwoman. Jane wrote nearly seven thousand words, defending Joanna. It had been pointed out at the Council meeting that in 1805 William Pitt, then Prime Minister, had ignored Joanna's order to release Richard Brothers from prison. Joanna "removed him by death" as she did Lord Roslyn, who held similar views. Under the premiership of Charles Fox, Brothers was set free, but ironically this didn't help Fox who died on September 13 and is buried next to Pitt at Westminster. The Council unanimously decided that if Joanna had still been alive, and able to read their document about her, "she would condemn us all to a bottomless pit of misery."

In 1824 Jane wrote a book about her own communications but believers rated it as merely "interesting". There was still a lot of curiosity about *Joanna's Box*, still in her custody. "The prophecies are not in an iron chest," stressed Jane, "but in a box of common wood." She was now sealing her own writings and putting them in the *Box* alongside Joanna's prophecies.

By the end of 1823, Jane was bedridden and being looked after by Ann Underwood, who also had taken on the task of answering letters and enquiries. During their final years, there were petty quarrels between the two old women. Whenever Ann spoke her mind, revealing her common sense by voicing her doubts, Jane became petulant, accusing her of being possessed by the Devil. Jane even discussed the problem with her divine guide. "Since the death of Joanna, Underwood has not been happy," it was pointed out to her. "Satan has worked as powerfully upon her to prejudice and blind her mind against thee, as he did upon Sharp." She reported the conversation to Ann, who good-humouredly agreed it might be so. She had no wish to prolong the icy atmosphere at 17 Weston Place by denying it. Ann was very fond of Jane, but it seemed to her that her friend was gently going out of her mind.

Jane had now persuaded herself that Joanna's work - which she now confused with her own writings - would be examined, after all, on September 20, 1824 and she would be called forward before the end of the month. But during that winter, Jane's health got worse, her ramblings became wilder and eventually she died, in March 1825, without George IV contacting her. Her home at Weston Place was broken up and her possessions either sold or deposited with friends and relatives.

Ann Underwood and Dr. Owen Pughe packed her manuscripts and letters into a large tea chest. There were three other large boxes containing Joanna's writings, letters and miscellaneous papers, as well as the *Box of Prophecies*. Ann was old and, although the obvious choice to be custodian of the *Box*, she said her faith was not strong enough for the dubious honour.

She asked Thomas Foley if he would accept it and he was over the moon with pride. "With lively joy and gratitude to the Lord for this great blessing, I at once answered to say I would take the greatest care of them," wrote Foley in his diary on August 29, 1825. Consequently five boxes arrived at Old Swinford by coach and Foley was true to his word, to the point of absurdity. When his wife and some friends went on holiday to Plymouth, he refused to go with them - "Having the Ark of the New Covenant in my house, I dare not leave it," he declared stoutly.

After Joanna's death, Foley had maintained his belief in her, in Shiloh, in her *Box of Prophecies*, and in her mission, with naive and determined loyalty. Nothing, not his wife or his children, was ever allowed to come before his faith. He was as devoted to Jane, as he had been to Joanna, and was sure the divine spirit spoke through her and was prepared to obey her in all things. He expressed astonishment when Peter Morrison once refused to go on an errand for Jane to Stockport. "What is the reason he does not obey?" asked Foley with childish surprise. "For we know that obedience is better than sacrifice or than any vain imaginations of our own."

With his private income, he was able to continue his comfortable existence, suffering no real hardship bar mild harassment. Most of the time he didn't even realise he was being made fun of. Quite sure that, during his own lifetime, Joanna would return to earth with her son Shiloh, it was

238

Engraved by R. Cooper.

JOANNA SOUTHCOTT,
An Extraordinary Fanatic

This half-length portrait of Joanna was engraved by Richard Cooper, in 1822 - eight years after her death. He has made her look particularly sinister and unattractive. Being extremely vain about her appearance, she would not have liked it.

rumoured he kept a white, thoroughbred horse saddled in his stables ready for the Holy Child to ride off to the New Jerusalem.

His eccentricity often breached the point of madness, yet Foley was the only one of Joanna's seven disciples never to claim a divine experience. But, in his gullible way, he was always prepared to accept those of others. He was scrupulously honest, particularly to himself. Despite a tendency to go over the top, and a desperate desire to prove the truth of the Gospels, nothing would have induced him to say something that in his heart he believed untrue.

Perhaps this was why his faith in Joanna never wavered. He had made solemn oaths to God to obey her. To admit she was a fraud, or an impostor, was like admitting that the Scriptures were all lies, God was a myth and his own vows hollow. Therefore, having committed himself, he looked neither left nor right and stubbornly refused to listen to rational reasoning. In this way he continued at Old Swinford, with his tolerant wife and obedient children, absorbed in Joanna's writings and each day expecting a sign from God that the Day of Judgement was imminent.

John Scott, the solicitor who took part in the Neckinger Trial in 1804, sent a report that excited Foley. Scott was not the type to let his imagination run away with him. Yet he claimed he had seen Joanna's ghost. "I was laying in bed, half awake, when a sudden light came into the room and someone touched me on the shoulder and, looking round, I saw Joanna. She asked me if I had the manuscripts of the examination of witnesses at the Trial at Neckinger. She desired me to take care of them, for they would be wanted, and then disappeared. Upon which I began to consider whether or not I had been dreaming and began to doubt. But it was repeated a second time and a third time, which removed all my doubts and next morning I enclosed them in a paper, together with my Seal, and lodged them with a friend." Three days later, Scott said he lost all his books, letters and manuscripts in a fire at his home, but the papers about Joanna's Trial were safe with his friend.

Encouraged by this story, Foley waxed lyrical in a letter to James Mills, of Duke's Warehouse, Manchester: *"We are commanded by the Spirit of Truth to watch the Times, to watch the Seasons and to watch the Spirit and, whether it be true or not, to watch the Scriptures. Weigh the whole together, draw the link, lengthen the chain. See if one link will join with another. Compare the whole together. See if it adds link to link, chain to chain, like the dawning morning, higher and higher, brighter and brighter to the perfect day. Or, like a flower in bud, opening more and more until the full blown flower appears."*

The influential Foley family had not publicly disowned Thomas, but kept warily away from Old Swinford. Thomas wasn't aware he was an embarrassment to them. On July 22, 1824, he wrote cheerfully to his uncle, Lord Foley, at Witley Court, Stourbridge: "My Lord. When I returned home after a pleasant visit to Witley, I learned that Oliver and Harwood had fixed on Tuesday next to have a public dinner in your honour at the Talbot Hotel. It grieves me that I cannot make one of the party. Fourteen years ago I made a vow that I would not dine out at any public meeting, or accept any private invitation of pleasure at Stourbridge, or just around it, till after a certain event had taken place - and which has not yet been fulfilled. Still, I am certain it will come to pass, although I cannot fix the precise time - that being known only to the Almighty."

In the same letter, Foley invited his uncle to stay the night at Old Swinford Rectory. As an incentive, he added that he still had "a little quantity of De La Maine's Port in my cellar of twenty-five years old and, I hope, it is as highly flavoured as when I last had the happiness of seeing your Lordship at the Rectory". Lord Foley, still suspicious of his nephew's cranky ideas, politely declined.

Foley enthusiastically took charge of the distribution of Joanna's books and despatched by wagon from the Mitre Inn, Stourbridge, to James Mills' warehouse in Manchester, fifty copies of one of Joanna's early books. He also advised Mills that the communications to Jane Townley from Joanna's divine guide were "very weighty and highly interesting". There was a strong party in London, he said, doing everything in their power to put Jane Townley's visitations "entirely out of question".

James Mills was astonished when he heard that prints of Joanna's portrait were selling in Manchester for £1.11s.6d. "When they first came out at only 10d, I said the time would come that £20 to £50 would hardly purchase one," replied Foley with satisfaction. "Now the prints have already risen to nine times as much as they sold for at first. What will the prints sell for when it is proved to be the Lord's work?" Since Foley owned several copies of these valuable prints, he had every reason to feel smug.

As age crept up on him, Foley remained endearingly enthusiastic. He read Jane Townley's communications and saw sense in her theory that the only person in England with sufficient power to put into operation all *Southcottians* yearned for, was the King himself.

He wrote to Charles Taylor (Joanna's old favourite) in Exeter, advising him to read Jane's book dealing with George IV's role as the Shiloh. *"It is full of high thoughts and information. How I should rejoice with exciting*

*joy were our beloved Sovereign to see the works of Joanna Southcott in the
same light as we do. I only say from my heart that had he the voice of
Abraham then he would certainly embrace the Holy Cause and become the
greatest human monarch that ever sat upon the Throne."*

A Mrs. M. Waring was living in Jane Townley's old home at Weston
Place. From there she sent a distressing report about Dr. William Owen
Pughe, Jane Townley's doctor and secretary who, after her death, had made
it known he considered Joanna mad.

"His flesh seems to be unsound from bone to the shin all over him, and
so sore that he cannot bear anything to touch him," wrote Mrs. Waring.
"He is obliged to get up often in the night to shake his bed. His son has got
a down bed for him, but still he is in misery and the hollow of his hand,
from holding his walking stick, is in a dreadful state. Poor man! But I have
found that everyone that cannot believe in dear Mrs. Townley has had a
great affliction in some way."

This was a reference to King George IV, who appeared to be suffering
from the same illness as his father. Almost blind and tormented with
terrible pains in his hands and feet caused by gout, he also was said to have
dropsy - the illness that was popularly thought to have caused Joanna's
death. He died on June 26, 1830 - a bitter disappointment to Jane
Townley's followers.

But even his death was not enough to curb Foley's enthusiasm. He
concluded that it was a great pity the King had not recognised the
wonderful opportunity God had offered him, to become the greatest human
monarch ever to have sat upon an earthly throne.

Foley continued in boisterous health and unquenchable faith until he
suddenly dropped dead in September, 1835, aged 77. Without his belief in
Joanna, he might have led an empty, idle life like so many of the clever,
wealthy youths who had been at Cambridge with him. Instead, he was at
least able to devote himself to something he believed in, no matter how
misguided, which added spice and mystery to his life. Of all the people
who shadowed Joanna's life, he was the most appealing.

Joanna's other once loyal disciple, William Sharp, didn't withdraw from
the Mission but kept his distance. Not the type to suffer fools, he couldn't
bring himself to admit he had been made a fool of. As soon as was decently
possible, he handed *Joanna's Box* over to Jane Townley, along with any
other papers and relics he had. When Jane claimed she was in divine
communication, he told her candidly that he thought she was deluded. Jane
was upset when he refused to accept her as Joanna's earthly substitute, but
conveniently decided it was he who was deluded by the Devil. He put

himself out of favour at Weston Place, but remained on friendly terms with the more rational Ann Underwood.

He remained at Titchfield Street for a few years, engraving, painting and reading avidly. Because he was an amusing conversationalist, he was still invited to dinner parties. He became more and more eccentric. In his old age, he lost his hair on top of his head, but remained obsessively proud of the fringe of white locks which grew monkishly round the lower part of his skull. He refused to cut it and let it grow abundantly down the back of his head and over his shoulders. His crown was said to shine "remarkably silvery and beautiful" and he was very proud of it, refusing to wear a wig. Each morning, to prevent himself catching cold, he submerged his whole head in cold water.

Fond of good living, good food and good wine, he became fat and jolly as well as eccentric and eventually contracted gout. One of his charming theories was that every man's face resembled some creature and he enjoyed classifying his friends as Lions, Tigers, Bulls and Dogs, stipulating impishly that each man's character was invariably similar to the creature he resembled.

To earn a regular income he engraved portraits - but felt it was demeaning and once remarked that if people were so stupid as to give him large sums of money to engrave their awkward, unmeaning faces he could not help it, for he must live by his art.

Once he was pressed to engrave a portrait, from a painting, of the dead Prime Minister, William Pitt, whom he disliked intensely. He replied that no price could tempt him to perpetuate the memory of such a frightful-looking beast, for there was in him neither eagle, nor any particular beast, fish or bird, but rather an assemblage of everything disagreeable. He never applied his whimsical theory to Joanna, although she was sometimes likened to a fat-faced vulture on the watch for prey.

The idol he became enamoured by and prized more highly than he ever did Joanna Southcott, was William Hogarth, the engraver and painter - "the most extraordinary Painter that ever existed". He eventually sold his home in London and moved to Chiswick, where Hogarth lived and is now buried. It was Sharp's dearest wish to be buried in the same churchyard as the great man.

At Chiswick he lived very simply, eking out a living by doing occasional portraits and dining lavishly with friends. He died at his house in the early hours of Sunday morning, July 25, 1824, aged 74.

After Joanna's death her husband, John Smith, spend his final years in retirement at Rock Cottage, Blockley, cared for by Sarah, the child of his union with Joanna. He died on 22 December, 1829 aged 71, leaving her all his property and wealth, including Rock Cottage and the gold wedding ring containing a strand of Joanna's hair and other treasured mementoes.

Rock Cottage remained in the Smith family until 1873 when the owner, Jane Smith, died on the 22 February. According to a report in the *Evesham Journal* on Saturday, 22 March 1873, the house and all the contents were auctioned off, including many Southcottian relics such as a pair of satin shoes for the baby Shiloh embroidered in silver with the words "Prince of Salem" and "Priest of God", a short white satin cloak bordered with ermine made for Joanna, the famous patchwork quilt she made incorporating the curse on George III and the exquisite glass communion chalices made by John Pye.

John Smith is buried in Blockley churchyard. In the same plot is buried his daughter, Sarah Smith, who died on 25 January, 1858, his cousin George Troup and other members of the Smith family. Sadly (or perhaps mercifully) it seems likely Sarah was never told the truth of her birth for the inscription on the stone states that she was the daughter of John's brother, Samuel.

John Smith's Tombstone. Husband of Joanna and father of her child, he is buried with other members of his family in the graveyard at Blockley Parish Church.

The Rev. Thomas Foley
Third Custodian of Joanna's Box

Eccentric Vicar of Old Swinford and one of Joanna's most devoted disciples, Thomas Foley became custodian of Joanna's Box in 1825, after Jane Townley's death, and looked after it to the point of absurdity. *"Having the Ark of the New Covenant in my house, I dare not leave it,"* he told his wife and sent her and his family on holiday to Plymouth without him.

Samuel Jowett
Fifth Custodian of Joanna's Box

Samuel Jowett, of Bermantofts Hall, Leeds, became fifth custodian of Joanna's Box in 1861, after the death of Richard Foley. He and a friend went to fetch it from North Cadbury. Before loading it onto a train at the station, the Box was recorded as weighing 156-lb.

In a letter to his son, John, he said: *"The Box is nailed up as well as locked. We took a new cord with us to put round it for security."* Samuel died the same year and so only had custody of the Box for a few months.

Chapter 20

Turner & other Fanatics

The most bizarre of all Joanna's disciples was George Turner. When she was looking for a husband, it was he who came rushing excitedly from Leeds to say that a divine spirit had ordered him to marry her. A formidable looking man, with a large shaggy head covered with long, flowing white hair, and with piercing eyes and a blazing personality, he was the epitome of an *Old Testament* prophet. Joanna had always distrusted him, sensing he was dangerous and the one most likely to usurp her. His frequent attempts to prophesy she found irritating. On June 13, 1813, six months before she died, he wrote to say God had told him the war between Bonaparte and the Russians would cease. Joanna sharply informed him that she had also received a message from God and had been told the exact opposite

"But there is one thing in your favour that I marvel," she wrote scathingly. "It is that you should be ordered to send your news to me, before making it known to anyone else. This puzzles me, as it seems there are two spirits attending you - Satan and an Angel of Light to deceive you. But a good spirit interfered to prevent you from making it known to anyone but me."

He professed to be loyal to her and even when she died Turner's faith appeared intact. But within weeks, he was making a determined bid for leadership. Foley, Townley and others, knowing him to be a prattling, excitable extrovert with a wild imagination, ignored him.

When he claimed Joanna had paid him a visit (although remaining invisible) to say that God would speak through him, forlorn *Southcottians* took notice. Turner said Joanna's ghost stood unseen beside him, and described God: "Oh, the beauty of my Lord, the light around His throne. Who can declare the glory and the smiles streaming from His presence in holy life." Two days later he had another visit from her. This time she was visible. She said little but "her countenance was that of a happy being" and "her clothing I cannot describe, but it shone".

People in Yorkshire, Lancashire, Devon and other parts of the West Country were impressed, for they had felt bitterly let down by the non-appearance of Shiloh. Turner offered simple explanations and hope. He assured them Shiloh had been born before Joanna died, a temporal child who was alive and well somewhere in England. He was still only a baby but, when he was old enough, he would reveal himself. God had told him that as a result of the visitation of Joanna to George Turner, all other claims should be rejected - even Joanna Southcott's. For she had been ordered to lead and direct only things which happened during her lifetime and these ended with her death.

Turner published a dramatic announcement in the *Weekly Gazette.* "Earth! Earth! Hear the voice of the Lord. Prepare for the coming of Shiloh!" Having thus drummed up enthusiasm he made a rash prophecy - that the Day of Judgement would take place on January 26, 1817, when the sun would turn black and the stars fall from the sky and all who slighted God's prophet (Turner) would perish. Those who owned nothing would become Lords of the Land. Gullible people panicked, sold all their possessions and then gathered like hysterical vultures round wealthy houses, waiting for their owners to fall down dead so that they could claim their property. Carriages were even ordered to take believers to the coronation of the long expected Shiloh.

When the day arrived, nothing extraordinary happened, other than the fact that the Prince Regent, returning from opening Parliament in his carriage, was attacked by mobsters - which caused mild excitement. Turner hastily announced he had got the date wrong.

A committee was formed, headed by a Jew called Samuel Gompertz, for the Lost Tribes of Israel. It was claimed that he could tell which tribe anybody originated from so that when Shiloh, as King of the Jews, arrived there would be no confusion. Turner and members of the committee granted themselves salaries of up to £20,000. He became indiscreet, criticising the Treasury, the Horse Guards, the Royal Family and Parliament and ordering people not to pay rents, postage or taxes. He was arrested for high treason but declared insane and flung into a Quaker asylum. The Quakers believed that a quiet environment and lots of sympathy was the best cure for madness and so Turner was left very much alone, happily absorbed in planning Shiloh's new palace.

The walls were to be lined with gold, adorned with precious stones and 70,000 men would play musical instruments accompanied by 70,000 women singing. Shiloh would have 50,000 servants and his carriage was to be of pure gold. He went on to fantasise how God had ordered that His prophet, George Turner, was to be allowed 3,000 servants and a palace like Shiloh's and similar gardens and carriages.

In July 1820 he was pronounced sane and released and wasted no time regaining followers. A fondly held belief amongst Joanna's disciples was that, when she appeared again, by her side fully supporting her would be Joseph Pomeroy, the man she would dearly have loved to marry. Turner decided that, since Pomeroy would not co-operate, God had elected *him* to be Joanna's earthly husband and therefore father to Shiloh. He chose to ignore the fact, that just before she died, she married John Smith.

All who wished to be Brides of Shiloh, therefore, had to be married by him and he laid down a form of service. First the prospective bride was required to kiss Turner. Turner would return the kiss to show God had accepted her, and he would put his hand on her knee, symbolising she was ready to bow to heavenly commands. Her name was then entered into a Marriage Book. Turner, now old and lecherous, travelled throughout England by coach and the bizarre ceremony was enacted 1,556 times. Many a virgin maiden, fearful of God's wrath, allowed Turner to take further liberties than a few kisses and knee fondling.

A bizarre marriage supper took place at Westminster on August 30, when seven hundred gullible maidens, all dressed in blue, sat down to a feast (paid for by wealthy sponsors) of meat from "clean beasts" and puddings, pies, custards and plum cakes. There were at least three glasses of wine per person, so that Shiloh's health could be toasted liberally.

If he had hoped these festivities would dampen desire for Shiloh's arrival, Turner was mistaken. From all over England came demands that there should be no more delay. Reluctantly, he named a place and date - London, October 14, 1820. Shiloh was supposed to have been born when Joanna died in 1814. Therefore, he would arrive now as a boy of 6, but would be tall for his age. "He is not a god," stressed Turner, "but flesh and bone like other men."

It was a rash promise, but Turner must have had in mind a particular lad from the workhouse, because he was so specific in his description. He wouldn't have had Joanna's problem of having to produce a new-born baby. Once he'd committed himself, his enthusiasm knew no bounds. He described how the first fifteen years under Shiloh's rule would be an exciting struggle while the Holy Kingdom was established. Then would come the march to Jerusalem and the *Final Millennium*.

Believers surged to London in their thousands and crowded inside and outside the huge hall Turner had hired for the occasion. Journalists arrived to report the event. Hour by hour they waited patiently, confident that, after all these years, the Saviour would really arrive. The strange, tense atmosphere evoked visions. One person reported hearing angels singing and another said she had seen Shiloh inwardly. But the Boy Shiloh didn't turn up and Turner announced that God had deliberately disappointed them in order to test their faith.

He then invented an astonishing new tale. Shiloh's spirit had entered *his* own body and Turner was, in fact, Shiloh. But a dirty, ranting old man was no substitute for the golden youth people had been promised. Protests poured forth and Samuel Gompertz, as secretary of Turner's committee, had to hastily explain that Turner didn't actually mean he *was* the Shiloh, only that he was the adoptive father of the child, which meant he was entitled to use the same name. Until Shiloh actually arrived on the scene, Turner had divine permission to personate him. Since at some time God had said that Shiloh was to be presented as both spiritual and temporal, for the time being Turner was the visible character.

Just in case there were any lingering doubts, God issued a statement: "My son Shiloh did not appear on the 14th October as a child of flesh and bones. Neither is my servant, George Turner, Shiloh. I have placed him the adoptive father of My son, to attend him as a servant and to be spokesman to My children. Shiloh shall appear as a youth, a boy of 6 years. No other can have that character and he must appear to My children before he is revealed."

Having dealt smartly with that tricky situation Turner concentrated again on the Brides, stipulating only virgins could offer themselves to Shiloh. God had asked for sixty "Queens" (those under twenty) and eighty "Matrons" (those over twenty). They were to dedicate themselves to waiting upon Shiloh. If any of those listed married, then others would be chosen to take their place. These Brides, promised God, would receive rich inheritances from the holy kingdom. Eager maidens clamoured for the honour and Turner, being Shiloh's adoptive father and temporal manifestation, was therefore conveniently provided with dozens of desirable young women eager to please him in every way. But, despite his exalted position, he was short of funds, so God ordered believers to send him "your tokens of love" and to "increase My treasury by three hundred pounds".

Shiloh was to appear to Turner's followers before anyone else saw him, but God warned that next time He would not reveal where. Therefore, it was necessary for Turner to go on a long carriage journey, visiting towns all over the country. He was to always carry a bottle of milk and some bread to refresh the holy child. "My children must help you from place to place and pay the expenses. If there is any over, it must remain with thee and not be put into My treasury."

The suggestion was that Shiloh's spirit would travel with his father and occasionally materialise as a handsome youth. "You may go with My son, Shiloh, to Gravesend and Chatham, London, York, Northampton, Pontefract, Wakefield, Barnsley, Colne, Warrington, Tewkesbury and Ilfracombe, and I may direct you further. I lay no restraint upon thee, but shall bless those that receive My son Shiloh with kindness." So Turner set off again in the most luxurious of coaches, with a woman to comfort him. On March 10, he said the Lord told him to give ten days' notice of Shiloh's appearance and as he travelled around, he was to make use of the services of comely young women.

But there was no sign of Shiloh on the day specified and God explained if He had let Shiloh appear according to the expectations of the people, it would have been contrary to what He had promised - that He would bring forth Shiloh "in a way that will surprise all and that the faith of all would be tried".

By the middle of April, Turner found he had only £3.2s.7d. Again God ordered believers to send money to pay for Turner's expenses. Once the Kingdom of Heaven was established on earth, everyone, it was promised, would be paid double interest. The money poured in and soon Turner had the funds to continue his travels. He found a new woman, called Greenwood, to travel with and bought her a set of clothes in her favourite colour of blue, for the journey.

He then had the audacity to set a new date, May 20, for Shiloh's arrival When he didn't arrive, Turner was neither embarrassed nor remorseful. So! He was wrong again! It didn't worry him a bit. Shiloh would be coming soon, he said, and the people had to be patient. If anyone was to be pitied, it was himself, George Turner, who even God agreed had endured much suffering.

Turner had now been travelling for six months and covered over 3,000 miles. He was weary and not at all well. Stomach pains gripped him and the lurching of the carriage on the rough roads aggravated his condition. He rented a comfortable home in Leeds and went to bed and stayed there, but there was no relief. His pains got worse and soon Samuel Gompertz was obliged to issue a statement: "Mr. Turner has experienced a complaint accompanied with great pain, particularly when nature called. Blood and water are mingled together."

God said Turner's sickness would be temporary. "I have lowered thee that thou mayest endure unto the end. It is not My pleasure to afflict My children, but to try them that they may know that they must endure hardness like good soldiers and thou must know that I will afflict thee more. But be faithful and steadfast unto the end."

Each time he passed water, Turner writhed in agony and his stomach blew up like a balloon. On August 9, God told him: "Thy afflictions have been great, with an inflammation of the bladder, but thy affliction is greater to endure so that My pleasure may be known to thee."

Meanwhile, Turner's travelling bills were arriving and there was no money left to pay them. God asked for more money, this time through Gompertz. "Those that have much, send much! Those that have little, send little!"

As his illness became worse, Turner thought no more of Shiloh but only of how he could ease his pain. Finally he went into a coma and died a painful and humiliating death at the beginning of September, 1821. Shiloh's appearance on earth, at least as visualised by Turner, was indefinitely delayed.

Many of Joanna's followers had united with "false prophets that have lately risen up". A number were dangerously fanatical and opponents were often threatened with death and eternal damnation - much the same as Joanna had been wont to do. James Mills' wife wrote to Foley on February 9, 1830, warning him that one John Field was "soon to Old Swinford with his fourth book and if you do not adhere to it, you will be dead before next May". Mentioning reports that Joanna would soon return to earth to be married to "the man who the Lord has prepared for her" she enquired innocently whether "Mr. Pomeroy is still alive and if he is, how is his health?"

Colourful characters clamoured to replace Joanna and bask in her reflected glory. There was a mass of eager worshippers with no-one to worship and desperate for new or revived doctrines. Taking over from Joanna proved remarkably easy and a number of unpleasant would-be Saviours were astoundingly successful. Foley had been bombarded with letters from a lunatic fringe professing to have been in communication either with Joanna or her divine spirit. A woman calling herself Mary Joanna, the names of Foley's baby daughter who died shortly after being christened, wrote to him claiming she had been chosen to fulfil Joanna's mission.

A discharged sailor said he had read some of Joanna's writings and was intrigued by her claim that she had once seen the Devil, disguised as a black pig, destroyed in a furnace. He described how he gathered together a hundred men and women in a wood at Forest Hill and, after singing and praying, they released a squealing black pig which was savagely attacked by axes and sticks until it dropped dead.

A monstrous woman from Staverton called Mary Boon who had only one eye and a hare-lip which extended so far up her face it divided her nose into two parts, told Foley that Joanna had spoken through her. Almost illiterate, she dictated her communications to ex-London watchman, John Field, who was saying that in three years' time "there will not be a weed in the land, as they that do not believe him will be cut off." Mary Boon's religion was strict and stern. Every law in the Bible had to be obeyed no matter how inappropriate. She celebrated the Sabbath on a Saturday and, when spotted hanging out her washing on a Sunday, villagers were scandalised.

Then there was a tramp called Joseph Allman, who also called himself Zebulon and claimed to communicate with divine spirits. He wrote to Foley asking for funds for his cause, but to no avail. However, he struck lucky elsewhere when wealthy Captain William Woodley, of the Merchant Navy, sought advise from him for the sins of his youth. Woodley was so impressed by Allman that he became his benefactor, clothing him in rich garments and providing him with the latest, most fashionable coach so that he could travel round the country spreading the word.

The number of believers who had actually known Joanna was dwindling fast. As the original followers aged, they passed on all they knew to their children and grandchildren. When Joanna was alive, she would have been remarkably revered but, as the 19th century advanced, her enigmatic image grew out of all proportion. Mementos and souvenirs of Joanna abounded. Collectors clamoured to buy her autograph or original manuscripts.

As predicted by Foley, prints of her portrait fetched a high price and museums competed to acquire Joanna Southcott relics. *Kirby's Wonderful Museum* was particularly successful and bought many of the gifts donated by believers for the Shiloh. In order to pull in the crowds, they advertised her as a fanatic and impostor.

The main bone of contention amongst different groups was whether a spiritual child had actually been born in 1814 - immediately after Joanna died, and who was now alive and well living in hiding waiting for the Day of Judgement - or whether Joanna would at some future date return to finish giving birth to the promised Shiloh.

John Wroe was born in the village of Bowling, near Bradford, in 1782, his body badly deformed. Consequently, throughout childhood he was tormented and teased mercilessly. He had fits, which frightened villagers into believing he was possessed. He grew into a warped, ugly and vulgar man with a grudge against the church and society. Genuinely plagued with frightening visions, he gave babbling descriptions of what he saw. People were impressed and dubbed him a holy man.

Soon he began to believe it himself. After seeing a vision of Joanna with a child in her left arm, his reputation as a visionary was established and he began to make prophecies. He joined the Bradford *Southcottians* and, after George Turner's death, claimed the leadership, going from strength to strength. He even sailed to Spain to convert Catholics, but was promptly put on a ship back to England. Bizarre though it was, his sect flourished more strongly than the others. A tyrannical leader, his followers paid all his living expenses, including his extensive travel costs. He eventually died on a visit to Australia in 1863. Wroe was often ridiculed, particularly in Bradford and Wakefield. He criticised northerners for their lack of personal hygiene, which made him unpopular locally and at one time he was set upon by mobs and his beard half torn off, after which he prophesied grimly: **"They'll yet lie dead in heaps in Bradford."** A prophesy which, in recent years, has come chillingly true with the Bradford riots of the summer of 1995 and when Bradford City football stadium's main Valley Parade stand collapsed on May 11, 1985, crushing 56 fans to death in grim heaps and seriously injuring more than 200 others.

Then came John Ward, an Irish shoemaker blessed with native charm, eloquence and relentless energy. He spent a time in Newington Workhouse, where he had been sent for neglecting his family. He was a visionary in so far as he saw a way to escape his financial problems by setting himself up as a prophet. Renaming himself Zion Ward, he claimed Joanna's ghost visited him at Newington and then preached that he had once been the Devil but had been reborn as the Son of God, or Shiloh. Hundreds of respectable men and women were charmed by his Irish blarney and believed the rubbish he spoke were pearls of wisdom. His movement flourished until his health failed him and he died as a result of a stroke on March 12, 1837.

Joanna's close friends, Lucy and Robert Taylor, had remained faithful to her memory, as did their children, Charles, Fanny and Lavinia. Lavinia married David Jones, a Bradford printer and the couple devoted their lives to Joanna's mission.

In 1835, forty-three years after Joanna's 1792 visitation, they were hopeful her writings would at last be demanded by the Bishops, since the *Apocalypse* said that the Holy City would be trodden under foot for forty-two months. But nothing spectacular occurred and so for the next thirty years, Lavinia and her husband published twenty-one books, including unpublished manuscripts of Joanna's and a massive *Southcottian* hymn-book.

When Foley died in 1835, his son Richard, Vicar of North Cadbury, Somerset, took over the custodianship of Joanna's *Box*. Lavinia and David Jones jealously believed that they had more claim to it than he did. Lavinia was a determined woman and, when she found she couldn't persuade Richard to hand over the *Box,* decided to steal it. Dressed as a man, she walked into the Old Swinford Rectory, when Richard was out, and upstairs spotted an old deal box and thought she had struck lucky. An amused Richard Foley caught her creeping down the stairs, with the huge box balanced on her shoulders. He gleefully told her she was welcome to it - for it was not **THE BOX**, which was well hidden from the likes of her.

The claim that the *Box* has not been opened since Joanna's death is untrue. Jane Townley opened it often, to place her own writings side by side with Joanna's. And when Thomas Foley died, a large sum of money was thought to have been hidden somewhere in the house and the obvious place to look was in Joanna's *Box*. So Richard broke the straps, but found nothing but old manuscripts. He insisted he didn't break any of the seals and returned all the papers to the *Box*. Nonetheless Samuel Jowett came from the North to check the *Box* was intact and insisted that the original *Box* should be enclosed in a larger box, and this strapped up for added security.

Richard died in 1861 and Samuel Jowett became the new custodian. The *Box* was taken to North Cadbury Railway Station to be sent North. First its weight was recorded as 156-lbs. Jowett wrote that "the *Box* is nailed up as well as locked. We took a new cord with us to put round it for security".

Samuel died within months of Richard Foley and his son, John Marshall Jowett, of Apple Hall, Bradford, took charge. The Box remained in Bradford until 1898 - gathering dust and practically ignored except for a curious mouse that ate into one of the corners, making it necessary to enclose it in yet a larger box. John died in 1898 and his son, Edwin Armstrong Jowett, became the new custodian. It became an unwritten law

John Marshall Jowett
Sixth Custodian of Joanna's Box

John Jowett, of Apple Hall, Bradford, became sixth custodian in 1861, on his father's death. There was alarm when it was discovered that a mouse had gnawed its way into one corner of the Box, so it was encased in yet another larger box and thoroughly strapped and padlocked.

Edwin Armstrong Jowett
Seventh Custodian of Joanna's Box

Edwin Jowett became seventh custodian on the death of his father in 1898, when Edwin promised solemnly to preserve the "Treasured Writings" for posterity. To protect it from idle curiosity, it became an unwritten law that the location of the Box should be known to as few as possible and all sorts of false trails were laid to put people off the scent.

that information about the location of the *Box* be known to as few as possible and all sorts of false trails were laid to put people off the scent. Edwin kept the *Box* for many years in the modest bungalow he and his wife Emily retired to in Morecambe, which he called "Southcott".

A number of rich people became involved in promoting interest in the *Box*. John Pye, a well-known landscape engraver with a large fortune, spent his money on his two obsessions - the Royal Academy and formal recognition of Joanna and her work. It was he who, in 1804, made the two magnificent engraved glass Communion Chalices for Joanna, now on display at the Royal Albert Museum, Exeter.

Mrs. Anne Essam, a wealthy Hampton Court *Southcottian*, built a *Southcottian* chapel in her garden. She died in 1844, leaving all her wealth and property "to be dedicated to the printing, publishing and distributing of the writings of Joanna Southcott". Her family contested the Will on the grounds that Joanna's writings were indecent and immoral and that the Will was therefore void by the *Statute of Mortmain* - an ancient law forbidding the alienation of land to religious corporations.

Master of the Rolls, Sir John Romilly's assessment of Joanna when he gave judgement, is interesting to note: "Joanna Southcott is shown by her writings to have been a sincere Christian and her works, though confused and incoherent, are written with a view to extending the influence of Christianity. I cannot therefore invalidate the Will by reason of the tendency of the writings. She was, in my opinion, a foolish and ignorant woman of an enthusiastic turn of mind, who had long wished to become an instrument of God to promote some great good upon the earth. By constantly thinking of this, it became in her mind an engrossing and immovable idea until at last she came to believe that her wish was accomplished and that she had been selected by the Almighty for this purpose. Her personal disputations and conversations with the Devil, and her inter-communications with the spiritual world, I found very foolish but nothing likely to make people who read them immoral or irreligious."

However, he decided it did fall within the limits forbidden by the ancient law, and so the Court ruled in favour of Miss Essam's relatives and plans to produce an expensive edition of her works had to be shelved.

T. Hudson and the Birmingham *Southcottians* concentrated not on Shiloh, as did the more outrageous believers, but more realistically on getting *Joanna's Box* opened. Pye and his group and Hudson and his group were wealthy and sensible. But all sorts of strange people tried to jump on the bandwagon. Often they were from unsavoury backgrounds, such as the massively fat and repulsive Mrs. Ferrier, permanently drunk on rum who sat at the feet of an iron cast of Christ, throwing herself into trances and howling out messages of doom and despair.

In a back alley in Lambeth, an unpleasant woman in a dazzling robe posed as the "woman clothed with the sun". Chanting constantly, she sat on a stuffed black pig, which represented the Devil. Then there was the Wandsworth woman who hid behind a heavy veil and refused to reveal her name, but sent disciples out collecting names for a petition to destroy Satan.

But strangest of all was a mystery man, posing as a humble private in the 16th Regiment, who walked into the John Wroe headquarters in Chatham one day in 1875, unshaven and radiating a carefully cultivated air of mystery. He introduced himself as "The Stranger" but his real name was James White. Shortly afterwards he received divine orders to re-organise the Society. Leaders resented his interference and kicked him out. Undeterred he started a schism group, taking with him sixteen members, compiled a book called the *Flying Roll*, and proceeded to form a New Jerusalem in Chatham. From all over the world, people came to join him, selling their possessions and handing over their wealth to the new prophet.

He renamed himself Jezreel and bought twenty acres of land in Gillingham to build a terrace of houses for the faithful to live in, followed by a chain of shops. Soon he was director of an impressive number of thriving businesses - Jezreel Baker, Jezreel Butcher, Jezreel Greengrocer etc. He also built a successful college for Boys and Girls and treated himself and his wife, Esther, to a luxury house overlooking the Thames Estuary.

He went to Australia to spread the word, leaving his wife in charge of his empire. After a year, he returned with magnificent plans to build an enormous Temple on the brow of the hill above Gillingham - a hundred feet high, a hundred feet wide and a hundred feet long. The ground floor was to hold presses for printing his publications and there was to be a handsome Assembly Hall to seat 6,000 and the top storey was to house Jezreel's huge trading administration. Because he planned to use it throughout the *Final Millennium*, he built the palace to last, using cement instead of mortar for durability, with walls strengthened with ribs of steel girders.

Work started in October 1884 but, six months later, he died. His wife Esther had to manage his empire. She did a better job than her husband, bringing in various members of her family to help, opening new chapels, starting a monthly magazine and sending squads of believers knocking on doors all over the country, canvassing for support and funds. Under her management, the new building progressed - but she died three years after her husband, aged only 28. Her father took over, but didn't have the charisma of Esther and Jezreel and soon the Society was in dire straits under his bad management. The money ran out and the new Temple was never completed. But the teachings of John Wroe and James Jezreel survive today, in the *Panacea Society,* in Bedford, who believe that, together with Richard Brothers and Joanna Southcott, they form a series of prophets sent by God to prepare the world for the *Final Millennium.*

There were still those who held the unlikely view that Joseph Pomeroy, long since dead, would return at the same time as Joanna and the two would at last marry. John Vincent rejected the idea. On August 28, 1853, he wrote: "We are told why the Lord kept her single. To try and win him and in this was her obedience complete. She was ready to wed him and submitted to God's directions. But not so Pomeroy. He hadn't the courage to come forward in this manner. Had Pomeroy complied with the directions given him in 1813 (to marry Joanna) he would then have been an exalted character and I believe the Kingdom would have been established long since."

Towards the end of his life Pomeroy, despite enjoying good health, became terrified of catching an influenza virus that was rampant at the time, and confined himself to his bedroom, refusing to come downstairs. One day, however, a doctor friend called to enquire about his health. He ventured down out of politeness and within a few hours became ill and died. In his Will he asked to be buried in a stone coffin so that his dust should never run the risk of mingling with Joanna's. The lid of his coffin was fastened with iron bolts, let in with lead, to ensure his remains stayed put.

Southcottian Groups had become established in New Zealand, Australia, the United States, South Africa and Canada but, by the beginning of the twentieth century, interest began to wane. The surprising thing was that the Movement survived, not amongst the poor, but the wealthy and educated.

A strong feeling prevailed that the world had suddenly become wicked and unmanageable. As a result of modern weaponry wars were more horrific than any in history. Natural disasters occurred, which people read as signs from God.

Scientists such as Charles Darwin were producing blasphemous theories about the origins of Man and people felt uneasy without a reassuring promise of an afterlife. It was a relief to escape from this hopeless scientific view of creation, by turning to old fashioned, hellfire religion with its simple story of earth's divine creation.

Before examining how the Southcottians survived into the 20th century, it is interesting to note how Daniel Jones, a wealthy Quaker, from the Midlands, unwittingly summed up the effect Joanna Southcott had upon 19th century England.

"We have to see and duly appreciate the historical fact that we, who saw our King George III smitten with madness and driven from his throne in 1809, stand in the self-same relation to God as the Babylonians when their King Nebuchadnezzar was smitten and driven from his throne. Our King was kept in that state until his death.

"So, when King George III was slain in 1820, King George IV preserved the Kingdom until Joanna brought on his destruction in 1830. In the early days he married a Roman Catholic, Mrs. Fitzherbert, and in his last year he signed away the Protestant of his Kingdom in 1829. Within one year from this, God smote his hands and his feet, so that he died."

Towards the end of the 19th century, clever women read Joanna's writings and were interested. Feminism was about to emerge and women suffragettes were preparing to display incredible courage, demanding more freedom of expression. The time was ripe for a revival of interest in this strange, 18th century peasant woman.

Chapter 21

Revival of Interest

The *Southcottian* movement more or less died down and might never have got going again had it not been for four fey women - Alice Seymour, Helen Exeter, Rachel Fox and Mabel Barltrop. All four wrote brilliantly and seemed convincingly inspired. Each discovered Joanna independently and, as a result of their common interest, communicated with each other and thrived on each other's enthusiasm. It was directly due to them that Joanna's name survived into the 20th century.

Initially they were sceptical. Rachel Fox and Helen Exeter were particularly critical of Joanna, objecting to her "babbling verses" and long-winded prose. Yet some of the spiritual experiences claimed by these women rival those of Joanna.

The most bizarre of the four was Mabel, a clergyman's widow and mother of four. Once she latched on to Joanna she took the whole issue to heart and made herself ill. On hearing that the Bishops wouldn't open *Joanna's Box*, she went into hysterics and lost all sense of reality and her family committed her to a mental institution. During her time there she came into contact with Rachel Fox and Helen Exeter - amongst the few prepared to regard her as sane.

Alice Seymour was the first to rediscover Joanna. Born in 1855, she was a refined gentlewoman, descended from the Dukes of Somerset. Her parents were well-off members of John Wroe's Church, whose doctrine included a belief in Joanna's divine visitation. The family had some early editions of Joanna's printed pamphlets and the verses in particular enthralled her.

One October morning, in 1899, she woke with a powerful conviction that God wanted her to write a poem about the joys of the *Final Millennium*. Inspiration positively flowed and the final result was a long poem in seven sections, which she called *Radia*, published under the

Rock Cottage, Blockley, Glos.

Joanna shared this cottage, on and off, for ten years with John Smith and claimed it was where her son, Shiloh, was immaculately conceived. Alice Seymour bought it in 1919 and established it as the Headquarters of the Southcottian Society.

pseudonym Alec C. More, a pun on her own name. It was well received, particularly amongst educated women just beginning to make noises about equal rights and women's suffrage.

Alice was living in Plymouth, wealthy in her own right, having inherited several properties from her parents. She was an ardent feminist, believing passionately in better education for women, investing her money in a school for girls - Headland College, Plymouth - with herself as headmistress.

Alice struck up a friendship with the Rev. Walter Begley, of Hampstead, grandson of the Rev. Thomas Webster, one of Joanna's seven original disciples. His ambition was to revive interest in Joanna and so he was delighted that Alice shared his passion. The old man had inherited a collection of Joanna's pamphlets and original manuscripts. The two planned to write a book about Joanna but, before this could be done, he died in 1905. With his death, Alice's interest in Joanna intensified. The school no longer satisfied her. A much more splendid purpose seemed to be beckoning. In November 1907, God told her she must write the book herself. For weeks she considered it, unsure that she was up to the task. The thought of doing it, without Walter Begley, was daunting. People might have listened to him, but who would take notice of a woman with dubious talent? Then she read that the work begun by Joanna Southcott had to be finished by a woman. It dawned on her that nobody was as well qualified to do this as herself.

On December 8, 1907, she wrote: "Silence can hold me no longer. I am constrained to pick up my pen and begin to write a book and to publish to the world what a mistake has been made in rejecting, without examination, the writings of Joanna Southcott. If people knew of the vast mines of treasures God has laid bare to mankind in her writings, they would be impelled to dig deep themselves."

From that day on, with quaint sincerity, Alice devoted her life to God and "Mother Joanna", becoming jealously possessive of her. Even her verses, considered by most to be clumsy and uncouth, Alice convinced herself were cleverly constructed "some portions will bear comparison with the finest passages that have ever been written".

Alice travelled the country, buying anything remotely connected with Joanna. She acquired some original manuscripts from the Foley family which included Thomas Foley's diary, a great deal of contemporary correspondence and a rare copy of Joanna's handwriting. As well as manuscripts and pamphlets, she bought or was given relics - the engraved glass chalices by engraver John Pye, and the famous patchwork quilt made by Joanna which incorporated the dreadful curse upon George III.

In 1905 she missed an opportunity to buy a printed portrait of Joanna by William Sharp, from the Old Curiosity Shop, 33 Cranbourne Street, London. The *National Portrait Gallery* bought it! But, in 1913, she acquired the original copper plate on which engraver, William Sharp, etched Joanna Southcott's portrait from life. She sold prints from it, not for one guinea, as charged by Joanna in her lifetime, but at the bargain price of five shillings. The *National Portrait Gallery* put Joanna's portrait on display, labelling her an impostor. After Alice complained to the NPG committee, the word impostor was replaced with prophetess.

By 1909 she had published her book, *The Express*, in two volumes, sold her girls' school to a Mrs. Normington and retired to a cottage in Yelverton, Dartmoor. There she concentrated on more research, convinced that God had cut short the sixth millennium as a punishment to Satan and therefore it was likely that the *Final Millennium* would begin soon. She decided, like Joanna and Jane Townley before her, that she had been chosen to prepare the world for the coming of the New Messiah, Shiloh.

Alice retraced Joanna's movements, visiting every place she had ever been to. Amongst these was the village of Blockley, in the heart of the Cotswolds, where Joanna had lived at Rock Cottage during her last ten years. When Alice saw the cottage, with its strange Monkey Puzzle tree in the front and the odd, pyramid shaped windows, she fell in love with it. She knew at once that, more than anything in the world, she wanted to live there and establish it as the headquarters of the *Southcottians*. What better place to house the relics and papers she had collected, than the idyllic cottage where Joanna was said to have immaculately conceived Shiloh.

The owner was Ellen Bull, daughter-in-law of Nicholas Bull, of Saffron Walden, who had been a First Follower. The two women spent hours talking about Joanna. Ellen told stories she had heard as a child, from village folk who remembered when Joanna lived at Rock Cottage. On warm summer evenings she would apparently promenade along a paved walkway built over a fast running stream in Blockley High Street. It was the route she would have taken to the parish church, and it was then known amongst the villagers as "Joanna's Walk". Ellen also told Alice about a secret underground passage leading from the cottage to the old coach house.

Ellen died in 1912 and was buried in Blockley churchyard. By 1919 Alice had sold her home in Yelverton and moved into Rock Cottage, using the coach house as a store for her collection of Southcottian papers and relics. There she was joined by Mary Robertson, a jolly, sharp-witted Scotswoman, a graduate from St. Andrew's university who had been a member of Alice's teaching staff at Headland College. Amongst her helpers was Annie Veysey, a City Bank clerk, who came to Blockley most weekends, and John Muir Stitt and his wife, devotees of John Wroe and James Jezreel. The Stitt family owned a printing works in Clockhouse Lane, Ashford, Middlesex and it was from here that Alice's first *Southcottian* magazine was printed.

John Stitt was a handsome, kindly man. He and his wife were deeply committed to Joanna Southcott and Alice Seymour and were prepared to work long and hard for the Cause. His son, John Stitt junior, remembers Alice Seymour visiting them at Ashford. Once she brought with her an elaborately embroidered gown, which she said had been specially made for the Shiloh, and little John Stitt junior was made to stand on a chair while she dressed him up in it, to see what the holy child might have looked like.

Rachel Fox and Helen Exeter read her book, became curious and wrote to her. Through these two, Alice began writing to Mabel Barltrop, at the mental asylum where she was having treatment. Alice didn't approve of their involvement with spiritualism, pointing out to them that Joanna had discouraged Elias Carpenter's attempts to set up a Spiritualist Church. But they replied that it was too late, for they were already in touch with the spirits. Alice was particularly wary of Mabel Barltrop. Some of her claims and beliefs were so outrageous, Alice felt it was possible that she was influenced by the Devil. For this reason, she didn't want her own *Southcottian* group associated with Mabel's.

Rachel visited Alice in November, 1914, having read some of her leaflets about Joanna, and asked to know more. They spent four solid hours "plunged deeply into the mystery". Rachel noted later: "Miss Seymour is clearly inspired by her work. She said it was foretold that powerful helpers would be raised up in this tenth year of the work and seemed disposed to consider me as a harbinger of good things to come." Her talk with Alice convinced her and on November 19, 1914, at midnight, she wrote ecstatically: "Joanna Southcott has the key to the mystery of the *Revelation.*"

Born in 1858, Rachel Fox was sensitive and intelligent, descended from generations of Quakers. At 26 she married a Falmouth clergyman, whose great grandfather, George Fox, founded the Quaker Society in 1647. They had three sons and four daughters, and her life was fairly ordinary until tragedy struck when Rachel was thirty six. Her first born son died of typhoid fever at the age of ten. For a time she was inconsolable. Then she decided that to immerse herself in sorrow was unfair to the rest of her family. So she turned to writing as a consolation. One morning, as she sat down to write, she said her pen began to move of its own accord across the paper and the result was a wistful verse from her dead son, admonishing her for shutting him from her thoughts.

"Have you forgotten me, Mother,
Since three years we parted?
Oh! How sad you looked then, Mother.
And seemed so lonely hearted.
While I seemed lifted from pain,
And endless weary dreaming,
Into motherly arms again -
A place of heavenly seeming.
HE thought by taking me up here,
You would not let your gaze grow dim,
He sends this message to you, Mother.
If you think less of me, won't you think less of Him?"

With tears streaming, Rachel read the verse over and over to herself, and then wrote beneath it:

"Thank you darling, for your message,
From the Heavenly Home above.
It shall do its work and draw me closer,
This very hour, unto His love."

Rachel reflected on "the mystery the loss of a first born child is to parents" and later said that both she and her son had good reason to rejoice in the separation "which at first was so hard to bear". Fifteen years later she visited a woman "with great psychic gifts, taught by her father to use them only for holy things" who put her in touch spiritually with her son. He told her he had only been "lent" to her to prepare her for some important work she had been singled out to do for God. Relieved, she wrote another verse to her dead son.

"You were ever God's dear token,
Hung upon our hearts to cheer,
And when on earth, the chain seemed broken,
His Spirit took the broken ends up there.

And though the link is out of sight,
It never can be sundered more.
But down the Spirit's ladder, as an angel bright,
Our boy shall enter at our chamber door."

From then on she was convinced her dead child was responsible for her "inspirational" writings. Rachel was told by her son's spirit to read the Apocalypse. Then a friend sent her leaflets containing some of Joanna Southcott's verses and asked for her opinion. Rachel had never heard of Joanna and replied that she thought there were modern revelations of far greater value which would be more likely to appeal to this generation.

"Although I can sympathise with this woman's call to write, I think she is too artless a person to be accepted by the present world with its wisdom. These writings of one hundred years ago, amused me rather than arrested my attention. The poetry is almost too quaint for sober perusal."

Despite her spiritual experiences regarding her dead son, Rachel said she was level headed and her life unremarkable. "The more ordinary our lives seem to be, the less food there will be for the sceptic."

Helen Exeter was born in 1851, daughter of an English General. When she was 16 her mother died, leaving seven children. Their father, at a loss to know what to do with his large, motherless family, married Helen off to a military friend and by the time she was seventeen she was a mother herself. "I was a half-educated child," she wrote wistfully. They settled in South Africa, where they and their growing family went through the horrors of the Boer War, living on a remote farm surrounded by the enemy.

When she first came into contact with Rachel Fox she was a widow, her children grown up and married, and she was living a reclusive life in a haunted house in the Natal, with a Kaffir servant who she believed was responsible for evil spirits surrounding them. Spending so much time alone, she became interested in spiritualism when, she said, several angels of God began to visit her regularly. She knew them all by name, the principal one being St. Andrew. Under his direction, she was writing a book about a spirit friend she called Media, "a child with almost unparalleled psychic gifts". St. Andrew had been assigned the job of rescuing her from the lower forces, for training, protection and utilising of her gifts.

Apparently a group of twelve good spirits had battled for twelve months with evil powers, who had tried to seize her gifts for their own ends. Helen told no one of these experiences for fear she would be thought mad. In 1913 a friend in England sent her a copy of a book written by Rachel, and she immediately recognised a kindred spirit. "Since I received your book," she wrote, "I can hardly tell you the joy it has given me. We are workers in the same field."

For the next two years, the two women corresponded, pouring out their innermost thoughts to each other. St. Andrew told Helen he approved of the friendship, having read Rachel Fox's books, and confirmed that her work was inspired by God. "Whether she knows it or not," said St. Andrew, "she is psychic and guided by a clever guide. Unto her will come one of the greatest blessings of the age."

He pointed out that Helen too had been chosen for a divine assignment, at present hindered by a terrible incursion of evil spirits whose only object was to prevent the work. There was also a band of astrals - nine in number - to guard her. All these powers came from an immeasurable distance. Helen was told she was enveloped in an atmosphere so dense that at times her angels couldn't penetrate and had to retreat.

St. Andrew continued: "You appear to be in a thick cloud, which beats around you, occasionally lifting, so that we see you as through rain or a moving white mist. This is a protective atmosphere which is thrown over you. It should be as clear as crystal, or like a rainbow, but the outer circle of evil which tries night and day to reach you, discolours this as if by dirty smoke and may give a feeling of heavy weight to the body."

She was warned that if she tried to leave the house, the evil would increase in her absence and when she returned she would find herself in great danger.

"My own belief," she confided to Rachel, "is that the chief object of the attack of evil is to disable me mentally and physically, in order to prevent me becoming an instrument of the Higher Powers."

One day St. Andrew told her that the spirit child Media's gifts were to be transferred to her. This new power was different from what she was accustomed to. "It is more gradual in coming, softer, fuller and really indescribable. A peculiar sense of tenderness and love and comfort is given and the message is more clear. In leaving me, it seems to melt slowly away as a snowflake in one's hand might do."

Despite her own astonishing experiences, she found the energy to leap to Joanna's defence. "I do wish the *Box* was opened, but never will twenty-four Bishops in these days of ecclesiastical opposition to spiritualism, combine to demand it, unless they do so to expose the fraud. Might we not gratefully suggest this?"

Envious of Helen's familiarity with the spirits, Rachel plagued her with questions, asking how she was able to distinguish between her various visitors. "How does St. Andrew make you feel his power differently from the others? I can't think how you can tell."

Helen replied: "It is, in a sense, as one distinguishes one voice or one touch from another when in darkness." Once, she said, Jesus Christ spoke to her.

It was the start of the First World War and her spirits daily brought her news of events leading up to the War, several days before they happened. "I have been told for weeks that a mighty spiritual warfare is being waged at the same time, and that the armies of the Lord meet in terrific conflict with the legions of the Prince of Darkness. The Heavenly Ones are continuously engaged in works of mercy for the souls and spirits of the slain and for the heart-broken women of the stricken countries and for those hideously maltreated." Some of the mightiest angels were assembling to deal with these atrocities and two of her favourite spirits, Hermaeces and Hesperion, were of that number and had departed three or four months previously on such a mission, although St. Andrew was still around to console the afflicted.

On November 15, 1914, Helen was told to write to the Archbishop of Canterbury asking him to open Joanna's Box, even though at the time she had no true convictions about her.

"I don't know what you will think of me when I tell you I cannot read Joanna's poetry. I try to overcome my distaste, but it is no use. Directly she returns to prose, the divine light shines forth again, though still marred in some degree by the style, which is hers and had to be used by the unseen, as speech might be forced through a tongue with an impediment."

On December 10, 1914, came a strong communication relating to "a spirit man-child that was to be born". Both she and Rachel were chosen vessels, but she hadn't been told how or why. When Rachel mentioned Helen's communication to Alice Seymour, she was warned that "it might be engineered by the lower world".

Wrote Helen: "These words are like arrows that pierced my heart. You cannot guess how wounded I have been by that suspicion in her mind. Is it not strange that she, who has stated that it was foretold that unlooked for support would be given, should thus slight it when it comes?"

She supposed Rachel was to bear the holy child but, on February 16, 1915, the spirits told her it was she, Helen, who had the honour. "That I, so unworthy, have been destined from the beginning of things to be the chosen vessel for this great marvel," she wrote passionately. "It seems such a presumption, yet some inner spring of life tells me I must believe and accept it. It makes me quake lest you should think me mad."

Rachel's spirit guide confirmed that one of them was to be the mother of John the Baptist and the other of the Prince of Peace, and they were to "share one another's holy secrets". Rachel was relieved, for she considered she had already given birth to John the Baptist (her dead son).

"I saw no way in which I could receive a holy child and bring him up. In your position this is feasible," she told Helen.

On March 25 she sent some writings of Joanna's to Helen saying: "These must speak for themselves. Joanna has a trying style at times. Her experiences are like those of the Hebrew prophets and not even they were quite on such familiar terms with God."

Helen eventually set sail for England, and arrived in June 1915 to stay with friends in Exeter. Soon after, Helen and Rachel discovered simultaneously that neither of them were to be Mother to a holy child, but both were to mother the mortal woman in whom the child was to be made manifest.

This was Mabel Barltrop, but she was in a lunatic asylum protesting: "I am perfectly, horribly sane but I am too full of dread to ever be myself again."

Chapter 22

The Panacea Society

Mabel Barltrop was born in 1866, the youngest of the four women. Mother of two sons and two daughters, she came from a family whose women were "remarkable for their brilliant mentality". As a young girl she had been a close friend of John Ruskin and other literary lions. Widow of an Anglican curate, the family home was in Bedford.

One day, while walking in the street, she was handed a leaflet, written by Alice Seymour, urging the Bishops to open *Joanna Southcott's Box*. It was the first time she had heard of Joanna Southcott. It made her angry to think that someone's writings were not being read because of the stubbornness of the Bishops.

She had influential friends in the Church and she wrote to everyone she knew, and those she didn't know, pleading with them to open the *Box*. "How can the Bishops be so cruel?   So terribly cruel?"

She had always been highly-strung, hovering on the point of insanity. The plight of *Joanna's Box* plunged her into deep mental despair. Unable to control her, her family had her committed. From the asylum, she continued to write vigorous letters to the Bishops. Some fell into the hands of her doctors, who decided her delusions were worsening and placed her in solitary confinement. Her letters were anguished pleas for understanding. It drove her to distraction that what she saw as the simple truth, could not be grasped even remotely by intelligent people.

"Don't write me warning letters," she wrote angrily to her friends.

Rachel heard of Mabel as a result of her own efforts to get the Box opened. She contacted her at the asylum and Mabel replied cautiously: "I am level-headed and have been guided carefully for a long time. I have four children, so I need to get home, but I feel I must be in the wilderness a little longer."

"Southcott",
Harwarden Avenue, Morecambe

For many years Joanna's Box was kept hidden in this modest bungalow in Morecambe, built for their retirement by Edwin Armstrong Jowett and his wife, Emily. They called their new home "Southcott" but, says his granddaughter, Emily Nicholson, few folk really knew why. The Box remained there until Edwin's death in 1926. At some time the final "t", in the name on the gate, fell off and had not been replaced when this snapshot was taken.

Her letters revealed her fiery spirit. "When I came into her life," said Rachel, "she was like a bird beating its wings against the bars of a cage, which prevented her soaring into the blue heavens."

Mabel wrote: "The Bishops think I am deranged and they are sheltering themselves for the present behind that belief. If my letters to them of the last fourteen weeks are those of a lunatic, all I can say is that it is a pity they are sane."

There was another burning issue obsessing her, apart from *Joanna's Box*. It was over a hundred years since Joanna's death and it seemed to her time Shiloh made an appearance. She accepted that he had been born spiritually in 1814 and had been hovering around all this time waiting to house himself in an earthly body.

On June 11, 1916, as war was raging in Europe, Mabel told Rachel: "It is not Joanna who is so important, as it is important to find the child." She wrote a poem for children:

> Oh Shiloh, thou our rest,
> Come on the Seventh Day.
> To living waters, pastures green,
> Lead thou the heavenly way.
> The Virgin Mother bore,
> The Christ the Jews refused.
> An Englishwoman bore the Child,
> Whom Gentiles will not choose.

She missed her own children and wrote impassioned letters to them . "I simply pine for home and all of you. But I had work to do which is nearly underway. Try to stand up for Mother through thick and thin, and know that God has been leading her Himself to do a bit of difficult work. Now I want you to try and picture what an awful thing this was for me, because I knew it was making me ill, spoiling all the great work, because I had no outlet and we *must* express ourselves.

"You would find, if you did not do things and only thought them, that your brain would get hot and disturbed. I want to be open with you. I have been shown that I have great mental activity and that my quick perceptions are of use to God."

Meanwhile, she was spiritually conducting the war. "I have steadily commanded the war alongside God. I ordered the evacuation of Belgium and the paper said next day that this was miraculous, for the general had not thought of movement in that area. I have ordered that Germany be reduced to States again without any combined military, naval, aerial, commercial, scientific, educational or political power, and that Turkey be eliminated from Europe and that Satan shall go to Hell!"

Shut up in a room alone she wrote that she was "daily faced with the awful dread of losing my mind. I begged, in writing, to lose anything but my reason. It is awful here. There is common talk about suicide and how to accomplish it. No one can understand who is not here, so don't try!"

Rachel was now writing to her regularly, like a mother dealing with a petulant child. "Relax and give your mind a chance to be perfectly restored," she urged. But Mabel was not prepared to relax - it was an alien state for her and detrimental to her spiritual work.

"I regard advice, when it is opposed to my vision, as being of the Devil," she warned Rachel tersely.

She tried "automatic writing" to try to contact Joanna's spirit and then, like a small child, apologised to Rachel for doing so. "I hope I did not do anything risky. I did not feel frightened. I think I should have been afraid if it was wrong. If I could only be sure I was not talking to myself. You see, I have such a terribly quick brain. It is awfully quick. I know things before I am wanted to."

Rachel sent some of Mabel's letters to Helen Exeter. After reading them, she wrote back: "She is abnormal, yet her brain is not only brilliant but sound. I think there is a danger of her being affected solely through her temperament, which is unbalanced and is a mass of quivering nerves. She is like a beautiful vessel of perfect lines, proceeding through storms in trackless waters without ballast and therefore ever in peril of capsizing. I think she would have more success if she were to write less sensational letters generally. All the same, her incisiveness and fervour are effective. A little veiling might enhance them and prevent jarring. However, I am not sure she can tone herself down and she might spoil it if she did!"

Using her influence, Rachel got Mabel released from the asylum on September 18, 1916. Mabel was frantically grateful. "I want you and Helen Exeter to consider me as a possession of yours, but I hope I shall not prove a white elephant."

Helen and Rachel had privately agreed to "take Mabel on", convinced she had some part in the work God had singled them out for, and they saw it as their divine task to make sure Mabel regained her sanity. "Her mind is as a field that hath been over-cultivated," Helen and Rachel were warned by their separate spirits. "Let her take counsel of her appointed human guides."

Like two anxious mothers, they exchanged letters of sympathy. "You are a gallant defender of poor Mabel," wrote Helen. "She hardly knows how strong a tower you are to her. I feel the motherly tenderness to her that I would for a poor sick child whom one saw battling with fears. Satan wants her for she possesses decided and brilliant gifts and we shall have to fight for her."

On April 23, 1917 came news that Mabel's eldest son had been killed fighting. "I had a lurking fear that our brilliant and versatile friend might go off balance," Rachel noted.

Although Helen Exeter was now in England, she and Mabel had never met despite their intimacy. But a tremendous rapport had built up between the three women, similar to that which had existed between Joanna Southcott, Ann Underwood and Jane Townley. Rachel and Helen, like Jane and Ann towards Joanna, were tolerant of Mabel's madness, believing it divinely inspired.

Mabel played one "mother" off against the other. Helen, who tried to keep her in line, particularly irritated her.

"I did not know Helen was so warm-tempered," complained Mabel to Rachel. "She has not sufficient belief in Joanna's visitation. She has blown her candle out. I am very sorry, as I believed she was going to get a great light on Joanna. It has nothing to do with holiness. Helen is as likely to get mixed up with a Satanic agency as I am. While Satan reigns, there is no perfect immunity. If this is not the case, then Joanna's visitation is full of errors."

She added slyly, "Thanks, Rachel, for *your* steady kindness throughout." Then she wrote in February, 1918, to Rachel. "You can help me by taking a firm stand with Helen once and for all. I feel her lack of understanding. It hurts!"

In an effort to iron out the irritation between them, Rachel suggested to Helen: "Mabel is an enigma to both of us and herself. The Lord has some method behind her madness, or in what seems her madness to us." Mabel was also jealous of Rachel's contact with Alice Seymour, who she felt was taking the credit for the renewal of interest in Joanna.

"Perhaps Miss Seymour's views are more acceptable to you and we shall have to go our separate paths for a bit, but it will make no difference - the parting will only be temporary and very harassing to me, while you will have to hurry violently after me and climb the hill alone, when we might as well ascend together."

Another time she wrote with exasperation: "You and Miss Seymour need the capacity to realise where the manger of the spiritual child may be found. I have been trying to make you see this for nearly eight weeks and it is very exhausting."

She had now convinced herself that Shiloh had become manifest in her own body and she *was* the Shiloh. What *they* thought was that she would one day give birth to Shiloh. By 1918 she had set up office at her home in Bedford, appointed a secretary and a treasurer and started gathering in the names of believers - aiming at 144,000, as stated in the *Book of Revelation.* She called herself **Octavia** because the shape of the number eight represented the body of a woman. In Revelation it was said there were eight angels, or prophets. She believed these included **Richard Brothers, Joanna, George Turner, John Wroe, James Jezreel, and Shaw.** She considered herself the eighth - the Shiloh - but said she did not know who was the seventh.

Like Joanna, she required believers to swear to obey her as God's representative. "Of course, this does not mean you are to be guided by me. I don't want to guide anyone. I am too tired."

Her campaign to persuade the Bishops to open the *Box* intensified and she wrote frantic letters to them. Rachel and Helen, fearing she would be considered mad, were concerned. "Her letters are too wordy, too much about her own feelings and conditions to have been purely received," said Rachel.

Rachel was friendly with two influential people, - Lady Portsmouth and the elderly Bishop William Boyd-Carpenter - once a favourite of Queen Victoria and now Canon of Westminster. These two were sympathetic, although not professing to be believers. Boyd-Carpenter was kindly and understanding, for it seemed to him that, if so many people genuinely wanted *Joanna's Box* opened, whatever the contents and whatever the reasons, it was only right that their wishes should be met. A letter came from him saying he had the names of 24 Bishops or their representatives, all willing to open the *Box*, in the Jerusalem Chamber at Lambeth, on March 6. "We hope this will all be carried through satisfactorily and that we are approaching the end of our labours," he added kindly.

But Mabel's mob had reckoned without the formidable Alice Seymour, the only person who seemed to know where the *Box* was, and she was not prepared to tell. She explained she had discussed the offer with the custodian and they had agreed that the arrangements did not comply with conditions stipulated by Joanna.

Rachel and Octavia were furious but there was nothing they could do about it. "We felt she should have made the Bishops and us more definitely acquainted with these conditions." Later Octavia apologised to Alice for her rudeness, but never really forgot the embarrassment Alice caused her and relations between the two groups have been strained ever since.

Boyd-Carpenter was disappointed after all his efforts. He felt the reasons Alice Seymour gave for declining to give up the *Box* were weak and unsatisfactory. "There seems no real desire to know the truth or face it," he complained. A few months later he died, aged 77.

Rachel decided to appeal to the King himself, not so much to get immediate action as to furnish him and the Queen with all the necessary information about Joanna. "What has once entered the mind may, under stress of circumstances, become active thought."

Helen Exeter was anxious to see her sons again and was making plans to return to South Africa. On August 28 she was allotted a place on the *Galway Castle*, sailing early in September. This was too soon for her and she declined but was informed that no other boat was going to South Africa that year. Helen had to accept and prepared to sail within ten days. She was told to keep details of the trip secret even from friends, for fear of German interception. Her spirit guides told her that all would be well.

To Octavia she wrote a tender note of farewell: "Though we have never met in the flesh, yet surely we have a closer tie and more mutual comprehension and affection than many who have lived for years together. I long to take you in my arms just once and hold you close."

Helen's spirits were wrong. All did not go well! Within hours of sailing, the *Galway Castle* was torpedoed by the Germans just off Plymouth. There were no survivors! Octavia generously elevated Helen to the position of the seventh angel, or prophet, in Heaven, then turned her attention to other matters. She was more concerned about Rachel discovering of her own accord that the Shiloh had taken over her body.

"You must prepare yourself to part with all and concentrate on our dual work," she wrote to Rachel. But when Rachel was slow to catch on her hints grew less subtle

"Dear Rachel - it's not anyone else! It's me! A very small me! A nervous and not at all heroic me! I know no other way in which to express this than by saying I am Joanna to all intents and purposes and the awful Trial is my Trial and the Book of the Trial is my description of it. I plead with you on behalf of the whole world, to recognise that on you and me, the burden lies. This being Satan's world for the remainder of the sixth thousand years, God can do practically nothing except through the intelligence of Woman."

It seemed to Octavia in her madness, that being Shiloh and being Joanna were one and the same thing. She was getting crazier and crazier. Since leaving the asylum she had developed agoraphobia but had decided she was a prisoner of the Lord and he had ordered her to stay within her house and garden. She was now preaching that Satan had been a son of God, the Chief Archangel, higher than Michael, who had fallen and through him evil evolved. Her ideas about the prophets were merging and Joanna was taking a minor role.

Mabel said to Rachel: "You remain a Joanna believer. I take the whole set of prophets as one. I take Joanna for comfort, and John Wroe for directions on the only thing that matters - the law of Christ."

Rachel was living a comparatively normal life surrounded by her children and grandchildren in Woodhouse Place, Falmouth. Sometimes Mabel/Octavia's way of looking at things seemed bizarre even to her. "I marvel how I was led to decide to stand by her during the hours in which I pondered over the matter and sometimes I really wished I could see a way to get out of it. For I have an intense shrinking from what I can only call the unknown quantity in Octavia's personality."

Bedford believers wouldn't let go of her. One wrote to her: "The fact is, Shiloh is here." So she considered whether Shiloh could be a woman and whether Shiloh could be Octavia. She at last wrote to Octavia telling her that the penny had dropped.

Mabel/Octavia was ecstatic. "We have known now for five weeks, but it is so much better that God should give you this understanding. I simply knew I was the woman who had to stand for Joanna today on behalf of the immortality of the body. But you are of a different calibre. You are placed to investigate and to dig and delve in order to be able to argue the matter."

It had now become obvious to Mabel/Octavia why she had suffered. "If I, in spirit, was actually confined in Joanna's flesh for ten months with the dragon, or devil, waiting to devour me, well it is no wonder I have attacks of dread and it is a good thing I have remembered that thirteen years ago, the fear of being shut up began. It is, I believe, a pre-natal influence obviously inexplicable to other people. Also, I have remembered that as a child I was always afraid to put my feet down in the bed lest the serpent should be there."

Now it was established that Shiloh had arrived and was in Mabel/Octavia's body, efforts were stepped up to increase the number of believers. Sealing had already begun - Mabel, who shall from now on be referred to as Octavia, had acquired a seal with the initial "**O**" on it. She aimed to seal 144,000 people who would help rule with Shiloh during the

Final Millennium - each 12,000 representing one of the 12 tribes of Israel. All over the world, people sold their property and possessions and flocked to Bedford. Dozens of large Victorian houses were bought near to Octavia's home to house the newcomers. New recruits donated all their wealth to Octavia, moved into their new quarters and prepared to devote the rest of their lives to the re-establishment of Jerusalem in Bedford.

Twelve disciples were chosen. Octavia ruled that Rachel could not be included because she would not leave her family to live in Bedford. It had been a toss-up as to whether Rachel would join Alice's group or Octavia's and in the end her motherly instincts came to the fore and she chose Mabel because she felt Alice was self-sufficient and needed her less. Also, Alice was too much of a gentlewoman to pressurise Rachel, whereas the Bedford Group were determined not to lose her and ruthlessly worked on her until she finally gave in.

Rachel's wistful yearning to know more about the spiritual side of mankind stemmed from the tragic death of her son. Otherwise a down-to-earth woman, this painful loss made her susceptible to suggestion. What woman wouldn't want to believe that her dead child continued to live in spirit? But her honest, rational soul continued to question when she suspected others of being carried away by the desire to believe in spiritual paradise. Her ultimate opinion of Joanna is worth mentioning: "She is one of those people held to be contemptible and base by the world, one whom it utterly despises, yet whose wisdom will confound and bring to naught the wisdom of men."

Alice inspired love and admiration amongst her converts, whereas Octavia filled her people with fear. They were almost too scared not to believe her. She had a powerful personality and would not be thwarted. Many followers were conscripted from the Suffragette Movement such as Alice Jones, once secretary of the Church League for Women's Suffrage, and Ellen Oliver, who had served a spell in Holloway for militant behaviour. An attractive aspect of Octavia's teaching was her promise of eternal mortal life. She told her people: "When Christ returns - He is due any moment now - those who are ready will remain on earth and reign with Him forever", and "all who subscribe their hands to become members of the Community must live as persons who do not expect to die".

She stepped up the campaign to get *Joanna's Box* opened. Samuel Galpin wrote from Standard Road, Hounslow, Middx, on August 17, 1923, to Alice Seymour in Blockley. "Like yourself, I have been perturbed at the persistent campaign of the so-called followers of Mrs. Joanna Southcott in petitioning the Bishops to open the *Box of Sacred Writings*. I was asked to become involved. I declined, as I knew that if I sent anything for publication to the newspapers, I should be deluged with letters on the subject and enquiries would be made as to where the *Box of Sacred Writings* was located."

Galpin was 79, and an authority on Joanna. He said it was plainly stated in the Writings that the Bishops should demand the *Box of Prophecies* voluntarily without any urging from the believers. He wrote sadly: "Where at present can we find 24 true believers, united together in one faith and belief?"

The Archbishop of Canterbury had written to Lady Portsmouth: *"You and Mrs. Fox assure me that there exists somewhere in Devon under the custody of a gentleman whose name is not known, a certain box which it is believed contains documents placed in it 100 years ago by Joanna Southcott. You assure me that a large number of people entertain a belief that the contents of this box would prove to have an extraordinary value and interest at the present time in connection with religious and international questions. I desire to say quite plainly that if a number of people believe that the Box contains papers of real interest which have been enclosed in it for a great many years, it ought to be opened. It is seldom that any papers that have been out of sight for 100 years are devoid of interest when they reappear and I think it is well that the mystery attending this subject should be brought to an end."*

Alice had bought Rock Cottage not just to satisfy a sentimental whim, but because she had a dream of establishing a haven where *Joanna's Box* could rest safely in a familiar place "surrounded by fields". The current custodian of the *Box*, Edwin Armstrong Jowett, who lived not in Devon but in Morecambe, accepted that she was divinely chosen to write about Joanna. There was therefore every chance that he might agree to the *Box* being transferred to Rock Cottage. She carried the hope in her heart up to her death.

According to John Stitt, son of John Muir Stitt and stepson of Anne Veysey Stitt, just after the First World War the elderly widow of a believer died. Her relatives announced they had found *Joanna's Box* in the attic and offered it for sale for £200.

Alice, who knew full well it was not genuine, pretended to be heartbroken when she failed to raise the money to buy it, claiming she had sunk all her savings into Rock Cottage. Octavia and her Bedford Group, rich as a result of obligatory donations, easily raised the cash and, to Alice's pretended distress, acquired the Box.

Alice wanted to divert attention from the whereabouts of the real *Box*. She even went to Bedford to discuss the matter with Octavia, who thought she now had the upper hand and there was even talk of the two groups merging. A set of rigid rules were drawn up, stipulating the conditions under which the *Box* should be opened. Alice didn't trust the Panaceans but, by humouring them, won their respect. It was a clever bit of acting on Alice's part. She knew where the genuine *Box* was and she hugged the secret to her, determined to protect it from the sort of sensational publicity Octavia seemed anxious to incite.

But Octavia soon realised she had been taken in and became more zealous in her efforts. Her rapidly expanding Community was now very rich. Huge donations were made regularly and she demanded tithes from her followers. The mystery of the *Box* was the essential factor for sustaining interest in her new movement and attracting new recruits. After she realised the box she had bought was a fake, she couldn't risk admitting it. To enhance the mystery, it was essential that people were encouraged to believe she was the new custodian.

There was plenty of cash available to finance the regular advertisements in the newspapers. Octavia hired sandwich-board men to parade London, proclaiming "The Bishops must open *Joanna's Box* to save England from ruin." The same message was plastered on the walls of the London Underground and a petition with 10,000 signatures was delivered to Lambeth Palace. A full-time press agent was hired to keep the *Box* permanently in the public eye.

In 1927 an ingenious character called Harry Price caused a stir by announcing he had anonymously been given the genuine *Joanna Southcott Box*. This remarkable man was obsessed by things mystical and he had dabbled in theatrical magic. His speciality was exposing fraudulent spiritualists. After the First World War there had been a surge of doubtful mediums with no qualms about exploiting thousands of gullible bereaved, anxious to be convinced they could be put in touch with their loved ones "on the other side".

In 1927 Price founded a National Laboratory for Psychical Research, which he was keen to publicise. He had been bombarded by requests from magicians, spiritualists and mediums, challenging him to try to prove their acts weren't genuine - for anyone in the occult business given the thumbs up by Harry Price was guaranteed success. But publicity had been poor and Price was looking for a really good stunt to launch his new laboratory.

When a bulky, metal-bound walnut box arrived at his office one morning by parcel post, with a note saying it was *Joanna Southcott's Box*, he knew it was what he had been praying for. It was much smaller than the genuine box was supposed to be, only eleven pounds in weight. Nevertheless, sunk into the lid was a mother of pearl plate engraved with the initials JS. Silk tapes were secured in five places with black seals bearing the young profile head of George III.

A note explained that it had been left to the writer by an old servant who had died. The servant and his sister, Ann and John Morgan, were the surviving children of Mrs. Rebecca Morgan, whose maiden name had been Pengarth. The story went that, as a young girl, Rebecca Pengarth had been the sole companion of Joanna Southcott between the years 1798 to 1814. On her death bed, Joanna had given the box to Rebecca with strict orders that it was only to be opened at a time of national distress, and in the presence of 24 bishops. It is an unlikely story. When she died Joanna was surrounded by dozens of close friends, journalists and doctors and there is no mention of a Rebecca Pengarth, nor is there in any of the hundreds of letters and notes and writings associated with Joanna. If Rebecca had been so close to Joanna, her name would at least have been mentioned.

On the other hand, Joanna loved creating mysteries and had a habit of placing papers and other objects into sealed containers. In her will, Joanna bequeathed at least 10 assorted boxes to believers and friends. So she might well have given one to a lowly servant.

The anonymous writer said he was leaving England that day for New York and wouldn't be back. He said Price could do whatever he wished with the box. Price had an insatiable thirst for publicity. He relished being in the limelight and, although he didn't really believe that the *Box* was genuine, decided he would squeeze as much publicity out of it as possible. A grand opening was arranged at the Church House, Westminster. Not only were all the bishops invited, but the national press, established spiritualists and clairvoyants and any member of the public who cared to come. He even put an advertisement in the *Times* saying that, if anyone else believed they had the genuine box, to bring it along and he would open it at the same time, free of charge. No one took up the offer, but the advert received the effect he wanted - more publicity.

On July 11, at 8pm, the hall at Church House was packed to bursting. The press arrived in force, but only one bishop - Dr. J. E. Hine, Bishop of Grantham. Alice Seymour and Octavia both received invitations. Octavia reacted in her usual, hysterical fashion, urging Alice to go with her to the meeting to protest. Alice said she would attend if she could be allowed to address the assembly on the subject of Joanna. Price declined. He didn't want his publicity ruined by articulacy and rationalism. Alice sent word she felt the event was a diverting and ludicrous stunt, but she would do nothing discourteous or aggressive. She sent Mary Robertson to observe the proceedings. Octavia sent a rowdy crowd of female activists.

Price was determined to make the event entertaining, since he had a full hall. He explained first who Joanna was and then Professor A. M. Lowe gave a humorous speech about mass psychology and the madness of crowds, with special reference to the "particular form of lunacy known as the Southcott movement". The Bedford contingent obliged by hissing on cue.

Harry Price opened the *Box* with a pair of shears and a jemmy and the Bishop of Grantham removed the contents, holding each item up so that all could see. Inside were fifty-six articles, including a collection of romantic novels, some of them rather rude - the *Surprises of Love*, or *An Adventure in Greenwich Park*, and *The Romance of the Evening*, or *Who would have thought it*? There were annotations by Joanna, in her handwriting. As Price remarked dryly, "a worldly collection for a religious ecstatic".

There was also a lottery ticket for 1796, a fob purse covered with steel beads containing silver and copper coins and tokens ranging from a William and Mary tuppeny Maundy piece to a halfpenny coach token - rare coins and certainly of Joanna's time. Other objects were even more odd. A rusty horse pistol; a miniature case; an ivory dice cup; a bone puzzle; a woman's embroidered night-cap; a pair of tortoise-shell and inlaid gold earrings and a set of brass money weights.

Price remarked wittily that, if someone had put the collection before him without telling him the history, he would have hazarded a guess that they belonged to some old gambler. As far as he was concerned, there was not a shadow of doubt the box was Joanna's. He felt it was a real *Joanna Box*, but one of many.

"The Southcottians do not want their box opened, in spite of their parrot cry to the Bishops to send for it," he suggested. "For the Southcottian movement today would not last a month unless they had at least one sealed box to whet the curiosity of their followers. In other words - **No Box! No Mystery! No Movement**! The Southcottians without their box would have as much go in them as a motor-car without an engine. But they will never get another Bishop to touch a *Joanna Box* with the proverbial pitchfork."

Harry Price said that, as a result of his stunt, he had so thoroughly exposed Southcottians in Blockley and in Bedford, as frauds and exploiters, that they would never be taken seriously again. However, he confessed a sneaking admiration for Joanna. "She was a genius in

Harry Price ceremonially cutting the iron bands at the "opening" of what he claimed to be Joanna Southcott's authentic box, at Church House, Westminster, July 11, 1927. The bearded man seated on his right is the Bishop of Grantham. On his left, standing, is Professor A.M.Lowe.

obtaining publicity - a publicity she can still command." High praise from the leading publicist of the time.

In his autobiography, *In Search of Truth*, he admits opening *Joanna's Box* was one of the biggest thrills of his life. It certainly assured him of an odd posterity. Encyclopaedias still refer to the *Box* he opened and regard it as conclusive evidence that Joanna was mad, ignoring the fact that it was a hoax. It has even been suggested that the contents were put together by Price himself. His massive collection of books on occult subjects, all the laboratory equipment and the fake box itself, is now housed at the University of London Library. He had every reason to be proud of his collection - he offered it to Adolf Hitler who was considering accepting it just before the start of the Second World War.

Alice, in the peace of the Cotswolds, retained a dignified silence and in her own ladylike way, continued to build up a following of her own. Octavia, on the other hand, ruled her new community with the authority of a Mother Superior and established rigid rules which she insisted had to be obeyed to the letter. Some were positively bizarre. "Sneezing, yawning and creaking shoes must be apologised for. Humming and singing are not permitted! Persons who laugh in an ugly way must be told about it."

Housekeeper, Emily Goodwin, who had been expelled from John Wroe's church because of her occult practices, took to falling into trances and emitting awesome divine messages. Octavia was not in the least offended, nor did she feel threatened. On the contrary, she was impressed and offered to hand over her leadership to Emily. But Emily refused, pointing out that she was only an instrument of God, whereas Octavia was His chosen representative.

Octavia had diabetes, although it had not been properly diagnosed. She regularly took medication for headaches and exhaustion and one day, as she sat in her room nursing an aching head, she poured herself a glass of water to swallow a tablet with, but dropped the tablet and it rolled under a cupboard. After searching for it, she gave up and drank the water by itself, praying that the headache would go of its own accord. This was her first attempt at spiritual healing and, to her surprise, it apparently worked.

After a few minutes of quiet concentration her head was clear of pain. So she announced to her followers that God had ordained to her the divine power to heal, and urged them to rely on her water cure in future, instead of doctors. She had so much success, she decided to share the cure with the rest of the world and she began advertising the miraculous Water Cure. "Healing for all! Without money, without price!" Not only was it a cure for any amount of diseases, but relieved mental anxiety and business worries too, as well as bringing good luck and good fortune.

There were strict procedures for the Cure. Helpers first prepared small squares of ordinary linen which Octavia breathed over "with the breath of prayer". The squares were distributed to clients, who were told to first dip them in a glass of water and then to either drink the water, or bathe a wound, sore or stiff joint in it. Sometimes it worked, sometimes it didn't, but there was no shortage of eager partakers of the cure and astonishing testimonies to its effectiveness were claimed. Some women even gave it secretly to their families. "My husband is much easier to live with now," wrote one satisfied customer. Another said her dog was now rid of a dreadful skin disease.

A believer wrote to say that at a meeting held in London, the divine water was sprinkled outside each door of the hall and, as a result, an enemy of Joanna found himself physically unable to cross the threshold. Octavia recognised what an important bait the cure was for boosting recruitment. "It is a panacea for all ailments," announced Octavia. Liking the sound of the word, she decided to call her community *The Panacea Society*.

Alice Seymour liked to tell a story about the *Panacea* treasurer, Mrs. Tagg. She had a cataract, and Octavia insisted she should dismiss her doctor and rely entirely on the water cure. Some years later, Alice bumped into her in London and Mrs. Tagg told her she had left the *Panacea Society* after she had gone blind in one eye. "I saw she was wearing an artificial one," said Alice. "So the healing, I fear, often failed."

By 1929 Octavia had 633 members, most of them living in the Community at Bedford, having donated all their wealth to Octavia and depending upon her completely, believing that through her they would attain immortal life. Mary Robertson was harsh in her condemnation of them, suggesting in her scathing Scottish manner that "they make passes over people and exercise an occult power and many who visit them come under this peculiar influence. Seances and strange rites are practised."

Even Alice Seymour was moved to make some untypically harsh remarks: "They are spurious healers foisting on credulous minds the belief that the Power of the Spirit can be conveyed into the body by a small piece of linen placed in ordinary drinking water."

The *Panacea Society's* property in Bedford expanded. The houses were painted the same drab green, even Octavia's own huge house, *The Haven*, which was reserved as a holy palace for the Shiloh (herself). She furnished it with antiques, lush drapes and carpets. In 1924 she pulled a master

How the *Panacea Society* got its name

THE PANACEA SOCIETY

(Registered with the Charity Commissioners)

SLOW BUT SURE

DELIVERANCE

not Miraculous, but by Treatment,
through Water and the Spirit,
"Without money and without price,"

—— FROM ——

Nerves, Rheumatism,
Eye, Ear, and Throat Troubles,
Mental Anxiety, Business Worries,
Faults of Disposition.

Protection can be secured in the Tribulations
and Perplexities that are preceding the
Coming of the Lord.

Do not write for particulars, but tell your complaints
and difficulties in as few words as possible. You need
not acknowledge our reply, but send the monthly report as
requested when you have had a month's treatment.
Please write your name [Rev., Dr., Esq., Mr., Mrs., or
Miss] your address and your list of complaints clearly,
and send your letter, enclosing an addressed envelope, to

C.S.S., THE PANACEA SOCIETY,
Bedford.

Mabel (Octavia) Barltrop believed she had divine authority to cure physical and mental illness by merely breathing over a piece of material to impregnate it with her powers. The patient was advised to soak the cloth in a glass of water and then drink it. "It is a panacea for all ailments," she said and, liking the sound of the word, decided to call her rapidly growing community in Bedford *The Panacea Society.* This "Miraculous Water Cure" is still on offer today advertised as "free of charge".

stroke over the Salford Museum, who had in their possession the crib made especially for the Shiloh in 1814, at a cost of £200, complete with its original furniture and coverings. It was donated to the Museum in 1860 by William Hows.

Octavia persuaded the curator to allow her to house the crib temporarily at Shiloh's new "palace" in Bedford, along with embroidered baby clothes, a silver christening spoon, a pair of Joanna's gloves and a silk scarf. The curator was under the impression the crib was going on show at a museum but, once she had it in her possession, Octavia hung on to it. All the Salford Museum have to remind them of their relic is a black and white photograph.

Octavia's illness got steadily worse and much of her time was spent in bed, although she still ruled the community with a rod of iron. In October, 1934, when she was 68, she was found dead in bed by Emily Goodwin. Her followers had believed her to be immortal and had been promised immortality for themselves. It was on the strength of this promise that many had handed over their worldly wealth. The unscrupulous Emily Goodwin took charge and decided to keep Octavia's death a secret from most of the members for a while, fearing they might lose faith and kick her out. Like Octavia, Emily regarded the water cure as a winner and had no wish to abandon it. So she too claimed divine authority to breathe over the bits of linen and continued to advertise the cure.

Mary Robertson pointed out that although Octavia sent out her healing waters all over the world and told people to rely upon it completely, she herself had been having treatment under a doctor. "Octavia couldn't even heal herself," she remarked with contempt.

Despite their differences, Alice and Octavia had been on amicable terms. Octavia, although niggled that she couldn't dominate Alice, respected her as an authority on Joanna. Octavia's children used to visit Alice regularly at Blockley and one daughter who, despite living in the community at Bedford, was particularly fond of Alice, confessed an uneasiness about her mother's beliefs. While she was alive, her children feared her but after her death lost no time in leaving Bedford, saying they couldn't abide Mrs. Goodwin.

Emily stepped up the publicity and collected 28,757 signatures for a petition demanding the opening of *Joanna's Box*. This was duly delivered to Lambeth Palace in the usual vulgar blaze of publicity, which made Alice cringe. The Archbishop's secretary sent out a message. "His Grace is unable to review the decision made after much thought many years ago."

Alice remained discreetly in Blockley, leading a respectable life with her group of dedicated helpers. They were not flamboyant, like the Bedford lot. Indeed, they couldn't afford to be! The Society was funded by members. From all over the world Southcottian converts sent postal orders of five or ten shillings to pay for copies of Alice's books or her magazine.

She reserved one afternoon a week for visitors. Graham Greene, the novelist, visited her there between the two World Wars. He found her eccentric and endearing and described Rock Cottage as a "strange high house, like Noah's Ark with a monkey puzzle tree and a step-ladder of terraces". The rooms, he said, were tiny and of the same shape and packed with Staffordshire ornaments. He was shown two patchwork quilts, which Miss Seymour told him were made by Joanna, and some locks of her hair and a communion glass engraved with "little ludicrous symbolical figures" and piles of manuscripts and pamphlets "some in Joanna's own handwriting".

She was old and innocent, he said, but terribly sure of herself and "took Joanna's life from the ghost's lips". Her eyes were clear pale-blue and she wore an old-fashioned dress of faded mauve and horn-rimmed glasses. While having tea, he watched with amusement as a mouse ran backwards and forwards in a cupboard behind Miss Seymour's back. "I could see it moving through a crack, between the tins of dry biscuits."

Hanging on the wall was a portrait of Joanna and Alice Seymour sat beneath it and talked with "complete confidence" about *The Millennium* which would come in the next fifty years and which he said she explained in mundane detail, confessing with a schoolgirl wistfulness "I've always wanted to see Jerusalem."

Alice was regarded fondly by the villagers as rather dotty but harmless. She and Mary Robertson kept very much to themselves, spending much of their time in the garden. Early one morning Alice looked out of her bedroom window, and said she saw a vision of a powerful-looking woman - "the most beautiful I have ever seen" - in a flowing white robe, her face towards the East.

"She looked stronger than the world and set on some great and eternal purpose, against which nothing could withstand. So like did she appear to a great Archangel that, instead of Michael, I called her Michelette." The vision kept her company for months. "She sat on the corner of my bed and on her face was a beautiful smile," wrote Alice.

In 1939 heavy bombing destroyed all of Alice Seymour's property in Plymouth, from which she derived her income. There were six houses, which were rented out, and the Headland College was on lease. So, during the war years, the two women were very poor and their friend, Emma Grayson, would send them food parcels from New Zealand. With little money coming in, Alice was unable to pay the bills and, indeed, was now incapable of managing her own affairs. Mary Robertson took charge of the finances and Alice would sign cheques without querying them. Her money rapidly dwindled. She was faced with the prospect of going into an old people's home, after selling her beloved Rock Cottage to pay her debts. Her mind had now almost completely gone and her relatives (non-believers) considered having her committed.

A devious woman, Annie Veysey, came to the rescue. She was one of the *Southcottian Society's* staunchest members but also one of its most formidable. She had been living in London with a mentally-ill brother, having retired from her job at Westminster Bank, Piccadilly, and already nervous about bombs shaking her house. She came to an arrangement with Alice's relatives to buy Rock Cottage, at a bargain price, in return for allowing Alice to live there for the rest of her days. The Society's committee and Alice's nephew, Harold Seymour, agreed that it seemed a sensible solution. Harold was getting fed up with constantly popping up to Blockley to sort out his aunt's petty domestic problems. So Annie sold up, bought Rock Cottage and moved in in 1941.

Despite agreeing to allow Alice to remain there, no such promise had been made about the faithful Mary Robertson and Annie lost no time in sending her packing. Relatives in Scotland were persuaded to take her in. Alice was now well into her eighties and so confused she had no idea of what was going on. So Mary tearfully said goodbye to Blockley and, not long afterwards, died without ever seeing her beloved Alice again.

Annie, at 51, was a spinster but attracted to John Muir Stitt, a fellow Southcottian who printed all the Southcottian literature at his works in Ashford, Middlesex. When his wife died, Annie set her cap at him and within months they were married and both had moved into Rock Cottage, sharing the task of looking after Alice.

So for her final seven years, Alice led a miserable life - confused and ill-treated by her benefactor, but at least ending her days in the home she loved. She died in 1947, aged 92.

Deryck Seymour, her great-nephew, visited Blockley shortly after his aunt's death. Annie Stitt went to great lengths to tell him how tenderly she had nursed Alice, adding: "If you've heard any stories in the village, about me ill-treating Miss Seymour, they're not true!"

Deryck Seymour, to his distress, found out otherwise.

Alice Seymour
(1855-1947)

When Graham Greene, the novelist, went to visit Alice at Blockley about the time this photograph was taken (1933), he described her as old and innocent but terribly sure of herself and "took Joanna's life from the ghost's lips". She talked to him "in complete confidence" about the Final Millennium which he said she explained in mundane detail .

Chapter 23

Blockley Southcottians

Annie and John Stitt became joint Heads of the *Southcottian Society* in Blockley. And what an odd couple they made! Annie, at 57, was full-faced and still reasonably attractive. John Muir Stitt was 70 and had been a widower for four years. Unworldly and vague, he was a kind man whose thick white hair grew to waist level, which he twisted into a startling knot at the nape of his neck. Most of his face was hidden behind a bushy white beard, making him look like a child's idea of God.

Annie had thought her new husband was rich and was disappointed to find he only had his pension to rely on. She decided her stepson had tricked his father out of his money. Her retarded brother, Cyril Veysey, also lived at Rock Cottage. He had an obsession with figures and would sit for hours at the table writing meaningless sums on the cloth. It was a strange, grim household and John Stitt soon regretted marrying Annie. Within a year he wrote to his son: "I can't stand it much longer. I'm coming home."

But Annie wouldn't let him! Rows erupted between them. Annie was exasperated with the piles of papers and once told her husband she would like to put them all on the fire and burn them. To which he replied scathingly: "Then I'll put you on top of them." Eventually, said John's son, they decided to have separate bedrooms.

Towards the end of her life, Alice Seymour had became senile, wandering around the house at night, banging doors and keeping everyone awake. She had to be watched constantly. According to John Stitt junior, Annie would put her to bed and lock the bedroom door at night. One morning, John Stitt came down and found the door unlocked and the poor old woman lying on her bed badly bruised. There was blood on the stairs and banisters and he thought she had escaped from her room and fallen downstairs during the night and just managed to crawl back to her bed. But his son was convinced Annie pushed her because, he claimed, she was fed up with looking after her and wanted to be rid of her.

Annie found guarding the *Southcottian* treasures a daunting task. There was the precious Banner which had to be laid across the *Box* when it was "demanded" by the Church of England Bishops, and there was the worry of the *Box* itself, rumoured to be hidden in a secret passage. Alice had always been secretive about the *Box* and Annie was probably never told its exact whereabouts. She came to believe it really *was* hidden somewhere in the cottage. The *Panaceans* had the same thought and were forever snooping about for clues. A woman came by car from the *Panacea* Headquarters in Bedford and asked Annie if she knew where the *Box* would be opened and was told in London.

Then, in 1957, Annie not only found out the truth about the *Box* but, to her immense surprise, became the reluctant custodian. When Cecil Jowett, of Cheadle, Cheshire, who had looked after the *Box* for over thirty years (having inherited the custodianship from his father, Edwin Armstrong Jowett), died, his wife, Maud Jowett, asked Annie, as the Head of the *Southcottian Society*, to take charge of it since they had no children to pass it on to.

Emily Nicholson, the Jowett's niece, was not a believer and knew little about Joanna Southcott. But she often went to stay with her uncle and aunt and once confessed: "It might sound like sacrilege, but as a child I played with the chains and locks on the *Box* and, indeed, it was my window seat while staying there."

Annie consulted fellow Southcottians and it was agreed that it was her duty to accept the *Box*. Southcottians in the States donated large sums of money towards the cost of safeguarding it. This new responsibility, however, affected Annie mentally. She became a recluse, nervous and obsessively suspicious of visitors and particularly scornful of the *Panaceans*.

When three ladies from Bedford called to see "any treasures" she had, she told them coldly: "They are not in the house, but in a place of safety. I do not keep the house open to the public, but only our own friends and believers."

Her husband and brother were now dead and she lived alone. One day she read a passage in one of Joanna's books, that no woman should be present on the day the *Box* was opened. This made her fearful and more and more uneasy about having the *Box* in the house.

Cecil K. Jowett
Eighth Custodian of Joanna's Box

    Cecil K. Jowett became custodian of Joanna's Box after his father, Edwin, died in 1926. He and his wife, Maud, were childless and so, when Cecil died in 1957, Maud was at a loss to know what to do with the Box.

    According to their niece, Emily Nicholson, her aunt decided to hand it over to the Southcottian Society, in Blockley. Emily, granddaughter of Edwin Jowett, said it required three or four men to remove the Box from an upstairs room, at her aunt's home at 3 Mount Grove, Cheadle, Cheshire. *"She was glad to see the back of the Box, which was heavy and cumbersome and a responsibility she said she could well do without."*

The Haven, Bedford, Beds

Originally the family home of Mabel (Octavia) Barltrop, who founded the Panacea Society between the two World Wars and now the Panacea Society Headquarters, it is reserved for Shiloh and Joanna to live in when they return to rule the world during the Final Millennium.

14 Toward St, Sunderland

Lily Duckett lived alone in this huge near-derelict old Masonic Hall, which she made the HQ of the Southcottian Society when she took over from Annie Stitt in 1971. It was finally condemned as unsafe and was demolished. Hundreds of old Southcottian books were either given away or destroyed.

So she went to London one day, with her daily help, Mrs. Fletcher, to see one of the curators at the British Museum. A large box was seen being loaded on to the train with them.

She wrote later to fellow Southcottian, Emma Grayson, in New Zealand: "I took the MSS etc., which a Barrister had been here to inspect, to the British Museum and gave it to them. They were thankful I did so, the directors wrote to tell me. **IT IS SAFE IN THEIR CARE AND WELL GUARDED ALL THE TIME NOW**! I knew if this house was bombed it may be lost for all time! The head man up in London took me to see the big table with 24 seats round it, where the Bishops will one day open the *Box*. I was so thankful I saw it! He was surprised that I gave it to them and refused to accept any money for it. I know it is safe all the time. In case of danger - it will be taken out of London to a place of safety within ten minutes."

This letter indicates indisputably that Annie took the *Box* to the British Museum Library for safekeeping, but Museum officials emphatically deny she offered it to them and admit only to Annie giving them two thick, hand-written volumes of manuscripts in 1966.

What is more likely is that she allowed the officials to sift the contents of the *Box* and take out the interesting documents. These would then have been bound into volumes for easier reading by interested parties. Having thoroughly examined the manuscripts, I can confirm that they are authentic and mostly in Ann Underwood's handwriting.

Without the impressive locks and chains round it, and its contents full of insignificant papers, the Box would have lost its distinction for it was never labelled because of the need for secrecy.

Now well over 80, Annie's mind was deteriorating fast. Wherever she looked, stacks of papers confronted her and the disorder distressed her. She tried to sort them out, burning those she felt were irrelevant in the kitchen fireplace. Her gardener, Harold Da Silva, remembers seeing stacks of papers arranged round the gas stove. The more she sorted, the more impossible the task became. As well as this, the appalling weather towards the end of 1966 got her down. It was bitterly cold and Blockley was snowbound. Annie was virtually a prisoner in her own home. More and more depressed by national events, on November 29, 1966, she complained of strikes, higher postage and unemployment. "It is certain Satan is doing his utmost everywhere to create disturbances and this is one of the signs we are near the end of his reign. I firmly believe it is a time of National Danger now."

She even distrusted people who had been kind to her. One of her hobbies was beekeeping. She bottled her own honey and took it to London to sell at the Young Women's Christian Association fund-raising events. She was on the committee and in her Will had left half her money to the Association. Local beekeeper, Mr. Turvey, had for years helped her with her bees and was upset when she accused him of stealing her honey bees by putting his Queen Bee into her hives to entice them away. At other times, she would wander through the village like a lost child, crying she had lost her mother and would bang on neighbours' doors in distress.

She wrote ominously to her friend, Miss Grayson: "Nothing in our lives happens by chance. This is why I came here and found Miss Seymour had the Banner in the house, in the large deed box. It must be used when the *Box* is opened. We took it by car to the Bank for safety and we have never had it home since then, as in case of fire or burglars it may easily be stolen. It is a sacred thing and I did not wish to risk losing it. Up to now God has shown His power by protecting us."

It is unlikely she kept the *Box* for more than a brief period at Rock Cottage. After taking over custodianship in 1957 she deposited it with all its contents, at the National Westminster Bank, Evesham, along with two other boxes containing the *Patchwork Quilt*, the *Southcottian Banner* and other relics, before eventually offering the *Box* to the British Museum. However, the responsibility drove her mad. She tortured herself wondering whether or not she had done the right thing in allowing the curators to separate apparently worthless papers from what *they* considered of interest.

She took to locking every room in the house and carrying a huge bunch of keys around with her, tied to her waist like a jailer. In her last three years she confined herself to the kitchen, sleeping at odd hours on one of the chairs, waking up sometimes in a blind panic convinced there were burglars. In the middle of the night, her keys jangling, she would go hunting through the house and usually returned to the kitchen with piles of papers on which she poured paraffin before setting them alight.

Her standards of hygiene slipped and she became dirty and smelly, no longer washing or changing her clothes. Visitors were rare but those she did allow in were obliged to remove piles of dusty papers in order to find a space to sit down. Since the only inside lavatory was upstairs, she used the flower beds to relieve herself. One person she trusted was Jean Cother, who worked at the Post Office and handed her her pension each week, which she thought was a gift. Jean, a state registered nurse, took advantage of Annie's trust to visit her at Rock Cottage and bathe and bandage her badly ulcerated legs.

One tantalising mystery which remains unsolved is why Annie suddenly decided to change her Will and leave the half of her estate she had promised to her favourite charity, the Young Women's Christian Association, to her solicitor, Henry Osborne Roberts, of Evesham, instead. The other half was pledged to the Vicar and Churchwardens of St. Hieritha Parish Church, Chittlehampton. After her death, the Will was contested by the **YWCA**, who had expected at least half of her money.

The Will was drawn up by Henry Roberts' own Evesham firm of solicitors and on 19 May 1967 was signed by Annie and witnessed by Evesham solicitor, Christopher Cox, and Mr. Bush, a clerk employed by Roberts' firm. At the time Annie's mental health was fast deteriorating, according to her doctor, Dr. Jean Haine, of Box Cottage, Blockley.

After Annie changed her Will in his favour, Roberts contacted local policeman, P.C. Bruce Smith, later Chief Inspector Smith of Gloucestershire Constabulary, and drew his attention to the fact that Annie was using paraffin to set fire to papers in the kitchen fireplace. He suggested it would be safer if the fireplace was blocked up and replaced with an electric fire with a guard. The constable was already aware there was a fire risk because on several occasions he had put out small fires after seeing smoke pouring from her kitchen window. An electric fire was consequently installed and Annie was instructed how she should switch it on and off. But she hadn't a clue and continued to poke papers through the guard onto the electric fire. And, although villagers had been warned she must not be allowed to buy any paraffin, a canister of it mysteriously appeared in her kitchen.

In July 1971, Roberts, and his wife, Margaret, planned a holiday on the Continent. Before departing, Roberts told his wife he'd arranged to call in to see Annie on business. Margaret described to me, on the telephone many years later, how she waited quietly in the kitchen while Roberts and Annie had their "talk". She said there was so much dust and dirt she preferred to stand rather than try to find a seat amongst the piles of papers and other rubbish. She appeared to have no inkling at that time that Annie had changed her Will in Roberts' favour. After their visit, the couple left immediately for their holiday.

It was while they were away, that the most dramatic event since Joanna Southcott claimed she conceived her holy child at Rock Cottage, happened in Blockley. Old Mrs. Yucksall first spotted it at 2 o'clock in the morning from her house on the hill at the top of Day's Lane. Tongues of fire were darting from the windows of Rock Cottage below, lighting up the night sky. She immediately rang the police station at the other end of the village.

In the early hours of the morning, July 26, 1971, the constable dragged himself from his bed to answer the phone. It wasn't very often, in this quiet village, that his duties deprived him of a good night's rest. He called the Fire Service before dressing hastily and cycling down the hill to Rock Cottage. The fire had already taken a hold and smoke belched from the windows. He tried to break in to save the old woman but was beaten back by the heat. Fire engines arrived from four different towns to deal with the blaze.

Dr. Jean Haine was woken abruptly by several explosions, which she said might have been window panes cracking. Seeing the flames, she raced over to the cottage in her nightie and peered through the kitchen window. Annie's body was on the floor with a little brass bell clutched in her hand, as if she was trying to raise the alarm.

Rock Cottage is in a unique position on the steep, western side of the valley, at the southern end of the village cut high into the rocky hillside. The fire, therefore, could be seen for miles. Villagers left their beds and thronged the narrow lane outside the cottage, fascinated by the rare spectacle.

From below, the burning cottage looked like the centrepiece of a theatrical stage, and local artist Hubert Williams brought his sketch pad to record the scene for posterity. The flames licked the strange, pyramid shaped windows and seemed to transform them into golden demonic eye-sockets. Flanked by tall trees and enhanced by the greyness of the granite stones of the house and walls, the effect was dramatic.

After getting the fire under control, the firemen pulled out anything which might serve to revive the flames. Charred mattresses, furniture and clothes were flung onto a pile to be disposed of later. Amongst these items were cardboard boxes crammed with papers. Next morning more villagers were attracted to the scene and there was no lack of observers when the Bank Manager and Trustee of Mrs. Stitt's estate, Mr. Wilfred Payne, arrived to survey the damage. Later Harold Da Silva, Mrs. Stitt's gardener, was engaged to clear away the debris. He was told to remove the smoking and dampened debris and fling it on to a heap.

Harold saw no value in the blackened papers, manuscripts and letters. But Norma Marshall, who lived opposite Rock Cottage, said there might be something interesting and asked to look through them. Harold said she might as well help herself, since it was all destined for the rubbish dump and all Payne and Roberts were concerned with was the antique furniture and silver.

Norma dragged several boxes from the still smoking pile. One contained papers in Joanna Southcott's handwriting and the Rev. Thomas Foley's own hand-written 1803 diary. As president of the *Blockley Antiquarian Society*, Norma was delighted and took them home to sort out. Though badly affected by the fire and the gallons of water which had been used to quench it, the papers were still readable. Norma Marshall and other members of the *Antiquarian Society* dried and cleaned the documents for inclusion in their collection of local history. Villager Dr. Arthur Exell, christened them "*The Rock Cottage Relics*".

Harold thought it would be a wicked shame to let things go to waste when no one wanted them. He was told he could salvage for himself whatever was on the rubbish pile. Harold wasn't interested in papers but, being a builder, knew the value of scrap metal. As he hunted around, he kicked aside a heavy piece of blackened copper. It wasn't until he got it home and his wife cleaned it up with Brasso, that it became clear it was a finely engraved picture of a plump old woman - William Sharp's original engraving of the famous picture of Joanna Southcott that he made in 1803. A copy hangs in the National Portrait Gallery, in London. Alice Seymour used to take rather poor copies off it after she bought it in 1913, from Foley's descendants.

The remains of Annie's body were found in the kitchen. It was decided she knew nothing of the fire. According to evidence at the inquest, she died of a heart attack - evidently before the flames got going because there was no sign of smoke in her lungs. Arrangements were made for her ashes to be buried in her family grave in St. Hieritha Churchyard, Chittlehampton, Devon, and not the lovely Blockley Churchyard, where John Smith, Joanna's husband, is buried near his close relative, George Troup, equerry to the Prince Regent and alongside half-a-dozen other Southcottians who had all once lived at Rock Cottage. Villagers refer to the group of graves as the Rock Cottage Stones.

Lily Duckett, head of the Southcottian Centre in Sunderland, arrived to take charge of the items stored in the Old Coach House at the bottom of the garden, which had escaped the fire. She stayed in the village for a fortnight, sorting everything out and a van was hired to take away at least 50 tons of papers, books and pamphlets.

There were also three impressive boxes, which Annie had deposited at Westminster Bank in Cheltenham. These contained relics, such as the patchwork quilt which Joanna had made with her own hands. Lily had nowhere safe to store them, so she offered them to the Royal Albert Museum, in Exeter.

Due to lack of space, they accepted only two which contained, amongst other things, the two fine, engraved communion chalices made by the engraver and landscape artist, John Pye, and presented to Joanna in 1803; the gold-embroidered jewelled banner designed to be laid on top of *Joanna's Box* in the ceremony preceding its opening by the Bishops; the patchwork quilt Joanna spent ten years making, sometimes working on it while receiving divine messages. The other box - Joanna's genuine *Box of Prophecies* - having already been sieved of its contents and now full of worthless papers and after first being refused by the Royal Albert Museum, Exeter, was offered again to the British Museum, who deny having it.

Lily Duckett became the new Head of the *Southcottian Society*, working from her home in Sunderland. She didn't question Henry Roberts' inheritance of half of Annie's wealth, valued at about £60,000, which included the remains of the cottage and its contents. Mrs. Daphne Brooch, General Director of the *Young Women's Christian Association,* Central Club, did! There had been suggestions that the solicitor, Roberts, had taken advantage of Annie's confused state. Mrs. Brooch told me she engaged a Queen's Counsel with a view to contesting the Will but in the end decided it would be too expensive to fight, and withdrew.

Shortly after the fire, Roberts bought himself a Rolls Royce and at the golf club sometimes, after a few drinks, he would tell friends how he had pulled off a "nice deal". Roberts retired from his firm of solicitors early, but lived only a few years to enjoy his inheritance. He died in 1977. Some who knew him well described him as a charming but devious gentleman, who deliberately set out to win Annie's heart and her riches.

Lily Duckett's home, in the depressed centre of Sunderland, was a marked contrast to Rock Cottage. She lived in one huge room at 14 Toward Street, Sunderland, a crumbling mansion built as a Masonic Headquarters, with two immense meeting halls complete with marble pillars and impressive platforms, where the elite of the area used to meet. Into these once grand halls, Miss Lily unloaded the tons of *Southcottian* literature she had brought from Blockley. Leaflets, pamphlets, books and boxes of old manuscripts and letters written in beautiful copperplate hand, were piled neatly amongst the rows of pews and above and below the wide platforms.

In another large room of the house, she slept, ate and worked, determined to spread the teachings of Joanna Southcott so that, when the

Day of Judgement arrived, at least some people would be prepared for it. Hardworking and devoted to the Cause, she sent literature to people in the USA, New Zealand, Australia, South Africa and South America.

It was a tremendous task she set herself. Her main enemies were not atheists and Satanists, but mice, damp and children. Mice constantly nibbled the papers, the damp steadily penetrated valuable old books and manuscripts, turning them green and mouldy, and children - knowing the only occupant of the house was an old lady - delighted in breaking into the basement and turning the neatly stacked pamphlets upside down on the stone floor. Lily had a small group of loyal helpers. There was Miss Belle Finn, a sweet lady with touching faith and a gentle disposition, and Miss Ann Vincent, formidable and rigid but nonetheless kind. Concerned for their friend's welfare, they persuaded her to move into a nursing home.

When I visited the derelict old house in February 1987, Miss Finn warned me to "prepare myself for a shock". She took me down to the basement hall and I was greeted by the bizarre sight of tons of literature, including many handsome hardback books - some printed 200 years ago - heaped in impossible chaos on the floor and shelves. The house was scheduled for demolition and Miss Finn and Miss Vincent had the daunting task of removing the tons of papers. *The Panacea Society* took a few lorry loads. Miss Seymour had never approved of the Society, agreed little Miss Finn, but "it doesn't matter how the Word is spread, as long as it gets around". I was invited to fill the boot of my car with "anything I cared to salvage" - an offer I gladly accepted.

The old house in Toward Street has since been pulled down and the current Head of the *Southcottian Society*, Dorothy Weyers, who lives in South London, keeps believers world-wide informed about anything of interest regarding Joanna Southcott.

In Gittisham, Devon, where Joanna was reared, there is no visible indication that she was ever associated with the village. Winsor Cottage doesn't have a plaque on the wall, acknowledging that she and her family once lived there. The old dairy, where Joanna and her sister Susanna churned the butter, is now used as a laundry room and the secret garden she called her Gethsemane, is still evident. The cottage is protected from the road by a mound of heaped up earth topped with a thick hedge, giving the occupants privacy from the narrow lane leading past the property and into the village. The present owner is proud of the fact that Joanna Southcott once lived there and wouldn't be upset if he found her still haunting the place, unlike the tenants of Taleford Farm, Ottery St. Mary, where Joanna was born and spent the first year of her life, who won't have her name mentioned.

The Panaceans continue to advertise for the Bishops to open *Joanna's Box*, but in fact don't have a clue about what has happened to it and, in a letter to Alice Seymour's nephew, Deryck, they admit they haven't got it themselves.

The fate of the actual Box itself is by no means certain. If the British Museum did finally accept it from Lily Duckett in 1971, they would have been unlikely to have valued it highly, papers of historical interest having been sifted by them years earlier and bound into two impressive volumes. Without its distinctive locks and chains and full of mundane rubbish, there would be nothing to positively identify it as *Joanna Southcott's Box*. Not meriting precious museum storage space, it would either have been disposed of years ago or else be gathering dust in some remote vault of the museum, indistinguishable from any other old box.

In view of the fact that the *Box* is supposed to hold papers which will provide solutions to the world's problems and explain what will happen when the *Final Millennium* begins, many feel its one-time contents, now in the comparatively safe custody of the British Museum Library, should be examined urgently by the Bishops.

But the late Dr. Arthur Exell, Blockley's much respected historian, told me he hoped the *Box* would never be found, nor its contents examined. "Let us hope it remains hidden away," he said with simple wisdom. "Some mysteries should remain unsolved. Some quests are best unsuccessful. Some discoveries only lead to disillusion!"

BANNER OF ISRAEL

Banner depicting Joanna as "The Woman Clothed with the Sun" (Rev. ch.12, v.1), designed to be laid on top of Joanna's Box of Prophecies prior to its opening by the Bishops. It is embroidered with gold thread and studded with semi-precious jewels. In the custody of the Royal Albert Museum, Exeter.

Joanna's Box of Prophecies
How it Grew Bigger and Bigger

William Sharp brought the Box from Exeter in 1801 and enclosed it in a large case sealed with seven seals. Jane Townley took charge of it in 1816 and said it was only made of common wood and added her own "divinely inspired" prophecies. Richard Foley opened it after his father died, to see if there was money hidden inside. As the Box assumed more importance and gained symbolic inference, it grew bigger and bigger. In 1861 Samuel Jowett recorded it as weighing 156-lbs

	Custodians
First Custodian	**1801-1816** William Sharp
Second Custodian	**1816-1825** Jane Townley
Third Custodian	**1825-1839** Thomas Foley
Fourth Custodian	**1839-1861** Richard Foley.
Fifth Custodian	**1861-1861** Samuel Jowett, of Burmantofts Hall, who died the year he got custody of the Box.
Sixth Custodian	**1861-1898** John Marshall Jowett, of Apple Hall, Bradford.
Seventh Custodian	**1898-1926** Edwin Armstrong Jowett, of Southcott, Harwarden Ave, Morecambe.
Eighth Custodian	**1926-1957** Cecil K. Jowett of Cheadle, Cheshire.
Ninth Custodian	**1957-** Maud Jowett (Cecil's wife). Didn't like the responsibility and gave it to Southcottian Society.
Tenth Custodian	**1957** Annie Stitt, of Rock Cottage, Blockley, who deposited it briefly with her bank.
Present Custodians	British Museum Library accepted it from Annie Stitt. They sieved the contents and bound anything of interest into two volumes.

Bibliography

G.R.Balleine, Past Finding Out.

T.P.Foley, Letters & Communications of Joanna Southcott.

T.P.Foley, His Diary 1802

C.Lane, Life of Joanna Southcott.

Alice Seymour, The Express.

Alice Seymour, Express Leaflets.

Alice Seymour, The Voice in the Wilderness

A.W.Exell, The Rock Cottage Relics.

Blockley Antiquarian Society, Joanna Southcott Collection

Rachel Fox, The Finding of Shiloh.

Harry Price, Leaves from a Psychic's Case Book

George Turner, Letters and Diaries.

J.F.C.Harrison, The Second Coming.

E.Hoyle, Southcottian Society, New Zealand

Joanna Southcott, Her Writings

James Jezreel, The Flying Roll

INDEX OF PEOPLE AND PLACES

Museums

Newspapers

People